Five Star Vision

TO MY FATHER

"Memories keep those we love close to us forever."

FIVE STAR VISION

BY

STEPHEN Y BOHDAN

VERSO RESEARCH
PUBLISHING

Copyright © Stephen Y Bohdan
Drawings © Alison Aldred

First published in 1998 by
Verso Research Publishing, World Trade Centre, 8 Exchange Quay,
Salford Quays, Manchester M5 3EJ

The right of Stephen Y Bohdan Wilk to be identified as the author of the work has been asserted herein in accordance with the Copyright, Designs and Patents Act 1988

All rights reserved. This book is sold subject to the condition that it shall not, by way of trade or otherwise, be lent, resold, hired out or otherwise circulated without the publisher's prior consent in any form of binding or cover other than that in which it is published and without a similar condition including this condition being imposed on the subsequent purchaser.

A CIP catalogue record for this book is available from the British Library

ISBN 0 9532328 0 8

Typeset by Amolibros, Watchet, Somerset

Printed and bound by T J International, Padstow, England

CONTENTS

Preface		vii
Introduction	Your Vision And The Truth	xi
Chapter 1	The Marvel That Is The Human Eye	1
Chapter 2	Unravelling The Mystery Of Vision	20
Chapter 3	Is Reading Bad For Our Eyes?	33
Chapter 4	Glasses - A Pyrrhic Victory? And Is Laser Surgery Safe?	43
Chapter 5	Is It True That Our Eyes Always Function Perfectly?	50
Chapter 6	Knowing Our Perceptions Is Knowing How To See! ...We All Have The Power Of Prediction	53
Chapter 7	Getting Started -The Magic Eye!	75
Chapter 8	The Essence Of Relaxation	83
Chapter 9	The Aligned Eye And The Rectifying Force Of Central Alignment	96
Chapter 10	Building Your Momentum	104
Chapter 11	Your Belief And Your Vision	108
Chapter 12	Accept The Benefits Of Central Alignment!	113
Chapter 13	Creating Better Mobility And Increasing Your Power Of Perception	121
Chapter 14	Shifting	131
Chapter 15	The Snellen Chart	143
Chapter 16	Submodalities	156
Chapter 17	How Memory And Imagination Will Improve Your Vision	168
Chapter 18	Imagination - The Powerhouse Of Good Vision	179
Chapter 19	Presbyopia - Old Sight: Can We Stop Its March?	189
Chapter 20	Applying **CAPE** As A Principle Of Good Vision	192
Epilogue		200
Appendix A	Vitamins: The Food Of Good Vision	201
Appendix B	Dry Eye	204
Appendix C	A Self-induced State Relaxer	205
Glossary		208

LIST OF ILLUSTRATIONS & ACKNOWLEDGEMENTS

Illustrations are inset after page 110

1. Eye Muscle Massage Exercises
2. Eye Muscle Massage Exercises
3. Eye Muscle Massage Exercises
4. Eye Muscle Massage Exercises
5. View of retina through an Opthalmoscope
6. Short Sight
7. Astigmatism
8. Long Sight
9. Normal
10. The Magic Eye
11. The Image Encapsulated In The Magic Eye

Photograph number 5 is copyright Steve Allen.
Photograph numbers 1, 2, 3 and 4 are copyright Vincent Devine, AMPA, 428 Hilton Lane, Walkden, Manchester.
Photograph numbers 6, 7, 8 and 9 are copyright Reader's Digest Association Ltd. How is it done. © 1990
Photographs 10 and 11 are copyright Magic Eye Inc.
Drawings included in the book are copyright Alison Aldred.

Note to readers

If no visual correction chart is enclosed with this book, please apply for your free copy by sending your name, address and a large stamped, addressed envelope to:

Verso Research Publishing
World Trade Centre
8 Exchange Quay
Salford Quays
Manchester M5 3EJ
United Kingdom

PREFACE

My eyesight had been less than perfect for a number of years. I had done a lot of reading intensive work and I originally found that my eyesight began deteriorating in about 1987. By 1988 I had simply progressed along the normal route. I visited the opticians and was prescribed glasses and contact lenses. I was just like anyone else who finds themselves in this situation. At first wearing glasses and contact lenses was not a major concern for me. It was the day I noticed that my vision seemed to be getting worse that really alarmed me. Looking at some fairly large words printed on a sign, I was shocked to see I could no longer make these words out with clarity. I knew I was standing at a reasonable distance, one from which I *should* be able to see words of that size immediately. The sharpness of the letters, 'their outline' had disappeared and the depth and quality of colour was very poor. I knew I was already short-sighted but on this particular day I noticed that my eyesight had definitely become worse. It was deteriorating. I did not need an eyesight test to tell me what I already knew. As the conscious awareness suddenly began to dawn on me, I was hit by this unexpected realisation. My feelings turned into major shock.

This deterioration in my eyesight hit me with far more impact than finding out for the first time that I needed glasses. **I expected my eyesight to remain more or less 'as it was'.** I was totally unprepared for such a further and shockingly noticeable deterioration.

Giving myself excuses for poor sight!

I considered the situation. I was thirty-seven years old. Perhaps I just had to accept that it was not unusual or even unexpected for someone of my age to experience deteriorating eyesight. Then I reconsidered my situation. In reality, what I was trying to do, was to *give myself an excuse* for the deterioration in the quality of my vision.

I made a decision and started a remarkable journey!

I don't know what it was that prompted me but in that instant I made a decision. I decided that **I was not going to accept poor eyesight** and that I was not going to be reliant upon glasses or contact lenses any longer. **I was going to do something about my deteriorating eyesight**. I did not know exactly what at that moment but I had **made up my mind**. I felt a gut instinct. It was telling me that there must be something I could do to reverse the process. After all, until very recently my sight had been far better than I had just begun to experience. I reasoned that *something* must have caused the deterioration in my sight. This is how I started upon a remarkable journey - *a journey that would ultimately show me that I did have control over the power of my own eyesight*. I was about to discover that what is normally accepted to be an unconscious and uncontrollable process is in fact **subject to personal influence and *is* controllable consciously.**

I did not realise at the time that I was going to be exploring and applying new ways of using my brain and mind and indeed thinking in new ways. These new thinking processes have in fact had a powerful impact upon other areas of my life. They have begun to reframe my beliefs about what is possible and what is not possible.

We are taught either directly or indirectly that certain things about our eyes and our sight are possible or impossible. There tends to be an accepted belief that once our eyes begin to falter and our sight becomes worse, there is nothing we can do about it. The normal solution is glasses or contact lenses. These are not however a cure and in fact have the effect of stabilising an existing condition. They do not mean that your eyesight will not get worse. In reality it is often the case that over time eyesight *does get worse* when wearing glasses or contact lenses. This was the alarming experience that I had on this day.

A natural approach wins hands down!

The huge advantage with natural eyesight improvement and correction methods is the very fact that they are **completely natural**. After I had decided that I was going to take action to correct my eyesight, I was later to find out that natural eyesight correction does have a sound medical basis. I came across a natural eyesight management technology that has been in existence for some number of years and **which had been proven to work** with improvement and correction management carried out upon thousands of people. I additionally used a number of these methods to push me back finally into a state of normal vision. I found I was able to adopt these approaches and incorporate the understanding into what I had already begun to do. I found the techniques had a sound and solid basis and could be explained when considered against a background of modern psychology.

Do you need a teacher?

I did not use a teacher to help me achieve my results. Some people advocate that a teacher is required in order to benefit from natural eyesight correction methods. This may have been true previously. Indeed I found that much of the information available was not really suitable for the ordinary person. As a layman, I had a little difficulty understanding the technical terms used and some of the reasoning and basis of how the outlined methods worked. That is one of the main reasons for this book. To provide **a guide and understanding that anyone will be able to use** and **to allow you to receive the benefits** natural eyesight improvement and correction offers, without having to depend upon a teacher. There may be those who feel they would like the input a teacher can provide. No matter which way you finally decide to progress, this book will achieve its objective in giving you a solid understanding of the direction in which you are heading and helping you to achieve so much more quickly your objectives in regaining normal vision.

When I began my quest I had no idea how the eye functioned or indeed what action I would take to reverse the process of my defective vision. I began by making my own changes in the quality of my eyesight and these were spurred on when, during the course of my further investigations, I discovered two very important facts. Both are crucial to knowing and understanding how your eyesight can be improved.

Is defective sight a permanent condition?

I had always believed that once eyesight deteriorated that was it. It was a permanent condition. Nothing could be done about it and that is why glasses were prescribed. The general body of opinion of which I was aware had stated that 'such conditions were permanent'. Far-sightedness (hypermetropia), short-sightedness (myopia) and astigmatism were all classified as permanent changes that took place in the eye's function. It is a major distinction and obviously results in a whole new perspective to find out that these conditions are in fact changeable!

A unique and highly talented Ophthalmologist, William H Bates was the first to reach this conclusion after thirty years research and investigation. His findings were first made available in 1919. Far from the eye being in a permanent state of incapacity, the eye can be shown how to work properly again. Dr Bates concluded that the not only could these conditions be corrected, he also demonstrated people are able to produce far sight, short sight and astigmatism at will! What this means is that if these conditions can be produced at will the same applies to correction, once we know how!

The second thing that Dr Bates concluded was that:

> "Correction of poor vision will be accomplished with the right mental approach".

This confirmed the approach that I was already taking. The link between good sight and thinking about good sight in the *'correct'* way became clear. So, the second crucial element in good vision is *'using the mental abilities you already have'* in the right way. Once you realise for yourself that good sight involves thinking about how you see, 'in the right way,' improvement follows very quickly.

The interesting thing is that although the methodology had been around for all this time it is practically unknown and certainly not advocated by the opticians I had visited. The question I asked myself was- "Why'? If it is possible to correct eyesight using completely natural methods, that are **both proven and effective,** why are so few people aware of this possibility? I am sure many, many, people would love to be aware of the fact that they do have a real choice and that **it is a choice that works and that will give you measurable results!**

Stephen Y Bohdan Wilk

INTRODUCTION

YOUR VISION AND THE TRUTH

"Truth. First it is ridiculed. Second, it is violently opposed. Finally, it is accepted as self evident."
Arthur Schopenhauer, German philosopher

Can you learn to see normally again?

Sight. Apart from those of us who unfortunately are born with some physical defect or suffer from some form of eye disease, we all know "how" to see, but the process of vision can become contaminated and corrupted. Some people may have worn optical aids for as long as they can remember. Perhaps they never really learnt how to use their sense of sight to full effect, before some form of eye trouble interrupted the natural development of the visual process. Perhaps you have had normal vision at some time and it has simply deteriorated? **This book will tell and show you how to begin restoring your own eyesight to normal. It will reveal how you can clean up and improve your own visual process.** The great and exciting thing is that you can start here and now, today!

The evidence that you can rectify defective sight! — naturally

It is an established fact that defective eyesight can be corrected by completely natural methods. **The evidence is very well documented.** In seems that in modern times, for one reason or another, (which we shall look at later), the established natural methods of eyesight correction have not been promoted. Dr William H Bates[1] carried out much experimental work in the field of natural eyesight correction. He also worked with thousands of people who regained normal vision using his visual re-education techniques. This book now links up some of the marvellous advances used in modern psychology with the techniques of Dr Bates, to provide you with an effective and practical way of regaining normal vision. It is my hope that many more people will now be able to take advantage of these methods of visual re-education.

What others have said about these methods

There have been many followers of this method. It is not new. Aldous Huxley (1894–1963), the eminent writer, benefited greatly from a program of visual re-education. There have been many other testimonials to the success of the methods. The *British Medical Journal* has carried editorial discussing the methods and concluding:

"...and Bates' method of visual education actually works."

The *Hutchinson Encyclopaedia* refers to the Bates' method and comments:

"The method is of proven effectiveness in relieving all refractive conditions, correcting squints, lazy eyes, and similar problems, but does not claim to treat eye disease."[2]

Actual proof that visual re-education works!

Let me share with you the fact that qualifies me to write about visual re-education. I have used the methods and techniques first put forward by Dr Bates and combined them with my own distinctions and other useful advances taken from modern psychology. The resulting combination is a potent way for you to bring about a measurable increase in the quality of your own eyesight. **Let me also share with you the results that I have achieved.**

I had worn glasses and contact lenses since 1988. My record is reproduced here. Unfortunately it does not show all my results going back to 1988. The history is however clear. My eyesight deteriorated in 1993. My right eye deteriorated again in 1994, with my left eye showing a slight improvement. These deteriorations were gradual and not as visibly noticeable as the deterioration I experienced in late 1996. This was the one that really moved me into taking action. Nearly ten years later, (on the 7 April 1997), when most people would expect their eyesight to be deteriorating, my right eye showed 0.25 and my left eye was normal - optically measured and tested by a fully qualified optician. The result was that "no prescription for spectacles was required". A remarkable result and an extract of the original and genuine test result is also printed here so that you can see for yourself what is possible. These are the results that I achieved and you too can improve and correct your own defective vision. **You can attain measurable increases in the quality of your eyesight,** following the techniques shown in this book.

Why have you not heard about visual re-education before?

It was only by chance that I happened across a method of visual re-education. It is a fact that 'visual re-education' is not actively promoted. There are a number of reasons for this, which will probably become self obvious. It is also a fact that most people are not well enough informed to

Stephen Y Bohdan is the writing/publishing name of Stephen Y Bohdan Wilk, shown as Stephen Wilk on the Eye Test History and Patient's Prescription

Rx Details for Stephen Wilk 30.9.94

with compliments
Broughton
                SPECTACLES
15.6.91   R -1.50
          L -1.75

5.6.93   R -1.50
          L -2.00

30.7.94   R -1.75 + 0.50 × 145
          L -1.75

DOLLOND & AITCHISON
The Opticians

708 Market Street
Manchester
M1 1PN
Tel. 0161 833 0469

NHS General Ophthalmic Services   GOS(P)

Patient's prescription /statement

Part A
To be completed by the patient

Patient's details

Surname: WILK
(Mr/Mrs/Miss/Ms)
Other names: STEVE
Address: [redacted]
         Timmend
         Wemley
Date of birth: 26/10/58

Information for patients

Read the rest of this form before you get your spectacles.
It tells you
- how to get your spectacles
- about help with the cost of your spectacles.

A prescription is valid for two years. If you have been given one, keep it in a safe place.

How to get your spectacles

If you are under 16 you must take this prescription to a registered optician.

If you are 16 or over you can take this prescription to a registered optician or anyone else who supplies spectacles.
Unregistered suppliers are not allowed to sell prescription spectacles to children or to adults known to be registered blind or partially sighted. Reading glasses may be sold to adults without the need for a prescription.

Help with the cost of spectacles

You can get help with the cost of spectacles for any of these reasons.
- You are under 16.
- You are a full time student under 19.
- You are getting, or are the partner of somebody who is getting Income Support or Family Credit.
- You are getting, or are the partner of somebody who is getting DWA and had capital of £8,000 or less when DWA was claimed.
- You are prescribed complex lenses.
- The Department of Social Security decides that you are on a low income.

If you think you are entitled to help for any of these reasons, ask the person who tested your sight for a voucher form GOS(V).

If you do not already have a certificate AG2 or AG3 for help with NHS charges and if you think that you are entitled to because you are on a low income, ask for form AG1. You must wait for a reply before buying your glasses.
Refunds are not given by the Department of Social Security afterwards.

War pensioners can also get help with spectacles if they are needed because of their pensioned disablement. Ask for a voucher form GOS(V).

You can find out more in leaflet G11 **NHS sight test and spectacle vouchers.** You can get this leaflet from your optician or your local Social Security office.

Part B
To be completed by the practitioner

Prescription details

	Sph	Cyl	Axis	Prism	Base		Sph	Cyl	Axis	Prism	Base	
R I G H T	-0.20					Distance	PLANO					L E F T
						Near						

I carried out a sight test today in accordance with the regulations with the following result:

☐ the prescription above was issued
☒ no prescription for spectacles was required
☐ the patient was referred to their GP
☐ no change was clinically necessary
☐ Tick if complex lenses for voucher purposes.

Name of practitioner (capitals): A.J. MORGAN
Practice address:
A. J. MORGAN F.B.C.O.
10..... ON DISTRICT CENTRE
L....... LTON
M....... M38 6AU
Tel. 5141

Signature: [signature]   Date: 7-4-97
Ophthalmic list number: 0084/121
Name of FPC receiving GOS(ST)A: [signature]

xiii

know that they have the choice of sight correction by re-educating their visual process. Most people experience some problem with their sight, visit the optician and actually *expect* to be told to wear glasses or contact lenses. Until you became aware that it is possible to correct defective sight by natural methods, what were your beliefs about eyesight, defective vision and whether it was possible to correct it? Stop for a moment and make a short list of things you know about your eyesight and any ways you know to improve it.

Things I know about eyesight   **Ways to improve my eyesight**

Take the time to think about the things on your list because many of the beliefs you have about your own eyesight and how to improve it will be challenged with new information. You may even be surprised at some of the things you will find out for yourself. As you look at your list now, ask yourself how the beliefs you hold about your eyesight could lead you to improving it? If like most people you find that your beliefs would not aid you in improving your **eyesight, this is the first secret we will share together.** Knowing and understanding the facts and ways in which your eyesight can improve naturally will help to provide you with a new empowering belief. A belief that will push you forward and into a new state of normal vision. As you begin to ask yourself new questions about your own beliefs and how they affect your eyesight, you will come to form new ways of thinking about your visual process. This book is about giving you a new choice! A way to 'tune up' your crucial sense of sight.

What does having good sight mean to you?

If you are like me, good sight is important to you for a number of reasons. The simple convenience of being able to look and see with out needing glasses or contact lenses is a marvellous feeling. We all know how inconvenient any type of optical aid can be. I personally used to find it a burden to come home after a social night out and have to start messing around with contact lenses, taking them out, cleaning them and being careful not to rip, drop or lose them.

What about the cost? How much have you spent on optical aids to date and how much do you anticipate spending, this year, next year, over five years, ten years or twenty years? I used to wear contact lenses as well as

Introduction

glasses. My contact lenses cost me between £300 and £360 per year, with my glasses costing approximately £100. Fair enough, the glasses would last me a couple of years, but even so, the cost soon begins to mount up. Over three years that's approximately £1150. Over twenty years you might be spending closer to £7000. What else could you do with this money? A holiday, extra savings, children's education, buy a small car or perhaps use for car running expenses? Think about all the money, time and inconvenience optical aids actually cost you!

What about the cost to your health? As you read through this book you will find that it is an accepted fact that glasses *do nothing to improve* the condition of the eyes or your health. It is more or less accepted that if anything glasses maintain a defective state of vision, which can only be detrimental to your health because one of your prime senses, 'sight', is not functioning as it should do! If you care about your health, (and quite apart from the financial saving to be made), you owe it to yourself to 'tune in your sense of sight'. Your sense of sight is of little use if you are not using it to full effect. Why accept a standard of sight below those standards you demand for yourself in other areas of your life? The fact you may have had defective vision for some years is no excuse. There is a reported case of a man of seventy who had worn glasses for more than forty years for short-sightedness and twenty years for reading and desk work. This man was able to correct his vision using these techniques. Ultimately he knew that he was entitled to a better standard of vision for himself and took the simple **step of deciding** that normal sight was no less than he should demand of himself. He achieved a marvellous result using natural eyesight improvement and correction management. Age or the length of time you have had defective vision is not a barrier to better sight. What is required from you is the desire and the belief in yourself that **you can improve the quality of your eyesight**. No one can give you that, it is something within yourself. It is something that will, however, grow, ripen and mature as you progress through this book.

How many people do you know who have improved the quality of their sight? How many people have had defective vision and corrected it to normal? It really is a remarkable personal achievement to prove to yourself and to others, that you have control over your own power of sight. It does not take any special qualifications or certificates, only the ability to find out how your own eyesight works, as a complete visual process. There is a wonderful feeling of personal satisfaction in regaining your ability to see the world naturally and clearly and knowing that it is your very own personal achievement.

There will always be those people who view their sight in a pessimistic way. Maybe they have defects of vision greater than those I have already proved can be corrected. Such people may try to use this an excuse and so a reason why these techniques could not work for them. It is a fact that many types of visual defects have been corrected using Dr Bates' techniques. What if such a person was able to gain a measurable improvement in his sight, so that it was only half as bad? That may mean wearing thinner lenses or may be not needing glasses in as many situations. What if such a person then used that improvement as a base from which to further improve his vision?

No doubt some critics, with their own interests to serve, may complain about the nature of the techniques or the formalising of qualifications in order to use the techniques. Others will argue that 'extensive clinical tests' must be carried out before anyone should begin benefiting. Personally, I would say that **the greatest qualification one can have is having achieved a result.** I have achieved quantifiable improvements in my own vision and this is the best qualification anyone can have. Certifications and qualifications often stifle creativity. In addition they can lead to narrow ways of thinking about problems and solutions. One can end up thinking in a mode and way that has been pre-determined by others. Why does the ophthalmic industry still not promote natural methods of sight correction?

Dr Bates broke away from traditional, restrictive ways of thinking about sight correction. The result was the foundation for an entirely new method of visual improvement and correction. Over the years these methods have been developed further by others. In addition, by adding some of the most useful, practical and workable developments in modern psychology, it helps further the development and effectiveness of the methods. These **developments** also help to explain the reason why many of Dr Bates' methods are so successful in treating poor sight. In addition they help to bring the methods up to date by making them **quicker and easier to use.**

People who frequently consider themselves experts, (although having good intentions), are often lacking in their own creativity and can be the cause of delayed progress and development, because of their adoption of outdated and restrictive views. Let's consider a recent illustration of how this can have a destructive effect. Tony Robbins is a highly successful individual who has led by example[3]. Some people have still criticised him despite the fact that he has created a multi-million dollar company and brought many practical, useful and beneficial personal development technologies to the ordinary person. His impact has been undeniable, yet Tony has no formal qualifications in what he teaches. This in fact has been his greatest asset. Tony has personal experience. He was able to take what he knew worked, something with which he had achieved results and show many other people how they too could gain the same benefits. The point is that if something works, then why not find out how and use it and why not let others gain the proven benefits as well?

As I said earlier we all know "how" to see. Over time different things can happen that interfere with our ability to see normally. Some of the things in this book may seem familiar. We often find that using what we

INTRODUCTION

already know, in new ways, can give us big advantages and better results. Good vision is really about doing what you do or should be doing 'naturally'. I make no apologies for saying that in some instances I am simply reminding you of what you already know in order that you can achieve the results that you want.

One point to constantly remind yourself of is that when ever you attempt to do something, to see something you can't normally see, or to do an exercise you may not be familiar with, the words "I can't…" are a description of a fact that is true only in the present moment. Carrying this description of your capabilities into your projected future will almost certainly guarantee that you will not achieve your objective. **Adopt the attitude that there is always a way to progress and that you will find it.** This book describes a model of what it is possible for you to achieve with your own visual capabilities.

Natural improvement and correction of sight

All the exercises in this book are completely natural and certainly cannot do you any harm. There is no physical interference with the eyes themselves. The techniques and exercises described work upon the eye muscles and the mind's perceptual abilities, which combined together form a vital part of the visual process. In the unlikely event of experiencing any pain from any exercise or technique, discontinue it immediately. It should also be common sense not to discard optical aids where these are required in order to perform work, driving or other tasks safely. Do not cease wearing optical aids in such circumstances until you are sure your eyes have been corrected. The best way to do this is to obtain an independent eye test from a qualified optician.

If you suffer from any form of serious eye complaint or disease then you should always rely upon and follow the advice of your doctor.

Book your eyesight test at the opticians!

The challenge for you the reader is actually to use the techniques and exercises described. Reading about them without doing the exercises will not improve your eyesight. The willingness to change, to view things in new ways, and using the techniques and practising the exercises *will* give you measurable improvements in the quality of your vision. My own improvements are facts that speak for themselves. As most people get older their eyesight deteriorates. I have improved mine. You can do the same easily and quickly if you turn on your own visual capabilities and skills. Follow the blueprint that you are provided with. You will soon be booking your own appointment with the optician for an eye test to confirm independently the improvements you have made!

Diagram 1 Approximate percentages of population requiring optical aids by age - UK

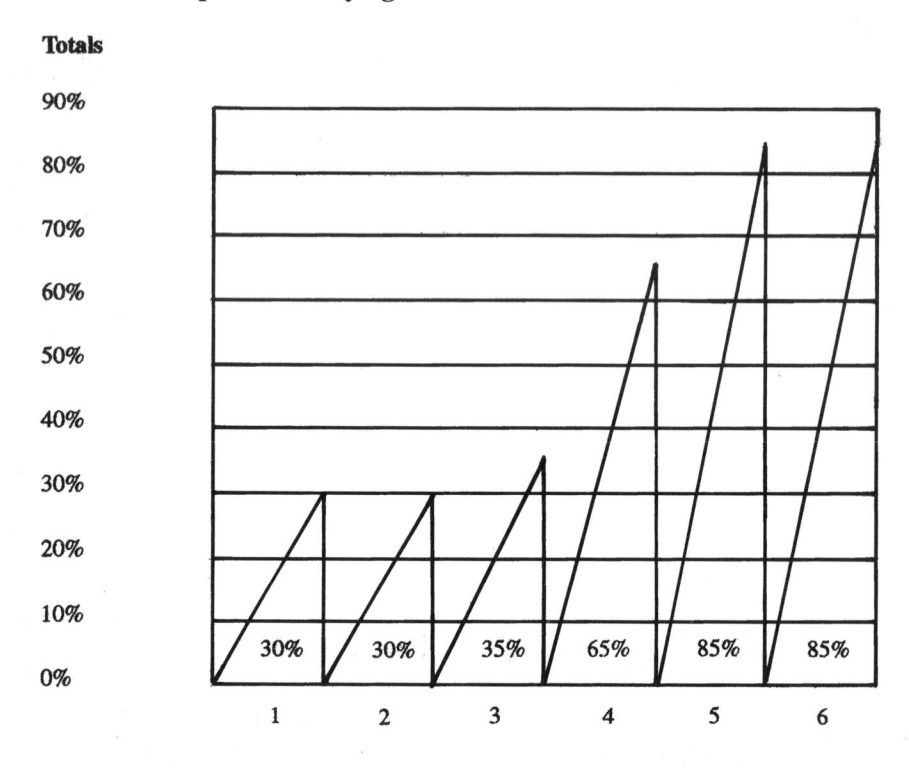

Totals

30%	30%	35%	65%	85%	85%
1	2	3	4	5	6

Age groups: 1=15 to 24   2=25 to 34   3=35 to 44   4=45 to 54   5=55 to 64   6=65+

So how did I come to make the remarkable discovery that it was possible to correct my sight by natural methods and how did I achieve these results? I will explain in later chapters how I began my own investigations into sight correction. Before I do that, the next chapter begins to look at the remarkable structure that is the human eye and how knowing about the make-up of the eye will help you in your vision correction program.

Finally, I believe it will soon become 'self evident' that visual re-education is and should be, the primary choice for improvement and correction of defective sight.

---

[1] As already indicated these finding were first reported in 1919.
[2] *Hutchinsons Encyclopaedia,* Helicon Publishing Ltd, 1994.
[3] Tony Robbins is a famous American personal development coach and trainer.

CHAPTER 1

THE MARVEL THAT IS THE HUMAN EYE!

"As a man is, so he sees.
As the eye is formed, such are its powers".
William Blake, English poet (1757 –1827)

Have you ever stopped to consider just how remarkable the human eye actually is? You may have heard many people in the past compare the eye to a camera. This however fails to do justice to the remarkable design of the eye. It is very useful to understand something of the structure and make-up of the eye. Knowing how your eyes work is the first step toward eyesight correction. An overview will help provide the necessary grounding from which you can step into the next level and aid an understanding of some of the exercises that follow later in the book.

The lens of the eye starts to develop in about the sixth week of life of the embryo. The lens itself actually develops from the outermost layer of the embryo, which is still transparent at this stage. The eye forms as a clump of cells in the surface tissue, thickens and finally falls back toward the developing optic vesicle. The optic vesicle is in fact a protrusion of the brain, which later forms the main part of the eye. Not many people are aware that the cells in the eyes are derived from the same embryonic tissue as the brain and this explains many of the eye's unique qualities.

Diagram 1   Lens development

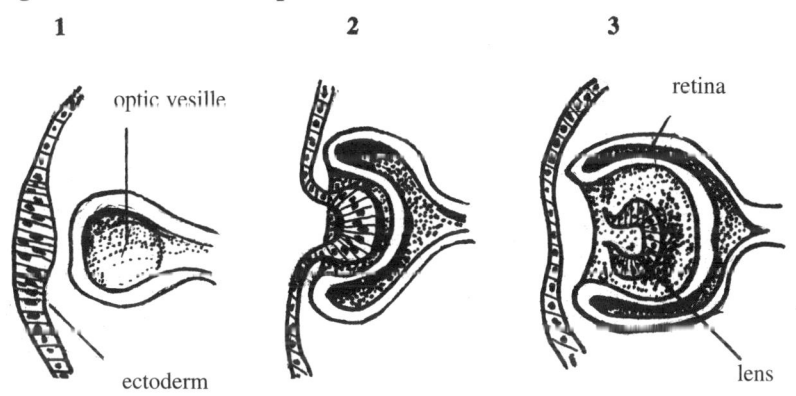

The lens develops from the outer layer of the ectoderm (embryo)

As the developing cells multiply, they come to form the lens fibres that are then deposited in layers. As the eye develops, it forms three layers in total.
  i) Light will eventually enter the eye firstly through the cornea (this is a transparent covering).
  ii) The 'sclera' is the white of the eye (a tough fibrous outer covering of the globe or eyeball), and
  iii) the choroid membrane which contains blood vessels to nourish the eye.

Diagram 2 shows the three layers of the wall of the eye

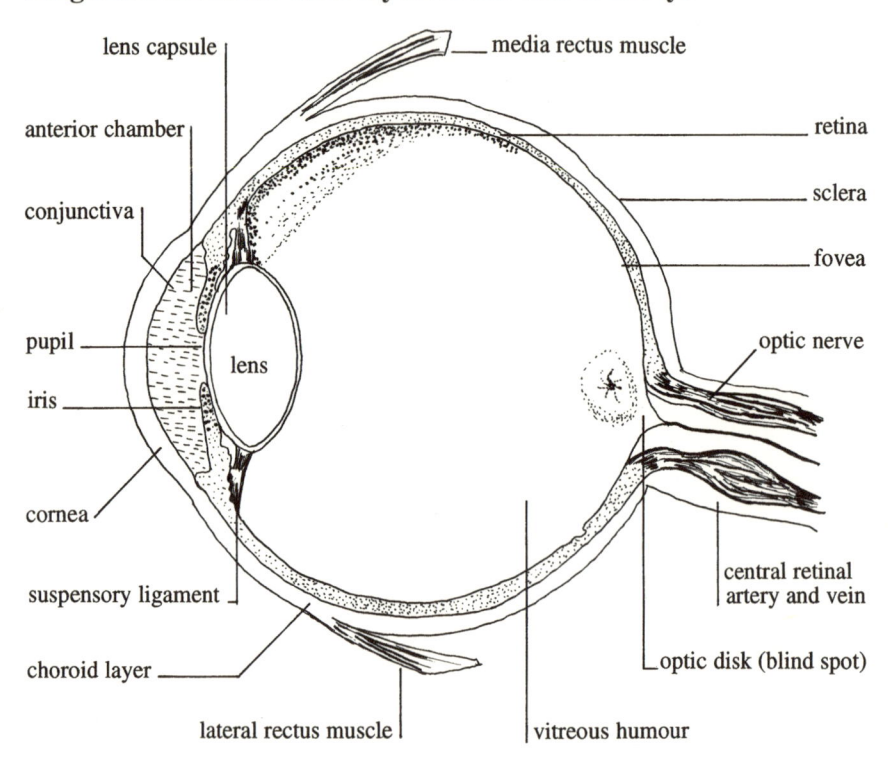

1) The sclera changes at the front of the eye, to form the clear cornea. This is the window to the eye. The sclera is opaque behind the cornea. From the sclera the rectus and oblique muscles emerge.
2) Immediately underneath the sclera is the middle layer of the eye, (the uvea). This choroid layer (also known as the vascular layer), is a plentiful network of blood vessels that provide nutrients to the eye. This pigmented coat absorbs light and actually stops light 'leakage' and 'scattering' within the eye itself. At the rear of the

eye, this layer lines the sclera. At the front of the eye however, this layer is separated from the cornea to form the iris and ciliary body. The iris is made opaque by pigment (colouring) and the iris itself surrounds the pupil. It is the density of the pigment, which is responsible for the colour of the iris, which in turn gives us our eye colour.[1] The iris contains the radial and circular muscles that actually control the diameter of the pupil and this controls the amount of light entering the eye. This is important because if the environment is dark, the pupil is enlarged to admit more light. If the environment is bright, the pupil is made smaller. These reactions are involuntary and we have no control over these muscles The iris can also react in response to emotional state, which can then affect pupil size. Precious gem and jewel traders have known this for centuries, as they used to judge the worth of a stone upon the reaction reflected by changes in a trader's pupil size.

The iris muscle fibres are reflexly controlled by fibres of the third (III) cranial nerve.

Diagram 3 The cranial nerves

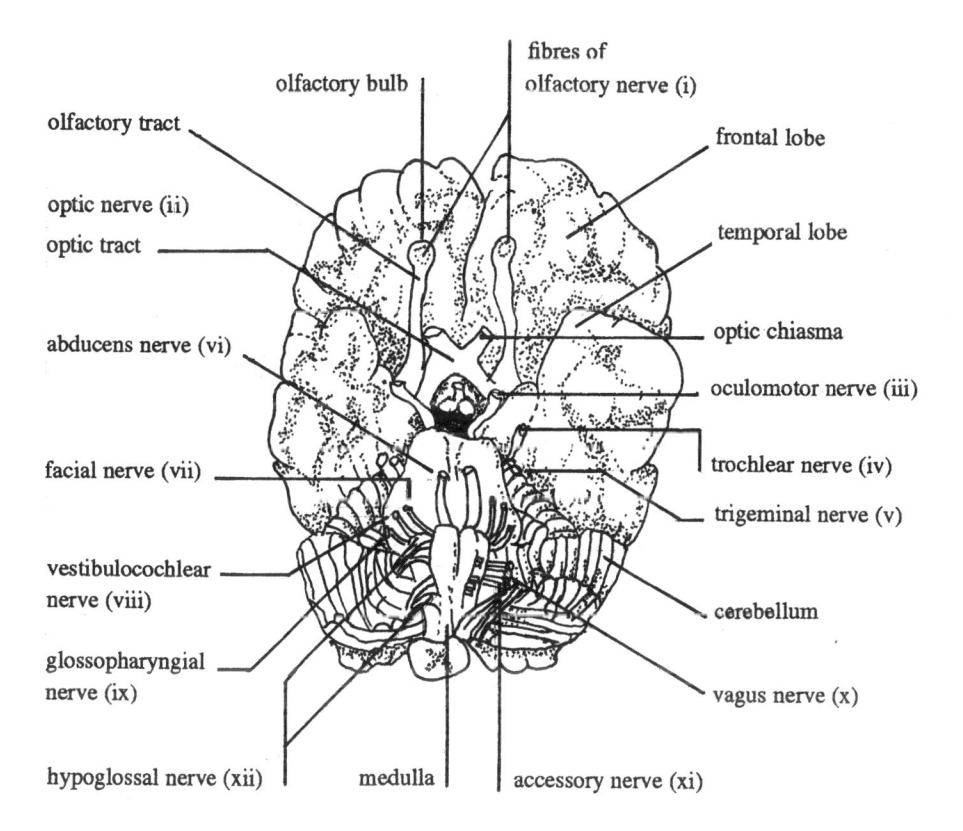

Diagram 3a Close-up section

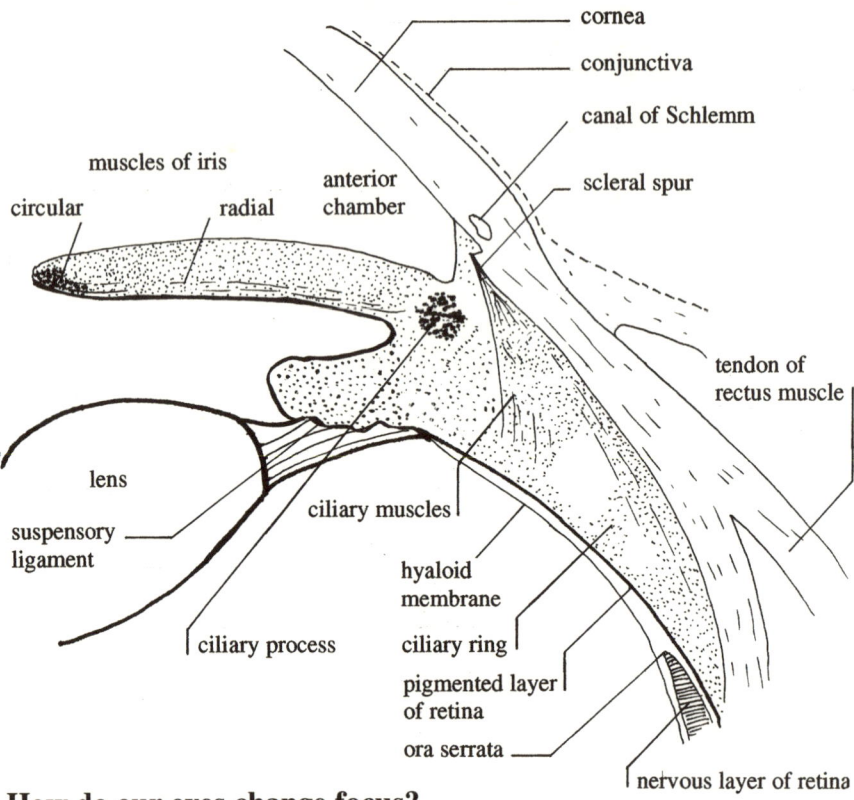

[Diagram of eye cross-section with labels: cornea, conjunctiva, canal of Schlemm, scleral spur, tendon of rectus muscle, muscles of iris (circular, radial), anterior chamber, lens, suspensory ligament, ciliary process, ciliary muscles, hyaloid membrane, ciliary ring, pigmented layer of retina, ora serrata, nervous layer of retina]

How do our eyes change focus?

Have you ever wondered how our eyes change their focus? This is an area that has brought up a divergence of viewpoints. It is within this divergence that the answer to correcting your vision hides. The old traditional view is that most important to the process of focus is the crystalline lens that lies just behind the iris. This view holds that it is this lens that is primarily responsible for and which enables the eye to change its focus. Composed of a large number of layers, almost like an onion, it is surrounded by an elastic capsule, otherwise known as the 'capsular bag'. Elastic type fibres known as the 'zonule' or suspensory ligament support this whole amazing structure. These ligaments suspend the lens from the ciliary body, which contains the circular and meridional muscles. It is these bundles of muscle fibre that when contracted change the shape of the lens and so alter the lenses focal power. It will be seen that the muscles in the eye play a crucial role in governing normal vision. We shall be exploring further exactly how they do this.

When light actually passes through the lens of the eye it is focused on the retina at the rear of the eye. It is the retina, with its receptor light sensitive cells, that then relays the information, by way of electrical impulse, through the optic nerve to the brain.

Diagram 4 Light entering the eye

Most of the bending of light (refraction) happens at the cornea. The lens also bends light but to a lesser extent. It carries out more of an image sharpening process.

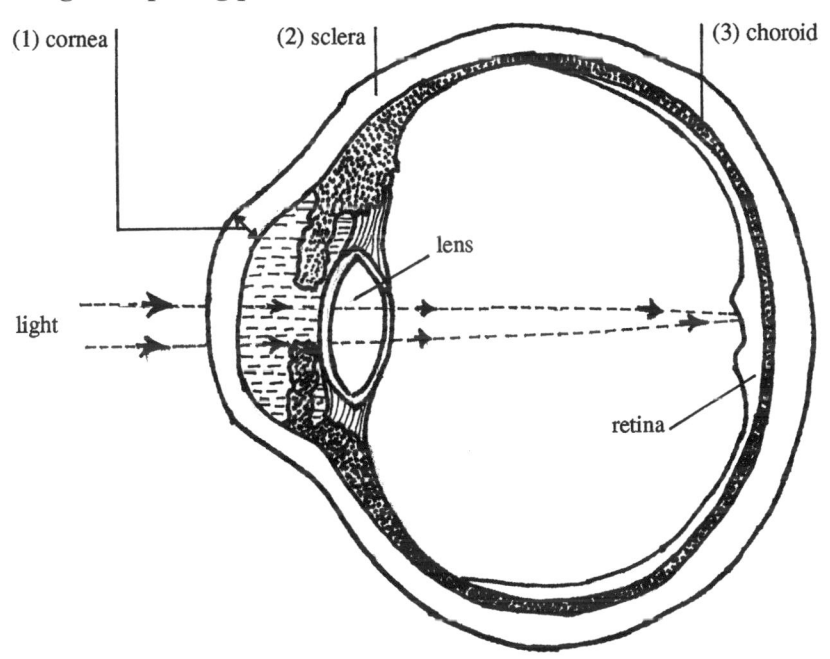

(1) cornea   (2) sclera   (3) choroid

light

lens

retina

How does the amount of light entering the eye affect your vision?

Here is a small exercise to show the importance of the amount of light entering the eye. Take a pencil and a piece of paper about six inches by six inches. Make a funnel out the paper by wrapping the paper around the pencil. Take an object that you cannot see well and look at it through the funnelled paper. Do you notice that the quality of what you see has improved? By this I mean the small area of the object that you can actually see through the funnel. It is usually better to look at some type of writing or sign. You should notice a difference. No matter how small the difference is, be alert to it and be aware that something as simple as the amount of light entering the eye can affect the quality of the eye's vision.

Five Star Vision

You may say to yourself that you can't walk around with a funnel of paper held to your eye so what good is this? It demonstrates one of the essential principles for correcting your vision. The vision of the eye depends to a great degree upon the muscles that control the eye's functions. Once these muscles are exercised and given a 'daily workout', they begin to strengthen and improve. With these improvements comes an increase in the power of your vision.

Let's go back to the ciliary body and the muscles it contains, namely the circular and meridional muscles that affect the tension on the suspensory ligaments. The old traditional view holds an importance for these muscles as it states they bring about 'accommodation' of the eyes, to focus objects at different distances. The difference in viewpoint concerns mainly the importance of the role these muscles play. The old traditional view is that accommodation actually involves the ability to 'change the shape of the lens in the eye' in order to be able to focus clearly. This view states that the normal situation is, that at rest, distant objects are in focus. When the ciliary muscles contract however, this causes tension in the suspensory ligament and as it reduces the lens swells. This is one picture of the process of accommodation that brings objects at the near point into focus. Like a normal lens, the periphery is less well focused than the centre of the lens and for this reason when the pupil is smaller, such as in bright light, vision is more acute and accurate.

There is no question that under normal conditions when the eye is 'unaccommodated', distant objects are focused on the retina but near objects are out of focus. When the eye is 'accommodated' near objects are in focus but distant objects are out of focus[2]. You will be learning later exactly how to take advantage of the eye's natural structure and operation as a way of correcting your own vision.

Diagram 5 Accommodation

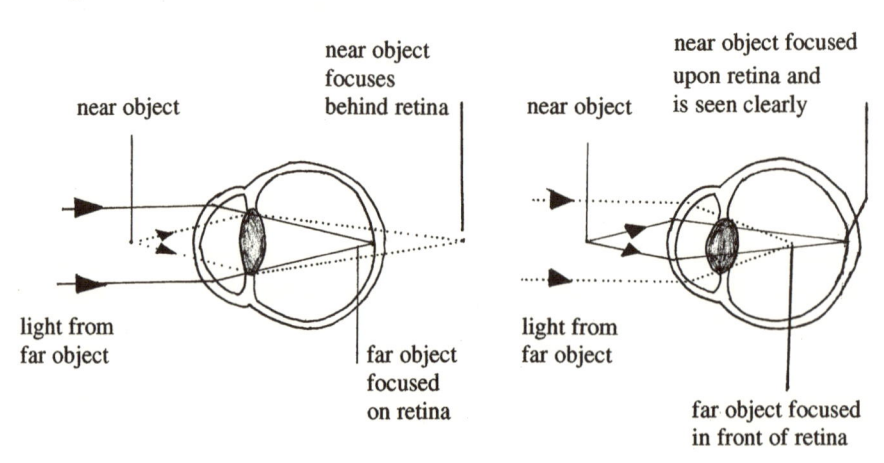

When is our vision at its sharpest?

Did you know that your vision is actually sharpest at the age of one-year-old? It has been regarded as an established fact that during early years of development, sight difficulties can often be compensated for by what has been attributed to the strong action of the ciliary muscles[3]. As the curvature of the lens is adjusted, focusing on near or far objects takes place. Other factors also come into play as you will see, but it is when the ciliary muscles weaken that the lens in the eye often cannot be made thick enough to focus on close objects. Keeping the eye muscles in strong condition is therefore vital. This will form a central element of your 'daily eye workout'.

The six muscles of the eye

Diagram 6

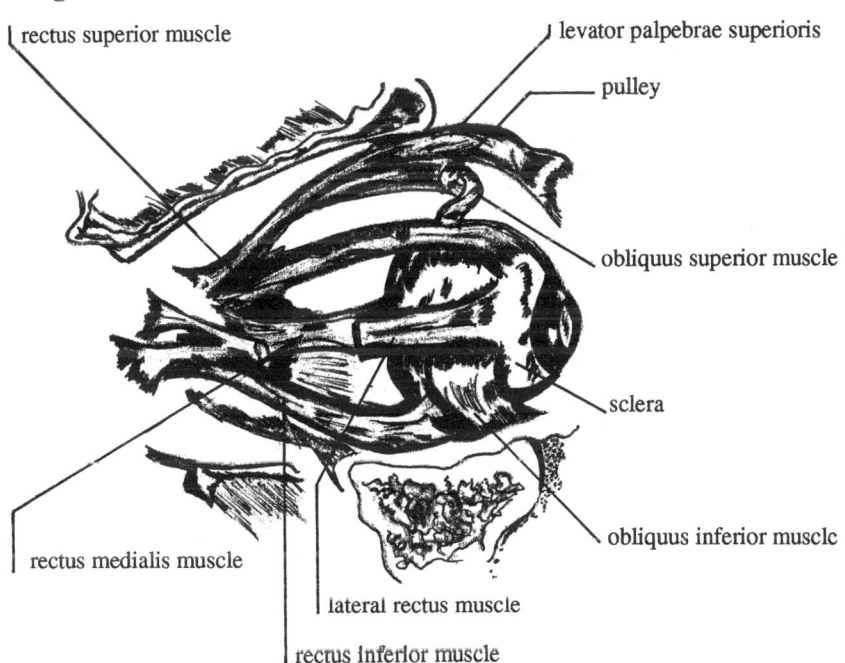

Labels: rectus superior muscle; levator palpebrae superioris; pulley; obliquus superior muscle; sclera; obliquus inferior muscle; rectus medialis muscle; lateral rectus muscle; rectus inferior muscle

Six muscles move each eye. The cranial nerves (diagram 3) give precise control over eyeball movement. The position of the eyeball is extremely important for focusing both at the near and far point.

There are two main groups that these muscles fall into:

> *oblique* inferior oblique. These move the eye downward and out. (IV nerve)
> superior oblique. These move the eye upwards and out. (III nerve)

7

rectus   superior rectus. These move the eyeball upwards. (III nerve)
inferior rectus. These move the eyeball downwards. (III nerve)
medial rectus. These move the eyeball inwards. (III nerve)
lateral rectus. These move the eyeball outwards. (IV nerve)

There can be little doubt as to the importance attached to the eye muscles in the visual process. Realising that you can begin improving your sight by strengthening your eye muscles is the first point to grasp. This is the first step on the road to sight correction. Dr Bates was the first person to recognise this fact based upon his research. He concluded that the two external muscles of the eye, the inferior and superior obliques induced the focus of the eyes (accommodation). The point where Dr Bates departs from the traditional view of the eye's ability to focus is in the function of the lens. Dr Bates concluded that the process of accommodation or focusing was brought about by a change in the shape of the eyeball, (rather than a change in the shape of the lens).

In other words, good or bad sight, short-sight or far-sight are the result of the entire eyeball changing shape - lengthening to read print in a magazine or book and shortening (from front to back) to see objects that are further away or at a distance. This was the process of accommodation, as Dr Bates proposed it. To prove the point he showed that the removal of a patient's lens (as in a cataract operation) was not a bar to re-training a patient's eye to see again at both the near and far point. A lenseless pinhole camera takes pictures in the same way. Dr Bates concluded that the lens of the eye was therefore irrelevant (or at least secondary) to the process of focusing the eye and it certainly was not the prime factor in accomplishing focus / accommodation.

Another way to view the process of the focusing of the eye is that the oblique muscles lengthen the eye for close vision and the rectus muscles flatten it for distant vision. The muscles work in a co-ordinated way to bring about focus and the shape of the eyeball is flexible, rather than fixed in shape. This is an important way of viewing the function of the eye because it leads to an entirely different approach to the question of how to correct defective sight[4].

Perhaps a somewhat surprising conclusion also reached by Dr Bates was that we have no voluntary control over these changes in the shape of the eyeball to bring about the process of focusing. These changes in shape are brought about by involuntary muscles. If this is the case how can we bring about sight correction? The answer lies in the 'co-ordination' of these muscles.

The eye muscles are no different to any other muscle within the body in so far as the way in which they function. The same principles apply. The fact they are classified as involuntary muscles means we do not ordinarily have direct conscious control over them. The result is that these muscles will behave normally when relaxed, but abnormally if tense. At least this is the case until you begin a program of visual re-education. The muscles we are concerned with are in fact extensions of the longer muscles attached to the outer part of the eyeball and have generally been referred to as 'the extrinsic involuntary muscles'.

It is important to realise that muscle co-ordination is the key. We can control voluntary muscles by moving our eyes from side to side or up and down. This however does not, on its own, bring about the process of focusing. If it did you would not have a problem with your vision as we can all do this. The involuntary muscles control adjustment and focusing of the eye and they do this in co-ordination with the voluntary muscles. Regaining the power over your co-ordination is what visual re-education is about and there are a number of factors that influence this process. Simply carrying out eye exercises on their own will not correct your eyesight. You need to appreciate the dynamic that occurs within the functioning of the visual process as a whole.

Have you ever seen a karate student performing a kata? These are a series of pre-set moves, each of which must be performed in a specific way. Each movement represents a different way of holding the body and muscles as a series of defensive moves and attacks against imaginary attackers. The difference between watching a white belt and a Dan grade carry out the same kata is noticeable even to the novice onlooker. The difference is shown by speed and grace of movement and the co-ordinated control over each movement within the kata. Yet kata is not karate. It is an element of karate. Being able to do a kata does not mean that a student can free spar in a karate contest. The kata is a building block upon which rests the totality of fighting moves that are karate. The moves from the kata train and co-ordinate the whole body, ready for putting together many different moves into a sparring contest. If someone wishes to learn karate, they are not taught the final result or sequence that is karate, they are taught all the things that will enable them to put this final result or sequence of skills together. The final result in karate is a master who is able to employ and use imaginatively, yet subconsciously, many individual skills combined in to a whole. The end result is a final skill that is something far greater than the many individual elements that it comprises. Certain things are only possible and can only be achieved by a Dan grade. These things are themselves based upon other established skills, which on the face if it would not seem to be directly used but which never the less support the higher level skill involved. When you watch a true karate master perform you will never sense a hint of nervous tension. A true master performs with total and absolute relaxation and this is the energy from which his skill flows.

Visual re-education is nowhere near as complex as learning karate, yet the same basic principles apply to the eye exercises. They are not an end in themselves, only a stepping stone we use in combination with other things, to step over and into a different place. Remember that maintaining relaxation during activity is the basis of any skill you can competently carry out. It is the true secret of any skill.

Consider the eye exercises that follow as a way of increasing co-ordination and control. Feeling a greater flow and range of response is the objective. Visual re-education is much like the karate kata. The aim is to acquire a combination of co-ordinated abilities that can be called upon at the appropriate time.

Other evidence that supports Dr Bates' findings — 'Orthokeratology'

That Dr Bates' conclusions are correct would seem to be supported when a new approach to sight correction known as 'orthokeratology' is considered. This is a way to control and reduce myopia (short-sightedness) by the use of contact lenses effectively to 'remould' the cornea. How does this work? Special lenses are made with a view to reducing the eye's optical imperfection. The cornea itself is of an 'elastic' nature and so generally returns to its original shape if changed. The idea is to wear lenses at night after the ideal corneal shape has been attained. Lenses, made from a rigid plastic material, are fitted in progressive stages to reshape the cornea towards less curvature and a more spherical shape. Eventually the aim is to stabilise a new corneal shape with lenses being worn overnight, part of the day or maybe every second or third day. The process can take anywhere between three and six months and apparently works best for conditions up to 3.0 diopters of myopia and 2.0 diopters of astigmatism.

The procedure can be time-consuming and it is not a permanent cure as there is the on-going cost of the lenses. What the procedure does show however is the principle that changing the shape of the cornea effects the ability to see clearly. The eyes' own natural way of doing this is through the eye muscles. Regain control over your eye muscles and you are on the road to improving your own sight! Exercises and ways of doing this will be demonstrated later.

Let's return to the structure of the eye:
3) The final layer of the eye is the retina. This inner layer is very delicate, containing the nerve and receptor cells that are responsible for passing on sight to the brain. These cells are known as the rods and cones. It is through a chemical process that we are able to receive light rays and then convert them into nerve impulses. A visible purple or 'rhodopsin' is contained at the tips of these rods. The interesting thing is that under the influence of light rhodopsin changes to 'lumirhodopsin'. Then a further transformation takes place by molecular rearrangement to

'metarhodopsin'. This is then able to divide into colourless retinine (associated to vitamin A) and opsin, which is a protein. While all this may seem a little technical, it is important and worthwhile to be aware of the marvellous way in which the eye works and sight is created. What happens next is extremely interesting because the reaction results in depolarisation, which is transmitted into the inner part of the rod and continues on through relay neurones and ganglion cells to the brain. We shall look at how the fascinating process of 'neurotransmission' works shortly.

Our vision is most sensitive at the fovea on the optic axis where the cones are concentrated. When we see in darkness rhodopsin is regenerated from retinine and opsin. Rhodopsin is actually a light-sensitive pigment that is broken down by light. Only a low intensity is required to generate an impulse that then passes to the brain. Have you ever noticed how it sometimes takes a little while to adjust when you enter a dark place after having been in a bright sunlight? This period of ' dark adaptation' is the result of rhodopsin that was changed by the light being re-synthesised. The cones actually stop working, the rhodopsin that was bleached by the light is formed and rod activity then increases.

Cones perform in a similar manner, except that they work only in bright light. Their pigment is iodopsin, which is not broken down by dim light. Located mainly at the fovea, they actually allow us to see colour. Divided into three types, cones contain a special opsin that is most active in response to light of wavelength 445nm (blue), 535nm (green), and 570nm (red). We need brighter light for colour vision and we see the whole visual spectrum by way of proportional stimulation. In other words, it depends upon the ratio and type of cones stimulated as to which impulses from the cones the brain interprets as colour. We will be looking later at some specific research connected to this area that will show you how to improve your vision.

The one place where the eye is not sensitive to light is the 'blind spot'. There are no rods or cones in this area where the optic nerve leaves the eye. The fact that the fovea centralis or 'yellow spot' is the most sensitive area of the eye to light can easily be demonstrated. Whenever you look at an image outside the area of the fovea, it does not look as distinct. For this reason, if you focus your eyes directly on an object, under normal conditions you will see it clearly, while surrounding objects show a lack of detail. This is in fact a central principle to correcting your own vision. The principle of 'central fixation[5]' is one that will be examined in detail and you will learn quickly and easily how to master the benefits it will give you.

Eye protection

The bony socket of the skull protects the eye itself. There is a layer of fat that cushions the eye in the socket and the eyelid, eyebrows and eyelashes give protection against outer dangers. There is also a thin membrane or transparent skin that acts as protection for the exposed surface of the eyeball and which also lines the eyelid. This is known as the conjunctiva.

Diagram 7 Eye protection

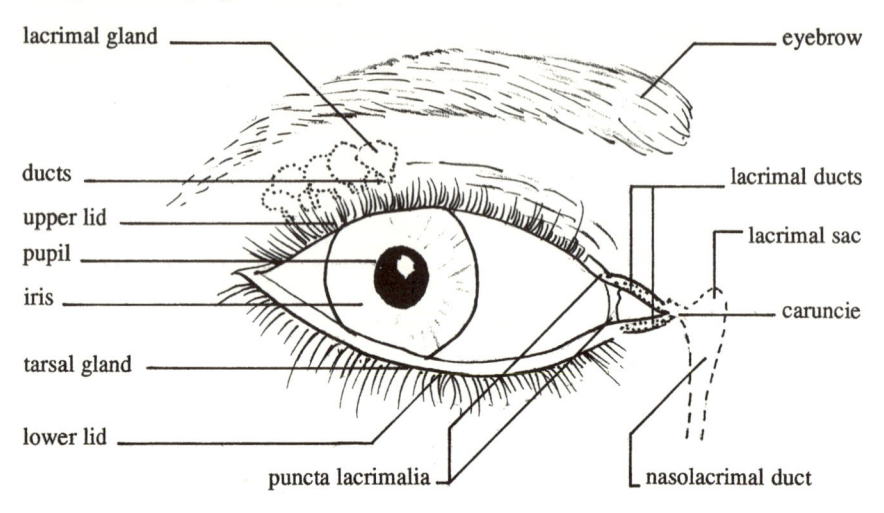

[Diagram showing the eye with labels: lacrimal gland, eyebrow, ducts, lacrimal ducts, upper lid, lacrimal sac, pupil, iris, caruncle, tarsal gland, lower lid, puncta lacrimalia, nasolacrimal duct]

Tears come from the tear (lachrymal) glands located in the outer corner of each socket or orbit of the eye. These secretions contain lysozyme, and are part of the blinking process that keeps the eye clean. This also helps to keep the conjunctiva moist. Excess fluid normally evaporates or drains away in to the nasal cavities. If you have ever had a time when a foreign body has got into your eye, maybe a piece of grit or sand, your whole lacrimal gland system powered up into overdrive. This refined defence system makes tears flood across your eye, as your eyelids seem to blink unceasingly. The irritant is usually quickly washed away.

Light and electrical impulses

As we know, the eye actually captures light and transforms it into electrical impulses that the brain then interprets as images. All other parts of the eye are formed around the retina[6] in order to;

   a) direct gaze as required,
   b) ensure the window to the eye is keep clear,
   c) control the amount of light entering the eye,
   d) make a sharp image of objects viewed.

Before we go on to look at exactly how images are formed there is another area of the eye we need to examine. The space in front of the lens is filled with a watery fluid called 'aqueous humour'. This space is called the anterior chamber and the aqueous humour is secreted by the ciliary body. It is the provision of nutrients from the aqueous fluid that nourish the cornea and the lens. (See Diagram 2).

It helps to think of the inside of the eye as being divided into two chambers, separated by the iris. The rear two-thirds of the eye, (the posterior chamber) has a semi-solid or 'jelly like' substance known as the vitreous humour. This substance is actually formed during embryonic development and will last for life. The vitreous humour helps to maintain the shape of the eyeball[7] and the position of the lens and retina as well as contributing to intraocular pressure. Between this and the anterior chamber lies the lens. These fluids also help to maintain the shape of the eyeball and also contribute with the lens in refracting light entering the pupil, as it forms a focused image on the retina, (the innermost layer of the eye).

The process by which we form images

The retina contains the sensitive nerve endings that actually convert the light that has been focused by the lens and other parts of the eye into electrical impulses. Light itself is the primary stimulus that starts the whole process. Light is made up of small particles called 'photons'. These photons travel in straight lines called 'rays'. So how do light rays help us to see objects? When a light ray strikes an object it rebounds from it and enters our eyes. As the light ray enters the eye it is refracted or 'bent' by the visual process. It is the cornea and lens and the shape of the eyeball itself that are responsible for bending light in this way and this leads to the rays being focused on the retina, where an image is formed.

Diagram 7a

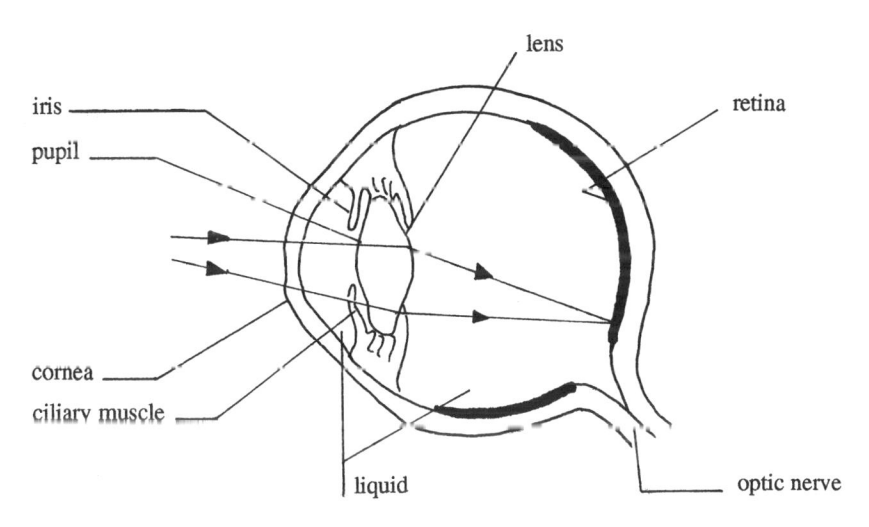

Imperfect images

What is extraordinary is that the images formed on the retina are 'imperfect'. The focusing process also does a very odd thing. It turns the image upside down and back to front.

In addition, the make-up of the retina means that images are left with 'holes' in them. The important thing is that it is the cerebrum, (a part of the brain - see below) that 'interprets' these images. How does it do this? It turns the images the right way up, corrects positioning by turning the image the right way around and fills in the 'holes'. It is important to be aware that it is the brain's 'interpretative' abilities that are responsible for a great many of the functions is producing vision. The other important point to be aware of is that the function of interpretation is 'learnt'. Although an object is seen the wrong way up, we 'learn' to see it the right way up as a learned experience. When vision is defective, the power of 'interpretation' has also become defective. You will be learning in later chapters how to regain control over your own power of interpretation and so your power of vision.

Your brain therefore makes images by using the electrical impulses that are transmitted to the vision centre in the brain by the optic nerve. This direct connection into the brain extends from the rear of the eyeball. So, what is the process by which these messages are transmitted to the brain? The question is of interest not only for purposes of our vision, but also to understand the way in which our whole nervous system works. How does our brain receive messages?

The human nervous system

Humans have a very complex nervous system which can be thought of as consisting of two parts, the central nervous system and the peripheral nervous system. The peripheral nervous system[8] links the central nervous system to all parts of the body. The 'cerebrum' in our brains is the centre of intelligence and controls our conscious activities. It also co-ordinates the impulses carried by sensory nerves such as the eye. Nerves are made up of large numbers of nerve cells known as 'neurones'. It is at this micro-level that we have to look to see how communication takes place. Each sensory nerve contains neurones that carry nerve impulses from receptors to the central nervous system. The nerve impulse actually passes down a neurone because of changes in electrical charges on the inside and outside of a neurone. This happens by depolarisation, which is the reversing of positive and negative charges located inside and outside the neurone. How are these electrical charges produced? Naturally, by ions present in the body, particularly sodium and potassium. This process occurs in the surface membrane of the neurone before, during and after an impulse passes along it.

THE MARVEL THAT IS THE HUMAN EYE

The procedure really is quite remarkable. At rest, the surface membrane of a neurone is polarised. This means there are more positive charges on the outside. When an impulse is started the balance of charges is reversed or 'depolarised'. This action continues along the neurone, until soon after re-polarisation occurs again. This is not the end of the journey. There are gaps at the end of each nerve cell known as 'synapses'. Impulses must be able to cross these gaps. This is achieved by the release of a chemical or 'neurotransmitter' to the target cell. This transmitter causes the depolarisation of the surface membrane of the target cell. Next, an enzyme breaks down the neurotransmitter very quickly after the impulse passes. This makes it ready to perform the same task again. It is in this remarkable and fascinating way that electrical impulses pass from the eyeball, through the optic nerve to the brain. This is the mechanics of how we see!

Before we leave the micro-elements that show how the eye functions let's look at a cross section through the retina. Diagram 8 shows a section through the retina.

Diagram 8 A section through the retinus structure

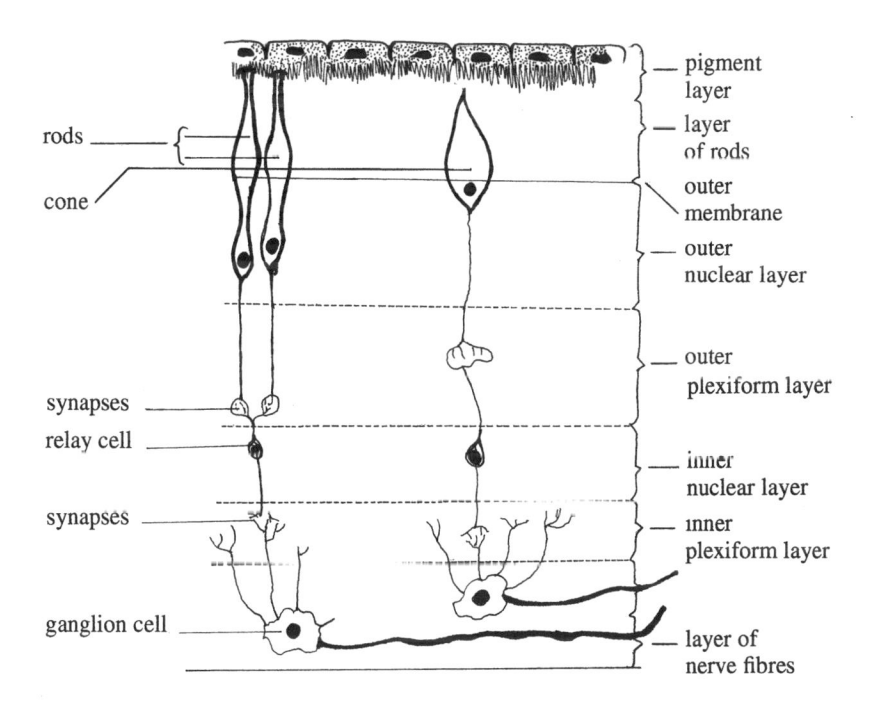

1 Light must pass through the neurones before it stimulates rods and cones.
2 The retina can distinguish detail more clearly as impulses are sent

down receptor neurones from different parts of an image. Each cone synapses with a single receptor neurone.
3　A single receptor neurone synapses with several rods. This means the retina is more sensitive to dim light.
4　Impulses from the rods and cones (also known as photoreceptors) are transmitted to the optic nerve fibres through the bipolar and ganglion cells.
5　The eye receives blood from the central artery via the central vein. Both run in the middle of the optic nerve.

Binocular vision

Our field of vision, the area seen by each eye, overlaps. Many of the things we see are seen at slightly different angles by both eyes. This is not shown in the final image as we see it, so how does this transformation take place? Consider that the images we see are stimulated on two retinas and this gives a 'stereoscopic' effect. What this actually does is allow our brains to judge depth or three-dimensional effect and also speed and distance when assessing objects. Try the difference for yourself by attempting to touch an object with one eye closed.

In accordance with the principle of 'contralateral representation', the nervous connections from the retina in the right half of the visual field are relayed to the visual cortex of the left cerebral hemisphere of the brain and vice versa. There is a slight difference to the normal principle as the optic nerves merge and cross at the optic chiasma. The nerves cross, yet only impulses from the medial retina cross over. Impulses from the lateral retina do not cross. This means each side of the optic cortex receives some impulses from both eyes.

Colour Blindness

We inherit normal colour vision as a dominant gene and if it is present, its specific features are shown on the 'X' chromosome. The 'X' chromosome is one of the sex chromosomes. Males have one 'X' and one 'Y' chromosome, whereas females have two 'X' chromosomes. You will remember that we have three types of cones, which means we are able to see colour. When one of these cones is missing, usually those affecting red or green, colour blindness results. Red - green colour blindness is inherited as a recessive gene. The condition most commonly effects males who only have one 'X' chromosome and who inherit the recessive gene. Women are more fortunate in this respect as they will only become colour blind if they inherit the recessive gene from both parents.

So what have you learnt?

Before we move forward in the next chapter to have an in-depth look at the properties of vision itself, the basics we have explored in this chapter about the structure of our eyes teaches you some very important things in understanding how to rectify your eyesight. Conventional thought is along the lines that permanent changes in the shape of the eye cause defective vision. Dr W Bates was the first to challenge this theory. His conclusions, after studying and researching many eye defects and diseases were that defective vision is due to 'functional aberration'. In other words, when the

Diagram 9 The optic nerves

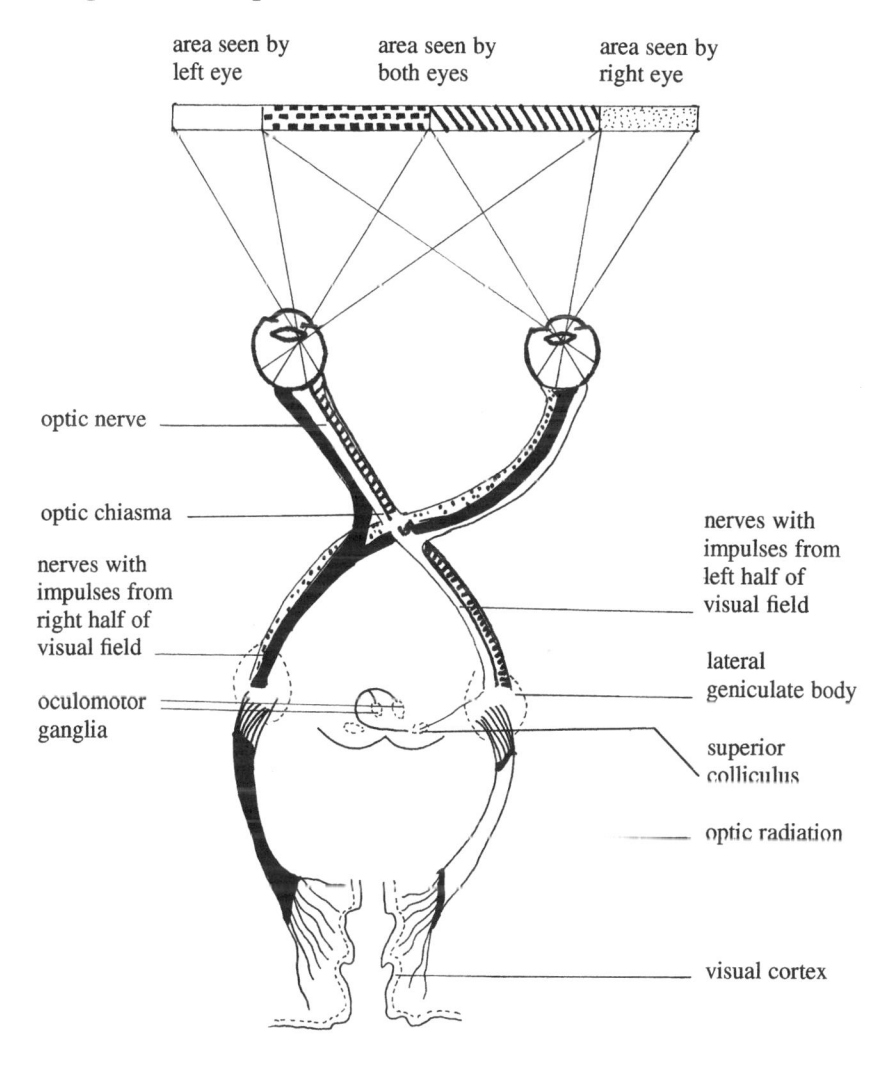

eye is used to look at an object, (as said earlier), it is the external muscles that surround the eyeball that are used to change the shape of the eye itself. So when a distant object is being viewed, the external muscles move the back of the eye towards the lens. When a close object is being viewed, the reverse happens. What this means is that it is muscular changes that alter the shape of the eyeball. Let's proceed on the following assumption for the time being. If an individual is short-sighted (myopic) or long-sighted (hypermetropic), they have eyeballs that have been misshapen by the actions of the external muscles that are functioning incorrectly. In order to 'maintain' a state of defective vision, a person has to be doing something specific! Unconsciously keeping the eyeball in a shape that makes viewing objects in that way difficult and/or interpreting information in an inconsistent way. This is not just supposition, as there is hard evidence from research that shows how easily any of us is able to do this. We shall take a look at this important and overlooked research shortly. The research is also important for another reason. It ties together the two prime factors in normal vision. Muscle control and 'perceptual control'. What do I mean by perceptual control? This is a crucial and fascinating area that we will be exploring in some depth later in the book. Once you have learned to control the way your own perception works, you will follow on by restoring your own vision to normal! *This is the power of your perception!*

Let's return to the external muscles of the eyeballs. Defective vision is a two-part process. It starts with external muscles of the eyeball being 'strained'. As soon as you begin to relieve these exertions and pressures, the eye muscles begin to function normally and vision begins to improve. The beauty of the restoration process is that improving the power of your perception also increases your visual ability, so improvements in each area become dynamic and self-generating.

Dr Bates has applied these principles to thousands of patients and many others have independently testified to their effectiveness. I have personally achieved the results shown earlier in the book. There is no doubt that these methods do work.

Another very important point to be aware of is that strained eye muscles and mental tension seem to be inextricably linked. Tangled together within the same thread, the job is to begin unravelling and separating them in order to correct them. The order of 'binding together' is that mental tension provides the food from which the physical strain in the eye muscles feeds. It can become a euphemism, all too common in today's society, to quote overwork, worry, fear and anxiety as the cause of many of our ills. The terms have become generalised and vague, yet when applied to defective vision, they really are the root cause of the defects that originate in our perceptions and manifest themselves as mental tension.

The fact is that there is now an increasingly powerful force of opinion moving toward a new interpretation of the eye's function and workings and the way in which defective sight can be corrected. So let's begin an exploration of the ways in which you can do something positive about these things. There are general and specific exercises that will train the parts of your visual function that really count. The parts that can achieve real results for you. So let's press forward and pierce into the mystery that is our vision.

---

[1] Research has shown that blue-eyed people have more sensitive corneas than brown-eyed people. There is a steady grading of eye sensitivity between bright blue-eyed people and those who have dark brown eyes who are much less sensitive to light.

[2] A very common problem is that people with defective vision try to focus upon everything at once. This problem will be considered later.

[3] New research referred to later in the book however challenges this view. 'Cellular Learning and the Theory of Emmetropia'.

[4] Herman Ludwig Ferdinand von Helmholtz (1821-1894) invented the opthalmoscope and wrote the *Treatise on Physiological Optics*. Although over one hundred years old it is still the basis for modern optics.

[5] Also now called 'central alignment'.

[6] The retina is made up of two layers. If these two layers become torn or separated a 'detached retina' occurs. This gives visual problems that can include blindness. The problem can be rectified by using a laser to join or 'weld' the two layers back together.

[7] If you have you ever wondered why the eye sometimes looks like it is bulging slightly there is a good reason for this. The eyeball itself is almost spherical with the front having a radius that is smaller than the curvature of the rest of the eye, which is normally about 2.5cm. This gives the impression that it is 'bulging' a little.

[8] The peripheral nervous system consists of nerves running to and from the central nervous system. There are two parts, those nerves controlling voluntary activities and those controlling involuntary or autonomic activities, e.g. blinking.

CHAPTER 2

UNRAVELLING THE MYSTERY OF VISION

> "You see things and you say 'WHY'? But I dream things that never were and I say 'why not?'"
> **George Bernard Shaw (1856–1950), playwright**

I touched upon light and its properties in the last chapter. Light is the prime energy that makes our visual process possible in the first place. So what is light and how does our sense of sight interact with it? What is the normal range of response for normal sight? It will help if we remind ourselves now of some of the basic but vital facts concerning light.

Light is a visible form of energy that we detect with our eyes. Some objects produce their own form of light and are 'luminous' sources of energy. This would include the sun, electric lamps etc. All other objects are illuminated by these forms of light and reflect into our eyes. That includes the page you are reading now and the words on it. The moon is another example. As we know, light travels in straight lines as waves of energy. You probably remember the experiments at school showing the motion of waves, like water waves on a pond and the ripple effect. Light travels in a similar wave motion.

The really incredible thing about light is its speed. It travels at 186,000 miles a second or 300,000 km/s. this is about a million times faster than the speed of sound. This is fast enough to travel around the world eight times in one second! You may recall that light takes about eight minutes to travel from the sun to earth. There is the old joke that asks; "what if the sun went out seven minutes ago?" – we actually see the sun as it was eight minutes ago! Herein lies another of the anomalies of vision. We do not see what we 'believe' we see. You will probably also recall that many other stars in the solar system are much further away than our own sun. The light from these stars can take 1000 million years to reach us. This means we are seeing these stars as they were 1000 million years ago! Some of these stars may even no longer exist. These qualities of light energy itself mean we would in such circumstances be seeing an optical illusion. The thing we *believe* we see no longer exists.

These are all basic facts we are familiar with. What is important are the implications of these facts and what they mean for our visual process. From what we have discovered about the structure of the eye and how we 'learn to see', you can begin questioning your own generalisations and beliefs about the way in which you see. Your visual process is actually a manipulation of certain patterns and criteria within the environment. This manipulation normally happens automatically and subconsciously. Know now that you can begin to control this natural manipulation process. As you learn to govern and control the process, rather than letting it rule your visual capabilities, you will find your vision improves quickly and easily.

Visible light that we can see and respond to has a wavelength of about 1/200th of a millimetre. Some wavelengths are shorter than this so we cannot see them. Examples include X–rays and gamma rays. Again, when a wavelength is longer than visible light, we cannot see it. Radio waves and heat waves fall into this category. Together these types of waves are called *electromagnetic waves*. As you think about your power of sight, bear in mind that visible light only forms a small part of the *electromagnetic spectrum*.

Diagram 1 showing electromagnetic spectrum

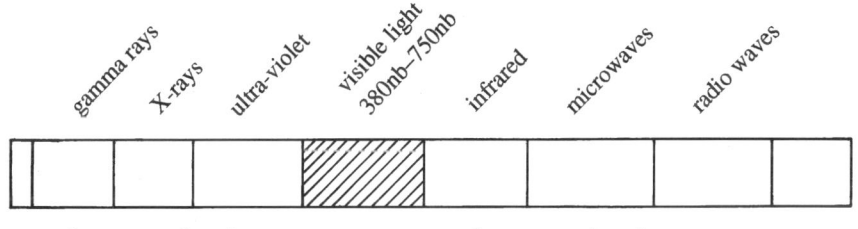

gamma rays | X-rays | ultra-violet | visible light 380nb-750nb | infrared | microwaves | radio waves

shorter wavelength   longer wavelength

Referring to the diagram above you will see the range into which visible light falls. Visible light itself is further divided into the colours of the visible spectrum. Do you remember the experiments at school where light was passed through a prism to show the colours? Exactly the same effect occurs when sunlight passes through raindrops, so creating the wonderful rainbow effect.

So what is colour?

What causes the colours in a rainbow? How do we see grass as green? We see objects as coloured when that particular wavelength colour is being reflected. So if we see the green leaves on a tree it is because the leaves are reflecting the green wavelength. Black as a colour is created by the total absorption of all wavelengths. White, however, is really a mixture of the several colours that can be split by the prism. So, the colours of the rainbow are caused by the *refraction* (bending when light passes from one property or medium to another) and dispersion of white light into the spectrum.

Knowing the properties of light is important for correcting your own eyesight. As you refresh your memory and remind yourself of the characteristics of light energy, consider the real facts about light when you consider what is said about sight correction. The real facts about light are not the way we normally think and interpret in order to form our sight. Returning to the prism, we know it shows the different wavelengths of light. When light enters a prism or other substance like glass, these wavelengths slow down, but each by a different amount. This results in refraction of different colours as they pass through the prism at different angles. Let's be a little more specific. Violet is the shortest wavelength and so it is slowed down the most. Its refraction is therefore through the largest angle. Red is a longer wavelength and so it slows down less. The result is that red is deviated through a smaller angle.

Diagram 2

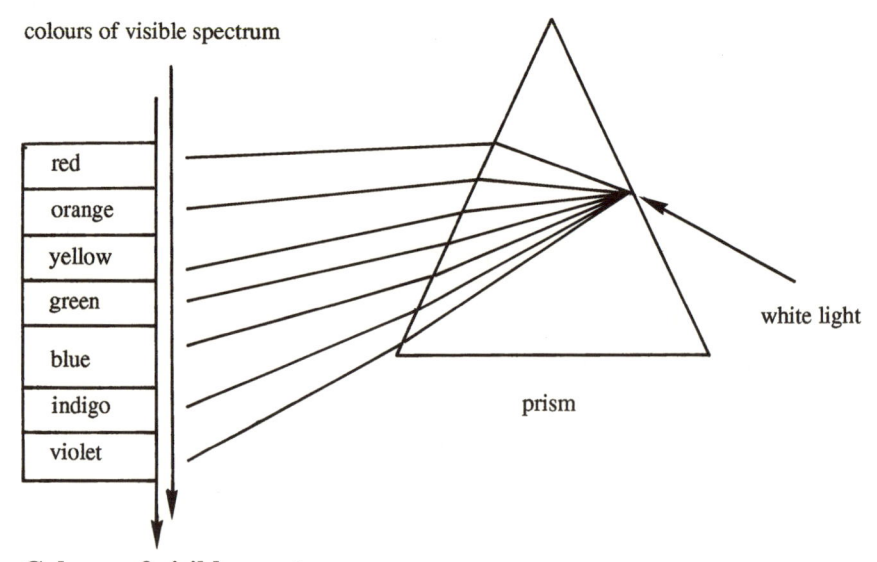

colours of visible spectrum

| red |
| orange |
| yellow |
| green |
| blue |
| indigo |
| violet |

white light

prism

Colours of visible spectrum

There are three primary colours that make up white. These are red, green and blue. The secondary colours are yellow, magenta and cyan. In appropriate combinations they also can make up white light. If you have ever wondered why shadows are sometimes formed, this is because rays of light continue to travel in straight lines, while others are stopped by an object. The type of shadow formed depends upon the source and the size of the generating light. Our sight has to contend with all manner of variations in light and this can often be responsible for changes in the quality of what we see. It is important to realise that we do not have perfect vision at all times or in all circumstances[1]. It is easy to form the false belief that our eyesight should be perfect all the times. People with defective vision tend to have this attitude. The example given earlier is a good one. We need to be taught and know as a fact, that our eyesight will not be perfect at the near point, when we are focusing upon objects at the far point. In the same way, our sight will not be perfect for objects seen at the far point, when we are focused upon an object at the near point. When our sight starts to deteriorate we subconsciously begin to lump everything together as 'evidence' of poor sight. We start to notice what we can't see. Consciously or subconsciously we soon fall into a self-generating loop of deteriorating eyesight. The fact is that as your vision deteriorates, you may begin to start doing things with your eyes and visual process that are impossible!

Let's return to the simple phenomena of a shadow. An understanding will be most helpful in appreciating some of the aims and effects of the correction exercises that follow later in the book.

There is an old experiment of a small electric lamp, a table tennis ball and a white screen. When the small lamp is turned on and the ball placed just in front of the light, a dark shadow is produced on the screen. The shadow has sharp defined edges.

Diagram 3

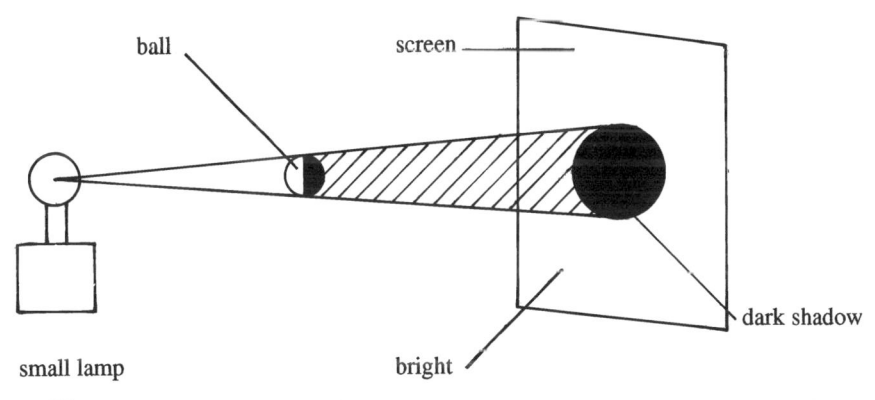

The same experiment with a large lamp produces a different effect entirely. Although the centre of the shadow still has a dark area, the surrounding edges now vary in brightness, from being very dark near the centre, to being very bright at the outer edges where more light can reach the area.

The same type of effect is produced when a shadow is produced on a clear sunny day. Contrast this with a shadow on a cloudy day. The 'characteristics' of the shadow differs in each case. This is all very simple, basic stuff, yet having attention drawn to these points specifically is important. Realising and knowing that we have different quality to our vision under different circumstances helps us to start identifying those situations, rather than just generalising and expecting our vision to be perfect at all times. You will learn about 'generalisation' and the impact it has upon your visual process in later chapters.

Diagram 4

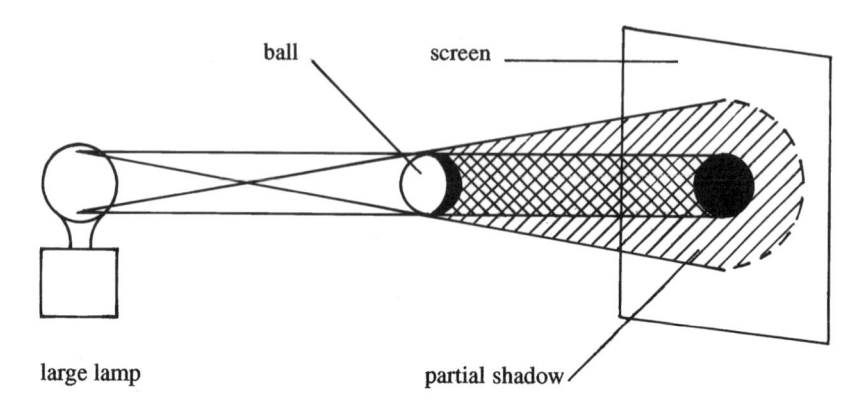

(Diagram showing a large lamp on the left, a ball, a screen, and a partial shadow cast on the screen.)

Refraction

Another property of light is refraction. This is the bending of light as it passes from one environment to another. A good example is placing a straw in a glass of water. The straw appears to bend as it enters the water. In the same way, swimming pools look shallower than they actually are. Although rays of light normally travel in a straight line they can be bent or refracted and the fact is that light travels more slowly through glass than it does through air. Lights speed is slowed to about two thirds as it passes through glass. A good comparison is a squad of soldiers marching on concrete and then moving onto mud. The speed of the march slows as the transfer takes place from one area to another. Walking on mud generally means that the speed of marching is reduced.

This is one of the crucial principles in the operation with our own eyes. Our eyes use refraction to bend light so that it is focused correctly upon the retina. This is where other components of the eye come into play. The cornea, aqueous humour, lens and vitreous humour all help to refract light. Our eye lens is of a biconvex nature and in conjunction with the shape of the eye itself, it means that the light is forced to converge onto a single point in the retina, the *focal point*. By comparison a biconcave lens results in divergence of light rays.

The process of sight actually involves us in 'focusing in', both on near and distant objects. Greater refraction occurs when we focus on a near object. As we already know, the image made on the retina is actually upside down and reversed. It is corrected by our special processing abilities in the

Diagram 5

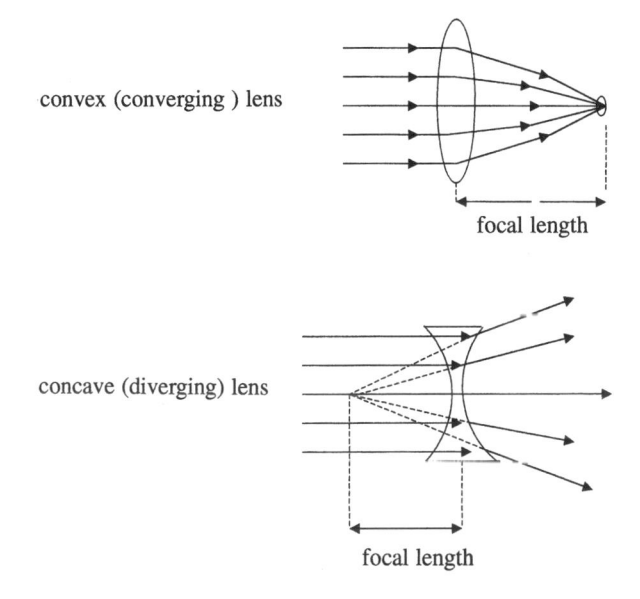

convex (converging) lens

focal length

concave (diverging) lens

focal length

central nervous system. Again we know that we 'learn' how to do this, although it is a totally subconscious process. **We now arrive at a very important point in understanding how we see and how we can learn to correct our vision.**

Diagram 6 Images become inverted. A convex lens like the one in our eyes turn an image upside down because the light that enters at the bottom part of the lens is refracted upwards and vice versa.

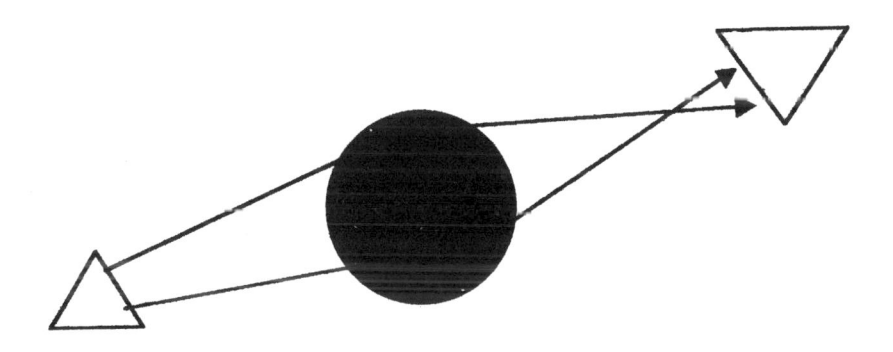

The review of light and its basic properties that we have looked at so far brings to our conscious attention the great number of variables that we normally combine and overcome in order to see any image. If you think about it, even when our sight is defective, we are still carrying out a wonderful array of operations that results in some form of sight. Placing corrective lenses in front of the eye can rectify the immediate problem of image definition, yet the rest of the subconscious process is still active.

A motivating force that will propel your own desire for normal vision!

As human beings we are extremely adaptable and we are never too old or too young to learn new things. As long ago as 1928 Theodore Erismann from the University of Innsbruck conducted an outstanding range of experiments to show not only how adaptable the human eye is, but also how adaptable our ability to learn new ways of perceiving can be.

Using a number of volunteers, Erismann constructed some special goggles that put a prism directly in front of each eye. He also managed to interchange the visual field by moving it from top to bottom or from left to right. In a further experiment he was able to provide a pair of glasses that enabled the volunteer to see only to the rear of his head. This gave the impression of having eyes in the back of the head!

The results that these experiments provided were truly quite remarkable from the perspective of our visual capabilities. The wearers found that within a couple of weeks their eyes had adapted! The report is that one volunteer wore these goggles transposing left to right for several weeks. The adaptation was so successful the wearer was able to drive his motorcycle through Innsbruck while wearing the goggles!

> "...The reasonable man adapts himself to the world. The unreasonable one persists in trying to adapt the world to himself. Therefore all progress depends upon the unreasonable man."

George Bernard Shaw (1856-1950), playwright

In a further experiment at the same university, Ivo Kholer reported the effects of volunteers wearing specially designed glasses that produced a blue-tinted environment for the wearer when he looked to the left. On looking to the right, a yellow tinted environment was created. Imagine wearing glasses like this for any period of time? The results are not what you would expect. The wearers found that not only did they mange to adapt to these glasses, the colour distortions also disappeared! The remarkable thing is that our visual process and perception allows us to adapt and to harmonise. **The wearers were able to introduce a corrective element and so neutralise the initially confusing effect of the glasses.**

Let's look at a further example of Kohler's work. **He proved that we are able to adjust our behaviour to account for 'new rules'.** By rules, we can give this a far broader meaning than usual and think of rules in terms of our 'subconscious rules for interpretation of our environment'. Kohler showed that our eyes will also adapt to variable as well as constant distortions. He took a pair of glasses and fitted the lenses with prisms. These prisms had their bases pointing to the right. You can imagine how this would totally distort anyone's whole sense of vision. The volunteers found when commencing the exercise that upon turning their head left and then glancing right, an image was produced that was steadily contracted. The reverse was true upon turning the head right and glancing left. The image would expand! Now not many people would expect to be able to live with that type of distortion.

The amazing thing is that after the first few weeks this distortion disappeared! The eyes somehow managed to adapt to their 'new world'. In actual fact, what happened is that a new learning process took place. In other words the visual process learned to 'expand' contracting images and to 'contract' expanding images, related to and determined by the position of the head and eyes. What was also reported was that when the glasses were removed, after having being worn for this period, the adaptation continued to operate! This volunteer continued to see the world in exactly the same way as he had done when first putting on these 'prism' glasses. Again the interesting point is that the effect did disappear, but only after a couple of days. Re-adaptation was made up on it becoming clear the 'new behaviour' was no longer required.

If **you are an perspicacious reader** you may already have begun challenging your beliefs about your own visual process and indeed you may be starting to **feel excited at the possibilities** that this research holds for you. If you are determined **to correct your own vision**, you will not have to do anything as bizarre as these volunteers had to experience. Your road to sight correction is far easier and simply requires a little discipline in your thinking. Your eyes and your perception are not stuck and capable of responding to situations in only one fixed pattern. Allow yourself to begin thinking of your complete visual process as an extremely adaptable and flexible endowment. Adopt this attitude now, as we shall be demolishing many of the myths that have prevented our culture as a whole from using natural methods of sight correction in the past.

The experiments we have just looked at prove and provide the evidence that your sense of sight will change its mechanics to become suitable in a specific situation or for a specific purpose. You will soon learn how to harness this natural power of harmonisation and synchronisation that is your genetic inheritance. **The ability to correct your sight lies within you.**

> "...sometimes a composition must be recast into a new form, after which it will perform perfectly..."

The traditional way of correcting defective sight

The way in which light is refracted through the eye has been the basis for eyesight correction for over one hundred years. The distance between the lens and the focal point in the eye is called the *focal length*. Under normal conditions the incoming light is refracted or bent according to the distance from the object we are looking at. More refraction occurs when we look at near objects. Diagram 7 below shows the differences when focusing upon two types of light sources.

Diagram 7

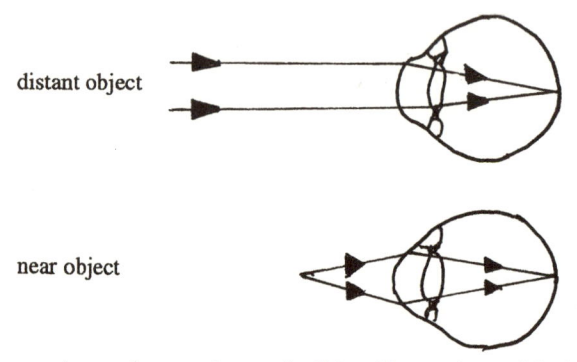

distant object

near object

As we know, the eyeball itself together with the lens will change shape to increase refraction when viewing a near object. The lens becomes more curved and under normal conditions the eyeball lengthens as the muscles react. This permits the lens to bulge and become more curved as the pull is reduced on the suspensor ligaments. By contrast, when we look at distant objects the ciliary muscles are relaxed which results in the suspensor ligaments pulling the lens flat. The rectus muscles also flatten to give the eyeball shape for distant vision. At such a moment there is little refraction taking place in the lens. When you are able to focus upon distant objects in this way the far point is at 'infinity'. This whole process is commonly known as accommodation, which we examined earlier.[2]

The near point is the closest point at which we are to see clearly by focusing on an object. Remember that part of the function involves the pupil constricting reflexly, thus reducing light entry and focusing it through the most curved part of the lens. It is a part of the ability of the lens to help increase refraction as part of the process of accommodation. Also required for focusing on near objects is automatic convergence of the eyeballs, which stops the production of two images that would otherwise cause double vision, (diplopia). If you ask someone to look at the end of their nose you will see how the eyes are caused to converge. The normal distance of near point vision for adults is usually about twenty-five centimetres from the eyes, for example if reading a book. You can evaluate your own near point by holding a book at arms' length and gradually moving it closer in order to find the distance at which you can focus clearly without straining your eyes. Make a note of this distance, as it can then be used as one of the measures with which to judge your overall improvements.

It is a fact that with age the lens loses some of its elasticity and so the ability to accommodate. The condition is known as *presbyopia*[3]. The lens can become less elastic and denser because the amount of fibres increase. While these changes may occur, *it is how they are interpreted that is important.* What we do about them. We are all familiar with the normal response, which is to prescribe optical lenses. From what you now know about the ability of your visual process to adapt, what if you become attuned to these changes that occur and use your own natural ways of adjusting to these changes? It is a fact that your visual process is always in a constant state of flux. The process of accommodation itself is always changing. If you really begin to think about it, it is lazy and totally unnatural to impose a fixed response or straight jacket solution upon your visual process, when what it actually needs to function correctly is 'flexibility'. As you move toward understanding this natural need for flexibility, you are able to behave in new and different ways that begin giving you real solutions to your eyesight problems. Part of the problem so far has been not knowing what your visual process requires and why. You will find that you will begin generating your own new solutions once you have the reasoning for doing so.

> "the assumption must be that those who can see value only in **tradition,** or versions of it, deny man's ability to adapt to changing circumstances"
>
> **Stephen Bayley**

Glasses and other optical aids do nothing to 'help' the existing visual problem you may have. By help I mean resolving the problem. Speak to anyone who has worn glasses for any length of time and the realisation is self evident. Glasses and other optical aids are a way of helping individuals *cope* with their visual problems, rather than finding a way of tackling the problem at its root cause. There is a world of difference in approach to the solution. We can either leave the cause of the visual problem in place and provide solutions to the difficulties thrown up or the problem can be dissolved at its roots, before it becomes a permanent feature. Take away the problem and there is no need for the traditional solutions on offer.

As you can see for yourself, the visual system is one that requires flexibility. Optical aids are in reality a way of sustaining a current muscle imbalance. It is a way of solidifying and maintaining the root cause of the problem. The eyes are actually being prevented from recovering because of the nature of the solution historically offered.

To hammer home the point let's just consider for a moment another conclusion that can be reached from the experiments done with the volunteers who wore the prism glasses. Their eyes adapted to these strange circumstances. If we contrast the wearing of optical aids, what this means is that although initially correcting the 'effects' of your problem, your eyesight will adapt to incorporate your problem. Why would any discerning, intelligent person want to accept, aggravate and eventually intensify their visual problem?

The answer lies, as has already been said, in becoming much more aware of your visual process and what the feedback that you receive actually means. If you have worn glasses or other optical aids for some time, your eyes became accustomed to artificial support over a period of time. Visual correction will be accomplished and maintained in exactly the same way.

Long-sightedness

Long-sightedness occurs when a person can focus on distant objects but not near objects. This can occur when the shape of the eyeball is too short (for the reasons already discussed) or perhaps the lens is too thin, which depends upon the ciliary muscles being squeezed. The rays of light are focused toward a point 'behind' the retina. The traditional solution was a converging (convex) lens. It is an ingenious solution that accounts for the natural properties of light energy. The rays of light from the object are converged so that the eye is in effect 'tricked'. As far as the eye is concerned the rays of light *appear* to be coming from a near point. In this way focusing on the correct part of the retina is made to take place.

The physiology of the eye means that it is working hardest, in real terms, for close vision. A factor we will look at again is the 'fixation' of the eye muscles. This is where the eye muscles become adjusted to a particular distance, and so causing a particular refractive problem. Think about reading as one common activity. When you read a book you will find that you always place it at a pre-determined distance that is comfortable for you. You may not have been conscious about this until now, but check it out for yourself. Continuous focusing in this (or any other position) soon leads to the eye muscles subconsciously adopting this specific physiology as 'normal'. Over time, the eye muscles begin to lose their ability to respond through their natural range, and so fail to retain the required degree of flexibility for normal vision. The muscles become weakened. Sight correction therefore involves giving your eyes an **easy daily 'eye workout'.** We shall be building a natural momentum for this as we progress forward through the process of visual correction.

Long-sighted people have a similar problem to that already described, as the eye becomes used to a physiology that focuses over a distance, it eventually begins to make viewing near objects difficult.

Eye muscles and perception

Some people ask how do we know how much muscle correction is required for our eyes before vision begins to improve? This is a question that does not really require a specific answer. As you will find out when we examine the power of your perception in Chapter 6, the two processes are dynamic and interactive. Each compliments the other and once these two aspects start working together properly, in a co-ordinated way, **improvement happens quicker than you would expect**. It is in effect utilising the known principles of the prism experiments carried out by Erismann and Kohler.

Diagram 8 Illustrations of refractive conditions and traditional forms of correction

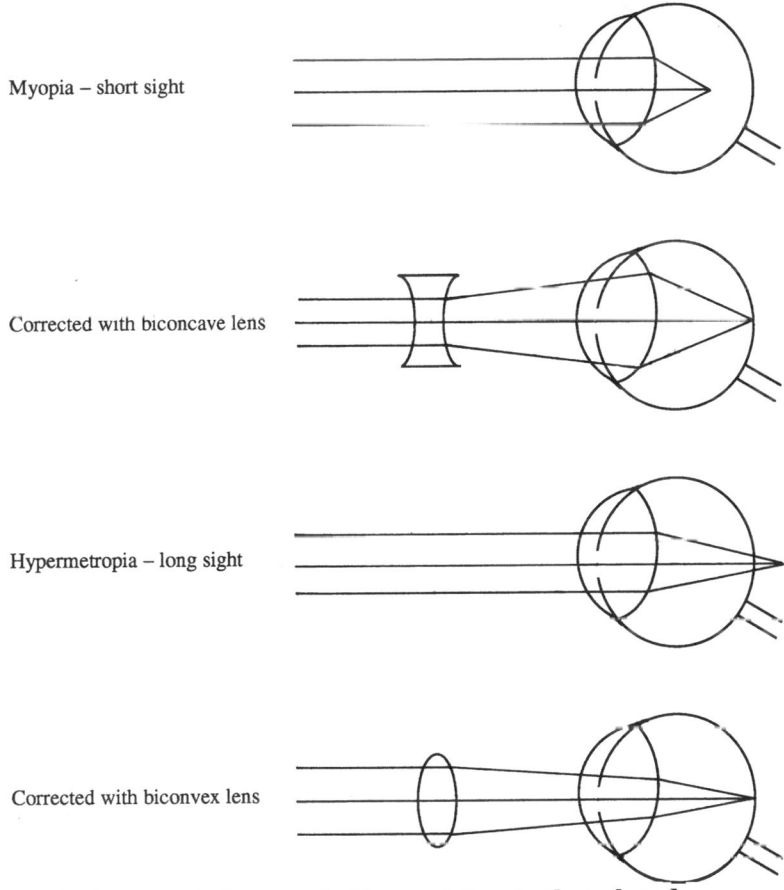

Myopia – short sight

Corrected with biconcave lens

Hypermetropia – long sight

Corrected with biconvex lens

Long-sighted people have a similar problem to that already described, as the eye becomes used to a physiology that focuses over a distance, it eventually begins to make viewing near objects difficult.

The food of good vision

You will recall that it is the rods and cones in the eyes that are responsible for converting light energy into electrical impulses. This can only happen if adequate amounts of the visual pigment that these rods and cones use is being produced. These pigments are formed from combinations of retinene, (a light sensitive molecule) and opsin (the protein). These elements are very important to good sight, in particular good night vision. A lack of these constituents can in severe cases result in blindness. Retinene is actually derived from vitamin A (retinol). A vitamin 'A' compound that is formulated with this defect accounted for is therefore extremely beneficial.

Your body is unable to make vitamin A naturally, so an external source in the required specific recommended quantities is vital and essential for good normal vision[4].

What other things are bad for our eyesight? We shall explore another myth in the next chapter and show you how to feel more confident about the way in which you use your eyes.

---

[1] The ideal of 20/20 vision is the standard by which eyesight is often measured. It should be realised that this is an 'academic' ideal. 20/20 vision is unlikely to be sustained under most conditions.

[2] See Chapter 1.

[3] Dr Bates suffered advanced presbyopia, (near vision failure corresponding to increasing age) and completely alleviated the condition when it occurred during his mid forties.

[4] See Appendix A.

CHAPTER 3

IS READING BAD FOR OUR EYES?

"Reading is to the mind what exercise is to the body."
Joseph Addison

Reading. We can all do it but have you ever stopped to consider just how we accomplish this amazingly complex task? More importantly have you ever thought about how reading can affect the quality of your eyesight? You may be surprised to find it does not affect it in the ways you may initially have expected! We also want to know more about the way in which we read because of the many parallel skills that can so easily have analogies drawn with our general ability to see. As we begin to consider our ability to read, we must also start to consider our power of memory, perception, speed of functioning and cognition. As our understanding in these areas develops, so **the speed at which our sight can be corrected increases.**

We have already looked at the basic facts and the way in which light energy enables light waves to bounce back off the page you are reading now, in order to allow your eye to see the black ink in which the letters are written.

You will also recall the importance of the eye muscles in the visual process and we shall be looking a little further at how reading can affect the functioning of these muscles. Reading forms an essential element of most people's lives, and 'old sight' (presbyopia or long sight[1]) is usually characterised by loss of the ability to read type without glasses. Numbers and letters are everywhere and play such an important part in our lives. We often measure the fact that our eyesight is defective by our 'inability' to read signs, books and other printed material.

The Snellen test chart (see Chapter 15) is itself based upon the ability to read. Many of the exercises presented later will involve a sharpening of your perceptions, which are based upon refinements in your recognition of written letters and numbers. Reading is therefore an important ingredient in your quest for better sight.

What do we know about reading?

Reading can be described as the ability to see and understand written language. It is a foundation skill essential to our development in today's society. Reading is a way of transmitting culture and information. Like many other activities it is a 'learned' skill. What distinguishes reading from other skills is that it must be taught. Soon after we learn to speak, most of us learn to read by making a connection between the words we see on the page and those we have learnt to say.

The letters and words that appear on the page are only symbols. If you think about this, the eye and the brain are carrying out a remarkably complex function, in unison, to accomplish this task. It is, however, the mind that has the responsibility for 'interpretation' of these symbols, that are the letters on the page, that form words and phrases. The interpretation happens because of a rapid recognition process based upon an individual's past experience. It is really a stimulation of ideas already present in the mind of the reader. If you have ever tried reading a foreign language that is unfamiliar, the symbols present no 'stimulus' for you. There is no connection between the sight of the symbol and any previous link in your mind.

Words and their meanings come to be recognised together and this is where your ability to perceive becomes important. Perception is something that is hard to define exactly as it can mean slightly different things in different situations. Perception may rely upon one sense or upon a combination of your senses. Perception is the 'activity' of the senses. For reading, this is generally the sense of sight, which can then stimulate other senses as we read.

We actually make sense of what we read after decoding the words by using our ability to 'comprehend'. This is more than a simple understanding of words, sentences and paragraphs. It is the ability to '**make a connection and relationship with what you already know and relate it to what you read**'. Reading is often about exciting the 'imagination', as a reader pictures what is read. What is the imagination? We will be going on to explore the imagination and its impact upon your sight in a later chapter.

Reading therefore involves our ability to see, comprehend, assimilate and then interpret. In this way we are able to build new ideas and concepts. So reading is in fact a very complex series of skills that we put together. Once we have learned to do it we take it for granted. It is important to explore the process of reading because it has many crossover points in the skills required for good vision. By this I am referring to powers of perception and interpretation in particular.

We read – but how do we know what words mean?

An interesting point to consider is the *'meaning'* of any given word. Much work has been done in this area and the way in which we are able to store meanings for any given word. Words are also anchors for stored experiences and each word will represent a different stored experience for each individual. No one word will mean exactly the same to any two people because of the fact that we all experience the world differently. We are all able to generalise meanings from words because this is what makes communication through words possible. If I say the word 'dog', you may have in mind a particular representation or picture of a dog remembered from your past, that gives this word 'meaning' to you. I may be thinking specifically about my Dalmatian dog from my childhood. The interpretation we both put on the same word differs, yet we are both able to make sense and understanding out of the word.

Our understanding of words can also change over time with the experiences we link to the words. You may have always thought of dogs as cuddly little creatures because you once owned a dog that was like that. Maybe you know someone who thinks of dogs in this way. If you then have a nasty experience where another dog gives you a severe and nasty bite, whenever the word 'dog' is mentioned this experience may be the one that is stimulated and through which you remember your meaning of the word 'dog'. This is what I would call an element of your perception. The process works incredibly quickly and usually without your conscious awareness.

This is only one example of the way in which **our perceptions can change**. If we assume for a moment that our perception works in a similar manner for all our skills, we can use the above example to begin understanding how our eyesight can change and deteriorate. Again, we shall examine and explore how our perception is one of the controlling elements of our sight in a later chapter. We shall also look at how **you can regain control over the power of your perception to aid your visual process.** Before we do that lets return to some of the fundamentals in the reading and 'seeing' process.

The European Organisation for Nuclear Research, CERN.[2] has estimated that to duplicate the function and sophistication of the human eyes would require a machine and equipment costing about $68 million dollars (£45 million pounds) and that this man-built 'eye' would be the size of a small house! When we consider the task that would be involved, it is easy to see why this is the case. The eye contains 130 million light receptors and each one of these is capable of taking in at least five photons[3] per second. The result is the eye's ability to distinguish over one million different colour types.

Sometimes it can be limiting to think of the eye only in terms of a camera. At other times it can be helpful because it is the closest analogy we have to aid our understanding of the eye. For a moment let's consider the eye to be like a complex and sophisticated camera. Have you ever seen a poorly taken photograph that snaps a moving object and the picture is all out of focus because the movement in the background makes the photograph a blur? The human eye has the ability to over come this problem. In order to see an object clearly the eye must hold the object still for a fraction of a second, before it moves on to the next object. In other words the eye does not hold an object 'still' continually in its field of vision, although this is the illusion that is created by the brain.

How does this translate to the reading process? When reading the eye will fix upon a few words at a time, 'photograph' them, register them and then move on to the next few words as the process is repeated. Slow readers read one or two words at a time, fixing upon the words for maybe one and a half seconds. A speed reader will take in three to six words per fixation, 'fix' on the words for a half or even a quarter of a second and keep their eyes focused on the page and their brains focused upon content of the page.

To put this into more perspective, a slow reader reads 100 words per minute, whereas a range reader can read up to 1000 words per minute or more! That's 16.6 words per second! That is what is possible.

Most of us come to believe that there are certain limitations both as to how fast it is possible to read and how much we can consequently comprehend. Antonio Di Marco Magliabechi (1633- 1714) was born in Florence. The Italian bibliophile was reputed to have remarkable skills that verged upon the superhuman. Magliabechi was able to almost immediately recognise, and remember, a whole book, after only a brief familiarisation. He was able to combine a special reading ability with phenomenal memorising techniques. It enabled him to remember entire books, including the punctuation!

Magliabechi was the librarian to Great Duke Cosmo III and he even developed a reputation for having read and memorised an entire library! Was he the greatest bookworm that ever lived? If he was, how did he come to achieve this?

We can now look at this element of the visual process in a little more detail in order to help our understanding. Our eyes have two main types of vision known as central vision and peripheral vision (or wide vision). The central focus is able to see clearly six words at a time horizontally *and* vertically.

There are approximately 260,000 light receivers available to us as we read. An estimated 220,000 are engaged in the process of peripheral vision. The reason for this is because the brain is aware of what is going on outside the central field of vision, being alert to danger and other things of interest. It is basically a part of the survival mechanism.

Interestingly this superior part of the visual field is very clear. The brain is able to pick things out of it with ease. Have you ever noticed when you buy a new car that you are able to suddenly pick out all similar models as you see them on the road, no matter where they are?

Research has been carried out which shows that everyone has a 'central eye', which is described as the brain! Our physical eyes focus centrally

Is Reading Bad For Our Eyes?

upon those objects the brain is paying attention to. It is a type of tunnel vision. In its natural state the brain is more alert, using its own internal massive eye to scan an entire range of data in the environment which enters through the lens of the eye. There are some times when our brains are focusing upon everything at once.

These are the visual skills developed by all the great artists, particularly those in visual arts and the martial arts. It was probably the same ability which Magliabechi developed allowing him to perform those remarkable skills. **The conclusion is that there are different ways of 'seeing'.** We need to know how to utilise them.

What should also now be clear is that reading is a very complex skill that uses many different parts of our capabilities, without us being consciously aware that all these different capabilities are actually being used. This is very much like the process of sight.

Reading and our eye muscles

From what we know about the structure of the eye and the eye muscles, we know how the eye focuses in order to see things both at a long distance and at the short or near distance. Muscles that have the same type of properties as any other muscle work the eye. Just think what happens if you spend any considerable amount of time reading. Think about this during your life - in school during your educational years and then maybe at university or college. Then there is work where we often have to read many documents and reports in order to do our job. How long do our eye muscles spend 'locked' into one type of viewing pattern, one where they are focused in a particular way?

This does not only apply to reading. Maybe your work involves special close up sight to perform a task. Hairdressing is an example. Even sitting playing a piano and reading the music involves 'locking' your visual focus into one set pattern that is maintained for an appreciable period of time. You may not always be conscious of it, but you have a preferred distance at which you 'feel' comfortable while viewing something. You will always place yourself in this same position to carry out the task. We are creatures of habit in more ways than one.

Computer work is another very common example and the dangers associated with strain of the eyes resulting from this type of work have already been recognised. The important point to be aware of is that it is a situation in which the eye muscles will be fixated in more or less one constant pattern of focus.

Research has shown that the majority of schoolchildren who fail the Snellen test[4] are myopic (short-sighted). What is also interesting is that these children are usually average or better than average students. In other words the majority of children who fail the test are children who are doing well at school, (usually doing a lot of reading and showing a lot of concentrated attention toward their work). The research also shows that children who pass the test and can see clearly at distances, are more likely to be those having problems that directly affect learning and reading abilities. Is there a connection between reading and sight-related problems? Do these difficulties emanate from a tendency to use the eye muscles in a fixed way or a fixed pattern?

It is known for example, with an ordinary muscle, that if it is exercised in a particular way the muscle can be shortened or given more mass. This is often found in certain weight-training techniques aiming to accomplish different things with a muscle or set of muscles. What if a similar thing is resulting with our eye muscles but without our conscious knowledge? This is where we reach an extremely interesting point.

We have already examined in Chapters 1 and 2 the traditional understanding of how the eye functions. The eye's ability to focus is traditionally viewed as being the result of the lens' ability to focus in response to the actions of the ciliary muscles. Medical textbooks today still quote the cause of defective vision, in particular long sight and short sight, (hypermetropia and myopia), as being due to the eyeball being too short or the eye lens to thin (hypermetropia) or the eyeball being too long and/or the lens too thick, (myopia). This explanation means that the shape of the eye as a whole does not change. Only the lens' shape changes to accomplish focus or accommodation. This view leads to the conclusion that defects of vision, particularly those that occur because of a change that takes place in the shape of the eyeball, are 'permanent'. Consider what has been said above about the eye muscles 'fixating' into a particular response and this view is quite reasonable. Examination would show the eyeball to be 'held in a particular shape' and so reflecting a particular 'state' of physiology.

Dr Bates progressed to a higher level. He asked himself a further question. What if the shape of the eye *did change* during the process of (accommodation) focusing? What would this mean? Dr Bates carried out many experiments that showed he was correct to ask this further question. He demonstrated that **the shape of the eye does change during the focusing process** because of the action of the external eye muscles on the eyeball. As we have already seen these muscles are usually just attributed with the ability to move the eyes in various directions, up, down, sideways etc. Dr Bates found these muscles can actually move the back of the eye towards the lens when a distant object is viewed. The shape is therefore shortened. When a near object is viewed, the shape is lengthened.

We already know that the eyeball being in a lengthened condition reflects myopia, (short sight). Hypermetropia, (long sight) and presbyopia (old sight) are conditions where the opposite is true and the eyeball is contracted along its longitudinal axis (i.e. the line between the lens and the retina). It becomes clear when looking at defective sight from this viewpoint that these defects of vision are due only to the faulty action of the external muscles of the eye. In other words, the eye is kept almost 'locked' into a particular position which produces the problem with vision, be it short sight or long sight.

If you think about it yourself, you will realise that if Dr Bates' findings are correct, then the traditional view is also correct *but only in so far* as it deals with the description of the 'condition' of the eye, *at the time of examination*. The change in the shape of the eyeball is not permanent. Dr Bates described many defects in vision as *'being brought about by strain upon the external muscles of the eye'*. The examples given above illustrate what he meant by this. In time this strain causes the eyeball to change its shape. To this extent the two descriptions of the visual process and the causes responsible for them are in alignment. It is simply that **the old traditional view** of the process of the eye's accommodation **fails to ask that further vital question**, which the brilliant Dr Bates was able to conceptualise and then implement. In the process he helped thousands of people regain normal vision.

There can be no doubt that Dr Bates' view is correct. The testimonials of success using his natural eyesight correction techniques are well documented. I have proven them to be correct myself.

This then is one of the fundamental principles upon which these natural eyesight methods achieve success. By first recognising that it is a special form of stress or tension that is operating upon the eye muscles, (of the nature outlined above). Relieving this stress or tension means the eyes are able to revert to their natural condition. The whole visual process is able to function properly again. As the relief and relaxation of these muscles occurs, many conditions of defective sight are automatically overcome. We shall be looking at this in further detail later.

How can I be so sure about this?

Quite apart from what you have already read above, we know what happens in the eyeball, the lens and how accommodation takes place. The muscles are a crucial part of the total dynamic process that is taking place. We also know from the work done by Erismann and Kholer[5] that it is possible to alter and change our perception. This means we can modify our visual process by a combination of correct muscle use and the retraining of our perception, (where this may also be necessary). Remember that if you have worn optical aids for some time or suffered defective sight that has not been corrected naturally, your visual process will already have made certain adjustments to compensate for your situation. **You can now use this knowledge to correct our own sight.**

We shall be looking in greater detail at glasses, where they came from and how they *really* affect our eyes in the next chapter.

So is reading bad for our eyesight?

We have all heard the stories about reading and how too much reading is bad for our eyes. That poor light is bad for us while reading and that it causes eyestrain. From what had been said above it will now be clear that this is only true where the eye muscles are used incorrectly within the visual process. Stop and notice what it is that you do while you read. By this I mean what you are aware of *while* you read. If you have never paid it attention before, now is the time to give it some serious consideration. Do you find your eyes move across the line of type as you read or are your eyes doing the minimum of work, almost 'staring' and trying to take in the whole line at once? Are you trying to do more than this and take in whole paragraphs and pages at once? In other words how flexible and 'mobile' are your eyes as you read? How much are you actually using and flexing your eye muscles as you read?

When I asked myself these questions I found that when I actually paid attention to how I was reading I was using my eyes in almost a 'fixation', with very little movement taking place. I also noticed I was always sat in a very similar manner, with a very similar body posture. The reading material was always placed at roughly the same distance in roughly the same way. All these factors simply 'reinforced' the poor way in which I was reading. It was as though reading involved me going through a certain ritual where I always did the same thing to 'prepare' and carry out my reading. As soon as I began to alter the way I read, I found that my vision started to improve. Once you are aware of the real way in which the eye functions naturally, it becomes almost common sense and the differences you will notice will prove to you that what you are doing is correct. You will begin to develop your own ways of giving your eyes mobility and flexibility. Your natural instincts start to kick in!

I found that regularly breaking my contact with the page and focusing on a more distant object was a huge benefit. Also, another method that helps a lot is to use a pencil as a marker that you follow across the page as you read. This has the almost instant effect of creating movement across the page as you read. Notice the difference in how your eyes physically perform. One you have re-trained your eyes in this way you will be able to drop the use of the pencil.

What if your vision is not good enough to read without glasses?

This book contains details of a number of exercises that will improve your vision as you progress. It may be necessary to return to certain parts of the book after you have read it and obtained an understanding of certain other things that follow.

If you cannot see the page to read without your glasses you must **decide to commit yourself now** to begin reading successfully without the aid of your glasses. Do this by reading a little every day to begin with, without the aid of glasses. This means relaxing and placing the page in front of you at a distance where you can make out at least the difference in colours on the page, i.e. black against a white background. It may be all a fuzz with no definition whatsoever. Your normal response at this stage may be that it is impossible to see anything clearly. This is exactly the time to show new resolve and belief in the fact that you will make progress, no matter how small that progress may appear at first.

An excellent way to prove to yourself that you can improve what you see is to use your peripheral vision. Hold a book at a reading distance of about twelve inches and notice any differences in the quality of what you see, when compared with your normal sight, when viewed straight on in the usual way. Peripheral vision is where you turn your eyes either completely left or completely right and look out of the extreme sides of your eyes. There will be a difference if you are alert and let yourself become aware of the smallest of differences in quality. It may be only that the depth of the black that looks deeper or it may be more definition, sharper edges or shape. Find your starting point, as you must find your own base point from which *you will build.*

No matter how bad you believe your sight to be, there is someone who has already had a similar condition which they have improved using natural correction techniques. Let's look at one particularly striking example. In one reported case the sufferer found at the age of four he had defective vision. At age five he was classified as having extreme myopia (short-sightedness) and was prescribed −ten diopters[6] glasses. These prescriptions gradually became stronger as the years progressed and by age seventeen the prescription was −eighteen diopters. By age twenty-six this spectacles' wearer was given the strongest glasses possible for him:

    Right eye   —20sph. —3 cyl.170
    Left eye   —20.5sph.—3 cyl.170

At the same time he was informed that he should give up reading and that there was nothing further that could be done for him. There was a danger of total blindness. Far from giving up this man continued with his life as best he could, but by age twenty-eight his eyes were at the stage where they would not last much longer. His sight was failing rapidly. Although he had some of the most powerful glasses available, he was experiencing head pains whenever he looked at anything closely. Traditional specialists were unable to help this man. His situation was such that he had no other choice available. When he came across the Bates' method he began to experience benefits almost immediately. He stopped wearing his glasses after twenty-three years and began the re-training of his visual process.

This man testifies that he could indeed hardly see anything at all when first discarding his glasses; however, after a few days he began to see improvement and in a short time was able to make his way around without his glasses. A remarkable improvement for someone so close to total blindness! Although he was not able to read immediately, this goal was also achieved within a moderately reasonable time period. The report confirms that after two and a half years he was still able to forget his glasses! The improvement was permanent.

Whilst my own eyesight has never approached these stages of deterioration, I find the report a remarkable testament to the power of the human visual process to correct itself and to its power of adaptation, if only it is given the chance. So no matter how good or bad you feel your own eyesight may be, know that you can improve it.

So is reading good for our eyesight?

Reading may be one of our greatest gifts but as far as our eyesight is concerned, it could, until now, also have been one of our greatest enemies! Our lack of awareness in the past about how reading can affect our whole visual process and so damage our sight has meant that its true nature as it affects our eyes has not been understood. The same principles apply to any other activity requiring 'fixed' patterns of focus for prolonged periods of time. Reading can be transformed into a beneficial activity for the visual process once we become aware of the correct methods of 'seeing' what we read.

It is appropriate to conclude here with a quote from Henry Miller (1891-1980), the US author.

> "There are lone figures armed only with ideas, sometimes with just one idea, who blast away whole epochs in which we are enwrapped like mummies. Some are powerful enough to resurrect the dead. Some steal on us unaware and put a spell over us which it takes centuries to throw off. Some put a curse on us, for our stupidity and inertia, and then it seems as if God himself were unable to lift it."

---

[1] Traditionally viewed to be due to loss of elasticity of the lens, which hardens and flattens its shape, in conjunction with other changes in the eyeball. One suspected cause is believed to be incorrect diet.
[2] An organisation set up in Switzerland to explore and measure the atom.
[3] A photon is a 'bundle' of light energy
[4] See Chapter 15
[5] Chapter 2
[6] A diopter is the optical measure of the eye's defect.

CHAPTER 4

GLASSES – A PYRRHIC VICTORY?
AND
IS LASER SURGERY SAFE?

No one knows for sure when spectacles were first invented. Rumour has it they were invented in the thirteenth century by a Florentine monk. It seems the original aim was for correction of farsightedness. There was not in fact much need for spectacles until books became widely available. It was about this time that vision problems also became more common place. In 1629, Charles I of England granted a royal charter to the 'Spectacle Makers' Guild', so their use had certainly became much more extensive at this time. The American writer Benjamin Franklin invented bifocal eyeglasses in 1784.

How do you view glasses or spectacles? Perhaps your views on them are changing. Some people have recently begun to look upon them as a fashion accessory and many Europeans view them in this way. Many people consider them to be a blessing, simply because they are entirely dependent upon them. Glasses have been held in a high esteem because they can alleviate the problem of poor vision. In one respect they can be regarded as one of the great achievements of the civilised world. There are arguments for saying that optical aids have done a good job. It is only when you begin to consider what natural alternatives are available that you come to see that glasses are in fact, in many ways, **a way of stopping your eyesight from getting better.** *Glasses create dependency.* It is probably the way in which glasses have been used[1] that now tarnishes them with this mark - that of being the perpetrators of maintaining defective vision for so many people and, in many cases, making their eyesight worse as time passes by.

Many other people naturally regard glasses as artificial, unbecoming, cumbersome and very inconvenient. They do very little for our sense of a strong self–image and in many cases they are the cause of attacks upon our self-esteem. Glasses are often associated with weakness, with 'puny' characters and 'bookworm' types. The inconvenience of optical aids is probably one of their major drawbacks. In truth they are a totally unnatural and unhealthy way of treating your eyes. It is only a lack of informed choice by the public that has kept spectacles in such an eminent position as the number one treatment for eyesight problems.

Glasses are an odd invention in some respects - glass lenses set in a frame and often worn *constantly* in front of the eye! It is true that spectacles, used correctly, can assist defective vision. For short sight a concave (spherical) lens is used and for long sight, a convex (spherical) lens. Astigmatism uses cylindrical lenses. Sometimes both types of lenses are combined into bifocals. These assist vision at a distance or for reading by combining the lenses of different curvatures in one piece of glass. The technology behind glasses is very clever, particularly as it uses and applies the known qualities of light and vision to trick our eyes.

The modern alternative to glasses is contact lenses. These were a marvellous invention. First referred to as a concept by Leonardo Da Vinci, it was not until 1887 that Adolf Fick actually invented the contact lens. Made of soft or hard plastic they are worn directly on the eye. They work in the same way as spectacles by assisting defective vision. First real uses were in the 1930s when special eye impressions were made, enabling the lenses to be made. It has been the modern technology advances in the nature of plastics that has made the soft lens more popular. These lenses can be worn for lengthy periods but they still do not cure defective vision. They also have their drawbacks. Prolonged use starves the eye of oxygen, which can cause enlarging of the blood vessels at the rear of the eye.

A common sensation when contact lenses are worn for too long a period is a 'misting up' of the visual field and a feeling of mild discomfort in the eye. Some disposable lenses try to overcome these problems but in the final analysis neither spectacles nor contact lenses actually cure defective vision or improve it to the point of normality. Inconvenience is still a major drawback, and many wearers refer to contact lenses as 'putting their eyes in'. Many people find that after a while, for one reason or another, they may become unable to wear contact lenses and they are then thrown back again upon glasses as the main alternative.

Laser surgery

Laser surgery appears to be the ultimate quick fix for defective eye problems. The procedure itself only takes about fifteen seconds per eye. Each eye is usually done separately for safety reasons so that in the event of the eye being damaged, only one eye is affected. Fifteen seconds to change your cornea forever!

There are numerous people who have had laser treatment and are quite happy with the results. Often these are people with low levels of myopia who experience the least problems. Other people have not been as happy with the results.

The fact is that the long-term effects of laser treatment are unknown. It is estimated that some five to seven per cent of patients can have immediate problems. It is the permanent nature of the procedure and its effects that gives most people cause for concern, should the procedure not work. We already know the basic facts regarding the eye and the reasons why short or long sight and astigmatism can occur.

For short-sighted patients the aim is to flatten the contours of the cornea and so reduce the bending of light. This places the focus upon the retina. For long sight, the aim is the opposite. Here the curve is flattened by firing the laser at several points around the cornea. The result is that the cornea shrinks and bulges slightly.

With the short sight correction method problems can include night-time halos, hazy vision, under or over-correction of sight and light sensitivity. For long sight results can include glare, subsequent long sight, or persistent short sight and cloudiness. Other symptoms can be a difference in the focusing ability of each eye, drooping eyelids and double vision. The end result can also mean that in some cases contact lenses cannot be worn.

Quite apart from these potential problems, there is the resulting pain from the procedure that can last forty-eight hours, with the eye taking up to three months finally to settle. A laser can result in the eye's surface being left badly scarred and with a resulting haze that means the person can no longer see clearly. There was a reported case of a young women who experienced distorted vision, halos and size increases of objects. The result was she was unable to see clearly to cross the road and was dependent upon people to help her.

In another reported case a woman had treatment that went wrong. She is now unable to go into bright sunlight or read without a magnifying glass. In addition she suffers intense pain. Her original problem was long sight and she wanted to discard her glasses because the frames gave her head pressure and headaches. The treatment has given her a whole new set of difficulties in which she includes destruction of the quality of her life and depression, while her eyesight is many times worse than originally. The very concerning point is that she expects to be like this for the rest of her life. It seems a massive risk to take when the results can be so unpredictable.

A recent review of surgeons carrying out laser treatment showed that the majority of medics themselves *do not* have the treatment. From among one hundred eye experts in PRK and LAZIC not one had taken the procedure. They still wore contact lenses and glasses.

Laser treatment for people with short sight has been described as an 'experimental procedure', and even 'doubly so' for people with long sight. The fact is that the long-term effects are not known. When the physiology of the eye is considered together with the findings of Dr Bates, that changes in the shape of the eye cause the problem in the first place due to 'functional difficulties', the concerns become very real. If the shape of the eye itself changes again at some time after the surgery, due to a change in muscle function, what will the results be in the long term? The laser treatment itself is irreversible.

Its seems then that there is no scientific way currently available to cure defective vision that is not free from some from of major health concern.

As we consider the ways in which changes of the eyeball shape can possibly affect vision we can place all current forms of eyesight correction in some perspective. Having looked briefly at laser treatment let's return to glasses. What happens if you take your glasses off and try moving forward without them?

Take off your glasses and begin progressing!

When we considered reading in Chapter 3 and how the eye really functions it became clear that the dynamic interaction of the visual process means that the effect of glasses over the long term becomes obvious. Glasses and other optical aids 'hold' the muscles in a state of incorrect functioning, whatever condition they are applied to. We touched up on the beliefs you held about glasses at the start of the book. It is still true today that most people believe defective vision is 'incurable' by natural methods and that the remedy is optical aids. If you now realise that wearing such optical aids is really **permanently preventing you** from remedying your eyesight troubles, would you still go for such an option? Why give yourself a handicap that you can so easily do without?

If you know changes that occur in your eyesight are not permanent and learn how to interpret the feedback your visual process gives you, **you will overcome and adapt**. It is one of man's greatest abilities. We shall go on to examine the idea of 'perfect vision' in the next chapter.

A simple test shows the characteristics of glasses and demonstrates some of the key features necessary for normal vision. Look at any natural colour through a strong convex or concave lens. A simple contrast of the difference when the same colour is seen with the naked eye shows the colour is less intense when viewed through the lens. As will be seen later, the perception of colour is also important to the perception of shape. **This means that both these crucial elements in the visual process are actually impeded by the use of lenses.**

It is true that until now, for many people, there has been no choice because they were unaware of the alternatives. The day I decided I was not prepared to accept deterioration in my vision demonstrated to me that although I had begun to wear glasses, **they did not cure my condition.** The fact was that I needed the strength increased in order to maintain 'normal' vision. This is the experience for most people. After wearing glasses for a time, you will often find that you cannot read or see properly what was previously clear beforehand *without* your glasses. Glasses create dependency and ultimately deterioration of your sight.

GLASSES - A PYRRHIC VICTORY? AND IS LASER SURGERY SAFE?

If we look a little closer at what is happening, the situation will become clearer. If you think about it glasses are usually given to correct the refractive or visual error which the eye is already producing. It is known that these refractive errors are never constant, even in a normal eye. What lenses or glasses therefore achieve is for your eye to be made to 'maintain' a position of refractive error, which would not otherwise be maintained naturally. The result is obviously that the condition of your eyes becomes worse over time.

Have you ever been wearing your glasses or contact lenses for some time and then found you were unable to wear them for some reason? You probably noticed that your vision without the aid of your glasses or lenses improved! It is a fact that vision improves to a greater or lesser degree in these circumstances.

Many people do not **notice** an adequate difference. This is one of the ways that you will learn to improve your vision. Improvements in vision do come about naturally and progressively. The fact is that *YOU HAVE TO NOTICE THEM.* You will learn quickly and easily to train to yourself to notice these improvements and to build upon each individual success.

Your eyesight has probably deteriorated over time, without you specifically noticing the deterioration until it reached a certain unacceptable level. Likewise the improvements will occur over a relative time period, with you noticing and building upon small improvements until normal vision is restored.

One crucial point to remember when using techniques to improve your vision is that you should always be setting yourself new targets. When you actually do your initial analysis of the current state of your vision, you may find that normal street signs have lettering that is simply a blur as you look from a reasonable distance. You may only be able to make out the sign. Without your glasses on you may not be able to see that there are letters on it! This is a common experience.

Over time you will begin to **notice small but marked improvements** in what you can actually see 'clearly'. The time will come when you can almost clearly and perfectly see the lettering on the sign that was initially not visible. When this time arrives, the thing to do is have a smaller sign in mind, at the same type of distance and with lettering that you cannot make out. In exactly the same way that the first sign looked, you may have difficulty even identifying if the sign has letters. As you begin to focus in and your vision improves you begin to make out the detail of this smaller sign. You will find that the lettering of the first sign is now clear and perfect.

Lettering approximately two inches high and two hundred feet away is ideal as a standard for the first sign. The secret is always to set yourself new improved targets! As you see you are about to achieve a visual target for something you could not originally see, move on to your next target. You will sail past your old target without even thinking about it! This method prevents you from becoming stuck in trying to measure improvement against a target that may otherwise take longer to achieve.

By focusing upon your new target you provide your brain with a subconscious presupposition. It is guaranteed to work provided your old target is within your reach. By this I mean that 'you know' you will achieve your old target and that you are extremely close to it. You will already have experienced perfect vision of the target but it is not yet a normal occurrence. In other words it still takes conscious effort to see it. You will find that by moving onto your next visual target at this time you are setting yourself a new challenge. As improvements occur here the old target will be surpassed.

As we consider finally the effect of glasses upon our eyes, this is probably best summed up by Dr Bates who says:

> "It has been demonstrated, however, that the lens is not a factor either in the production of accommodation or in the correction of errors of refraction. Therefore, under no circumstances can there be a strain of the ciliary muscle to be relieved. It has also been demonstrated that when the vision is normal no error of refraction is present, and the extrinsic (or external) muscles of the eyeball are at rest. Therefore there can be no strain of the extrinsic muscles to be relieved in these cases. When a strain of these muscles does exist, glasses may correct its effects upon the refraction, but the strain itself they cannot relieve. On the contrary, as has been shown, they must make it worse." [2]

It is important to remember that Dr Bates wrote for his peers and we all mean different things when we envisage 'strain'. I believe I have clarified exactly what the term means when applied to our visual process. One of the reasons some people have had difficulties in implementing the Bates' methods has been because of the lack of understanding of what exactly 'strain' meant. This had led in the past to people believing they needed a teacher to benefit from the Bates' method. The techniques presented now allow you to overcome that problem and implement sight correction for yourself. I have had no formal instruction from any third party in implementing my own sight correction, which demonstrates that the techniques can be easily applied once you have a clear understanding of exactly how to progress.

It is fair to say that given the choice most people would not wish to wear glasses. This reflects the natural instinctive condition of the human eye. Some people who suffer high degrees of short-sightedness or long-sightedness suffer great difficulties. Strong concave glasses make all objects seem smaller that they actually are, while convex glasses enlarge objects.

Of course there are the usual difficulties of dirt, condensation, finger marks, scratched lenses, breaking the frames and simply forgetting them!

So with all these disadvantages let's move forward toward implementing the new natural alternative. In order to achieve your objectives you must first be clear upon the quality of vision it is possible for you to achieve. What is normal vision and do you *expect* your eyes always to function perfectly? We shall consider these questions in the next chapter.

---

[1] The real purpose of glasses was not to create dependency. It is very frequent changes of lenses, with different strengths, that can actually aid a person's sight.

[2] Dr Bates, *Better Eyesight Without Glasses* (Souvenir Press), 37.

CHAPTER 5

IS IT TRUE THAT OUR EYES ALWAYS FUNCTION PERFECTLY?

What do you believe about the ability of your eyes to see? Do you believe that your eyes are, or should be, perfect working organs under normal conditions? What is normal vision and what are normal conditions?

We have already looked at those key characteristics of the way in which the eyes function and this helps us in part to answer these questions. We know what accommodation is, (the eye's focusing ability) and how it effects the process of sight. It is now necessary to look a little closer at the process of accommodation in order to explore what we understand by term 'normal vision'.

We have also seen the divergence of opinion regarding the process by which accommodation of the eye is achieved. In reality this is an academic distinction because what you are interested in is results and what works. The view I take is that the lens is complementary to the main focusing mechanism of the eye, as described by Dr Bates. So how does the eye know when to sharpen an image on the retina? How does the lens in the eye and the mechanism of shaping of the eyeball know what distance an object is at, in order to focus up on it? If the process is the same as occurs with other muscles in the body, it is the receptors that provide information about their activity. Similar receptors in the ciliary muscles and other eye muscles tighten and relax the appropriate parts of the eye, including the lens and so provide information about the distance of the objects being viewed. The interesting point is that this information would only be useful up to distances of approximately seven meters (if it was the lens alone that was responsible for accommodation) because research has shown lens accommodation to be negligible beyond that point. This is in alignment with what has already been said about the way in which the eye functions.

The eyeball reacts instantaneously to the stimuli from these muscles. This means that no visual or refractive state, whether normal or abnormal is ever permanent. It is a fact that very few people can maintain totally perfect vision for more than a few minutes at a time. In other words, *the ability to see is constantly subject to change.*

What is the difference between good sight and bad sight?

The difference between good sight and poor sight is the length of time for which a state of acceptable vision can be maintained. Research has shown that all persons with errors of sight have intervals during the day when normal vision is maintained. What has also been shown is that the actual form or nature of the error of sight changes.

So what does this information mean to you if you suffer from defective sight? If you have defective vision you simply fail to **notice these differences** because of a process known as *'generalisation deletion and distortion'*. This process and how you can begin benefiting from it will be investigated later.

Dr Bates was able to conclude that errors in the visualising process, (specifically errors of refraction), were not permanent and that errors of refraction could be produced at will. In the same way these errors can be eliminated temporarily in a few minutes and permanently (by continued attention).

The false belief that the eye is a perfect working organ

It seems that many people mistakenly believe that the eye should be regarded as something that will be in perfect working order under 'normal' conditions. When you think about it, where does this belief emanate from? The fact is that the eye functions continuously but 'inconsistently' under varying adverse conditions. This may include viewing objects or surroundings that are unfamiliar, poor lighting and even under strenuous or stressful conditions. The eye does not have 'normal' sight all the times. 'Normal sight' is in fact a rare phenomenon, even among people who are otherwise classified as having normal vision. As I have already said, 20/20 vision as the accepted 'norm' for a measure of eyesight is purely an academic distinction.

In a reported research finding carried out on several thousand school children in one year, it was found more than half had 'normal eyes', with sight which was perfect at all times. What was also found however was that not one of these children had perfect sight in each eye at all times of the day. Their sight might be perfect in the morning and imperfect in the afternoon or visa versa. The degree of imperfection was also found to be variable in terms of duration and conditions that resulted.

What this indicates is that our visual process, particularly refraction, is always changing. This is as true for adults as it is for children. It is interesting that during periods of sleep the refractive condition of the eye has rarely been found to be normal. People will often produce conditions of myopia, hypermetropia and astigmatism when they are asleep. Have you ever had the experience of waking in the morning with your eyes feeling more tired than at any other time of the day? This is due to these conditions being subconsciously produced while you were asleep.

You can prove to yourself what is said about changes continuously taking place in your refractive visual abilities. When your eye views any unfamiliar object, an error of refraction is always produced. You have probably experienced for yourself how a strong light or a pulse of rapid or changing light produces momentary defects in vision. Also consider the affect of noise. Although it is an auditory function and so one that we would expect to be unrelated to vision, noise can in fact effect vision in a normal eye[1]. Anyone will actually fail to see perfectly when subjected to a loud unexpected noise. You may be able to remember a time when you have experienced a similar event? By way of contrast a known sound will not lower the vision but an unfamiliar one always does so. In the same way conditions of mental and physical discomfort, stress, anger, anxiety and similar states will always produce a negative effect in the refractive ability of the eye. This means these things affect your visual capability. The effect of these things can be physically measured in the eye itself.

Variations in refraction of the eye are therefore a common occurrence and the myth that the eye always functions perfectly is untrue, even in eyes that are otherwise considered to have 'normal' vision. This will help you as you begin the correction of your own eyesight. It is important that you do not expect more from your eyes than they are capable of delivering. Obviously we all want our eyes to have good sight in as many situations as possible. The fact is though that our eyes do not function perfectly at all times. By understanding this you will be able to **notice more frequently the times that your eyes are functioning well** and concentrate upon improving the times and circumstances in which your eyesight could be better. The way in which you approach your visual problem and exactly *what* you expect on each occasion can make all the difference in achieving success.

So to recap, we have explored the physical make up of the eye, the way light is converted into sight by the eye, and the part played by the muscles in the eye as part of the entire visual process. Vision is actually created because of certain very clever tricks and ways of interpreting information that is carried out by your brain. The final element that combines all elements into good sight is our perception. What is our perception and how can re-training our perception help us achieve normal sight?

In the next chapter we will look at how our perception is made up and how the power of your perception can influence your sight.

---

[1] The senses are not mutually exclusive and have a certain degree of cross over sensitivity.

CHAPTER 6

"KNOWING OUR PERCEPTIONS IS KNOWING HOW TO SEE! ...WE ALL HAVE THE POWER OF PREDICTION"

"...perception is something we think we understand...until we try to understand it"
Duncan Dobson, psychologist

Perception is something that people have different views about. We have all heard of it and we all know we have it but what is it? How will understanding how your perception works help you correct your sight? How *does* your perception affect your vision?

Psychologists and others have attempted to define the meaning of perception and there are certain established facts concerning the way our perception works. The work of Erismann and Kohler[1] shows us that our perception of the world can be changed. Perception involves a great many factors but it is really about our **powers of prediction**! Perception is not just a visual phenomena, it involves all the senses and all our 'learnings' about the world. Our intelligence is applied to and is part of what makes our perceptions.

If we take this idea of perception a little further I would make a further distinction in the explanation of perception and divide perception into two categories, our perception of:
a) the 'outer' world and
b) our 'inner' worlds.
It will later become clear why it is important to make this distinction for purposes of our visual process.

Our ability to process the information we receive from the outside world and run it through the enabling features of our perceptual process is a fascinating insight into the workings of the human mind and brain. The further distinction we will look at, the perception of our 'inner world' is a world that can be stimulated simply by a thought. We then build a response to that thought within our minds. One example may be where there is a capability you would like to acquire. Whether you think you can develop any particular capability depends entirely upon how your inner world perception of yourself is constructed and what you connect it to. You hold a perception about yourself that governs all your actions and all your capabilities.

Diagram 1

Visual perception

As we explore how perception works let's first look at the make-up of our visual perception and how it is stimulated by the outside world. As I have already said, sometimes we are tempted to view the eye and the visual process, ('visual perception') in a similar way to a camera, and the production of a photograph. This can be a parallel that is useful on occasions. It can also be a limiting view because the visual element of perception is 'interpretative'. We shall now explore how this interpretative quality can help your visual process.

> 'PEOPLE ON THE
> THE BEACH
> *IN SUMMER*'

Expectation

Did you notice the repetition of the word *'the'* in the second line? Many people do not and what this demonstrates is that we often see what we expect to see, rather than what is actually there. This principle lies at the heart of your own ability to see clearly and normally. *'Expectation'* comes to form a major factor in the deterioration of normal eyesight. We shall be looking at exactly what this means later.

To illustrate the principle further, think of a photograph you have seen in the past showing unusual or weird perspectives of people or objects. Perhaps large hands or feet or large noses were the result of the camera being too close to the subject or perhaps at an unusual angle. We do not see it that way in our 'reality'. The camera however is unable to *make the adjustments* that the human brain makes automatically and unconsciously and which we take for granted. This simple example that we have all seen demonstrates *the eye's ability to lie,* which it can and frequently does do. As eyesight deteriorates, *the eye lies to the brain* in ways that we are unaware.

What have you found in Diagram 1? If you are not familiar with these type of patterns you may be asking yourself what there is to find? Do you see the word 'eye'? Some people see it immediately. They have seen this type of pattern before and this makes identifying similar patterns easy, using past experience as a guide. If you did not see it, what is the reason for that? Some people still do not see the word after being told it is there. This is because their mind has formed a habit of looking at things in only one or two ways in an effort to interpret information. You *expect* words written on white paper to be written in black ink. When you recalibrate and look for the word in white, you will see the word pop into immediate view. Every time you look at this from now on, you will always see the word 'eye'. The difference is a simple change in your perception.

This illustration is important in a number of ways. It shows that things may be available for you to see clearly but you simply do not see them that way. Also, as we explore perception you will come to find that the movement of the eye is crucial to good vision. 'Movement' for our purposes also involves those aspects of an object or image that you pay attention to *as* the movement takes place. As your eyes began to move over the pattern of the word 'eye' in a new way, based upon your new 'perception' of what to expect, you saw something different. No doubt you will be able to draw other parallels that are important to you, as we explore the make up of perception in more detail.

We have already looked at the way in which light is converted into sight. You will recall that light images are converted into patterns of nerve impulses, which are transmitted to the visual cortex. Light is received in the eye and then organised to produce 'vision'. We see the environment without thinking about it. In fact we carry out this complex process so quickly and naturally that we just accept it as the real world. **What we see is only an *'interpretation'* of the real world!** Within the power of interpretation lies a key for opening up your doorway to normal sight.

How do we see in three dimensions?

The eye allows the brain to see in three dimensions, although the make-up of the retina is only two-dimensional. You will recall earlier that we briefly looked at three-dimensional vision. It will help to look a little now at the process that allows us to do this, as it aids our later understanding of why movement is so important to the visual system. Research[2] carried out on animals has shown that cells in the visual cortex receive information from both eyes. These cells can be grouped into four separate classes. The research showed that an interesting thing happens when the *'gaze'* is fixed at any particular point. Certain cells are stimulated and an increased stimulus of these cells results if an object is positioned closely to the fixation point of gaze. The research also found that the stimulus decreases when the object is moved away. A complementary group of cells also reacted in exactly the opposite way, showing decreased stimulus when objects were presented near the *same* fixation point.

One conclusion from this is that 'near' and 'far' vision cells might be used to control eye movement. This would be as a result of near cells being caused to 'fire' by objects in front of the fixation point and being 'turned off' by stimuli behind it; far cells correspondingly reacting in the opposite way. These four types of cells each respond in different ways to a variety of images on the two retinas and are collectively known as *disparity detectors*.

How your vision works on a micro level

These *disparity detectors* provide us with an interesting insight into how vision is stimulated on a micro level. They show us the principle upon which some of these cells work. Knowing how these type of cells are stimulated helps us to understand the visual process and a later experiment that we shall look at builds upon what we have found here, to provide us with an even clearer picture. This research explains a little about how we come to appreciate depth as a quality of perception. Our perception of the outside world really comprises more than the determination of the 'depth' of individual objects. The images we receive are somehow combined with other qualities to produce a mental image that is totally three-dimensional.

Shape detectors

The left and right eye each have their own area of visual organisation, (the visual cortex), which research has shown to have a variety of cells types, each of which is characterised by its receptive abilities. Some of these cells have *circular receptive fields* whereas others are receptive to *lines*. These cells are stimulated or 'fire', when **a line of a specific orientation illuminates a particular part of the retina.** *A small change in the position or orientation of the line causes one cell to stop firing and another to start.* Other cells have different functions and the end result is that cells are able to 'code information' in a way that gives the brain data about the shape of objects[3]. What we can say now is that there are various levels of visual inquiry, which go to make up sight, the whole process being the combination of a number of very complex processes. We do not need an intimate understanding of all the complexities. We only need to know enough to manipulate the parts of the process that will give us the results we want.

Where does perception occur?

This is a question that has not yet been answered. We do not however need to know the answer to be able to use our perception properly. What we do know is that the various detectors and their activity are *related directly to the stimulation of the retina*. Perception itself has been described as a series of 'hypotheses'. In other words, we do more than ascertain our environment through the stimulation of 'feature detectors' in the eye. Your brain is presented with 'possibilities' based upon past experience.

Other elements of perception

If we look briefly at the elements that make up our perception of the outer world they include the ability to appreciate depth, colour, brightness, texture, speed, distance, etc.[4] It is a fact that in the main, most of our standard (but unappreciated) perception-building abilities function perfectly, even for those with poor sight. It is a focus upon one specific area of the perception-building process that will generate most results for correcting eyesight. This is your perception of movement. This is the crucial element of perception that usually goes wrong when poor vision is experienced.

Your perception of movement

Movement is crucially important to the function of natural eyesight. With this in mind we shall now look at what is known about the perception of movement and how you *should* use this feature of your perception.

A close examination of the qualities of our perception of movement has shown that perception involves more than the stimulation of 'movement detector cells'. As mentioned above, the brain is actually presented with possibilities upon which to base its perception, using past experience as its guide. The brain then takes specific features of an object and its environment to construct its 'hypothesis' of perception. The important point is that we 'learn' to interpret and perceive on the basis of our past experience.

You will recall in Chapter 1 that we looked at the structure and make-up of the eye. The eye is moved by the six muscles[5] that surround it. Dr Bates in his work decided to explore the accuracy of the eye's focus as the end result of the visual process. By working backwards from this point, (rather than viewing it as the starting point), Dr Bates was also able to conclude that the normal continuous movement of the eyes was important to vision. When this movement was upset, vision was always demonstrated to be poor. What continuous movement was Dr Bates referring to? Our eyes normally look to be in a steady position. They appear 'fixed' apart from when they are used to track or follow an object.

The answer is that when measured and calibrated against a person with normal vision, the eyes are or *should always be* in a continuous movement. This applies even when they are at rest. There is a distinction to be made between the movement of the eye as it views a moving object, when the eye movement will be smooth, and movement when the eye is *searching for an object*[6]. When searching for an object the movement is more of a rapid, jerking nature. This jerking movement is known as *saccades ('the flick of a sail' – derivation is French)*. It was when this movement was most abnormal that Dr Bates found vision to be most affected.

To be complete, there is in addition to these two main types of movement a further continuous type of small, high frequency tremor that characterises the eye's movement. These natural movements of the eye are vital to good vision, in particular the saccadic movement can be described as 'essential'. The mechanics of the eye is such that if an image is 'fixed' or 'optically stabilised' on the retina[7], vision will fade after a few seconds. This tells us much about the accuracy of Dr Bates' work. This is the equivalent of a 'fixed stare'. Dr Bates identified that this condition of subconscious 'staring' is the prime cause of poor vision. This is an important fact because it shows that the workings of the eye are such that the function and objective is to **keep the eyes moving.** The steady and regular movement that the eye must have has the effect of taking an image in a 'flow' across the specialist receptors in the eye. The reason that movement is so important is to prevent these receptors 'adapting' to an image and consequently ceasing to indicate the presence of an image, by failing to send the required signals to the brain. **Movement is therefore crucial to the eye's normal function**. The eye is constructed in a way that utilises the quality of movement. Re-educating the visual process simply involves taking advantage of the eye's natural abilities and characteristics. Once you are aware of this you will find that many of the exercises that follow make perfect sense.

You will see for yourself that poor sight does not mean the cells that require stimulation are damaged. **It means that they are not getting the stimulus of movement they require** in order to function. This is a major distinction to be aware of and it connects directly with Dr Bates' principle of 'central fixation' (which I have renamed **central alignment**)[8].

Some readers may think this gives rise to a strange anomaly. One of the later exercises uses the quality of a blank sheet of white paper to relax the eyes. If it is true that the centre of the paper provides no stimulation for the eye because the small movements of the eye detect no differences, no change in brightness, you may expect the effect to be exactly the same as when the eyes are 'optically stabilised'. One area of white is replaced with another that is exactly the same. Why does the brain continue to respond and produce an image when the result should be that the image simply fades away? The answer lies in the fact that the edges and borders of the paper will be the parts of the image that move around on the retina. This means the stimulus is constantly renewed but in a different way. Where large areas of the same intensity occur, no special information is given to the brain. Instead the borders and outline take on an increased importance and the large area of constant white intensity is then *inferred* by the central visual system. In other words it makes up the missing signals. The thing we see is not therefore what our eyes see. Controlled by our perception, our brains let us continue to see a white piece of paper.

Once we begin to add this knowledge to the known workings of the fovea centralis[9] or yellow spot, the process of vision becomes even more clearly defined. Central alignment is the whole basis of good vision. This means the point of immediate visual attention is always aligned with the fovea centralis. If you consider the cycle of operation, the movement of the eye is absolutely essential for central alignment to be maintained. The fovea must be continually stimulated. If at any time the eye adopts a 'fixed stare', the fovea loses its prowess as the centre of stimulation. It becomes no different, no more sensitive, than the surrounding retina. When this takes place vision problems of all types occur and the eye loses its ability to function efficiently.

The old historical response to the eyes' loss of ability to function correctly was glasses. If you consider the situation now, you will see for yourself that glasses cause the eye to maintain the defective condition. Glasses have the effect of providing clear vision, by tricking the visual system through the use of light. The real drawback of glasses is that the benefits of central alignment are no longer available to the eye. Glasses achieve clear vision *without* the focus upon central alignment. Focus is instead more diversified.

Have you ever taken off your glasses and found that you could see 'to a degree' but that all parts of your field of vision were not equally clear 'all at once'? Stop for a moment and try this. Become aware of exactly what you can see and how well. The reason you cannot see everything as clearly as with your glasses, is due to the fact that you have already lost the habit of central alignment and the ability to move the eyes in the natural constant movement they must have. In other words you are 'staring'. The ultimate effect of staring was shown above where the effects of optical stabilisation were explained. Looking at all parts of the visual field *equally* at the same time means that movement has been lost. Glasses allow you to do this at the expense of deepening your removal from your natural habit of central alignment. Glasses reinforce the eyes' new habit of 'staring[10]' and will consequently never allow your eyesight to recover because your visual system cannot carry out the natural viewing process during the time that glasses are worn. This is one of the ways in which glasses help to maintain a false belief. The belief becomes subconscious. Once a problem with sight is experienced and glasses are used to correct it, the glasses come to acquire their own in built re-enforcement system. You find that with glasses you see all parts of the visual field equally well at the same time. You never experience this without glasses because by this stage central alignment has already been lost to a greater or lesser degree. Think of it like this. The eyes without central alignment cannot track accurately, nor can they focus naturally. The object in the field of vision cannot be 'centralised' or 'aligned' onto the most sensitive point of the eye. This equally effects the muscular control of the eye as they strain to attain some form of vision. If glasses are used during the time that this strain is taking place, glasses simply ensure that the improper muscular condition is maintained.

We can look at the results of some interesting research into the way in which glasses or lenses actually effect the eye. Recent findings[11] show that the eyes of young chicks actually compensate and adjust in growth cycle when optical lenses are worn. If a situation is created where 'defocus' results because of the effect of the lenses, then the eye itself *elongates* where a negative lens (hyperopic defocus) is used and elongates where a positive lenses is used (myopic defocus). This shows that the growth of the eye itself is bi-directional. The lenses also effected the thickness of the choroid as it was shown the eye wearing a +15 diopter lens developed thicker choroids.[12] In effect this is a 'lens induced' change in the length of the eye. This means that the retina of the eye is able to appreciate circumstances of 'defocus' and regulates the eye's growth to correspond. This research has parallels with earlier research done into the theory of emmetropia[13] (which is the condition of a normal eye when parallel rays are focused exactly on the retina and vision is 'perfect').

This earlier research looked at the ability of 'cellular learning'. Various research has now begun to show and it is becoming apparent the growth of the eye is regulated by a 'physiological feedback loop'. Learning is taking place at a *cellular* level. The process is apparently that the retina stimulates hormone secretions in response to images on the retina, whether these images are clear or unclear. It is these secretions that slow or speed up the eyeball's growth rate. What this does is to regulate *axial length* and so the eye's focusing ability.

This research also shows a contrast between two extremes. If the visual process is completely disrupted, for example by constant darkness or strong lenses, the result is that refraction is highly irregular. In addition the growth pattern is shown to be inconsistent.

Where tests were done with weak lenses of four diopters or less and these were placed in front of the eye at certain stages in the growth process it was shown that:

> 'the development of the eye will change course to adapt to the altered condition'.

This evidence was then considered against the findings of Dr Bates and the comment was as follows:

> "If the information is extrapolated to humans (which is presumably the ultimate point of such research), the consequence is obviously that Dr Bates was far more right than even he ever

knew: Wearing glasses to 'correct defects' not only disrupts vision, it actually perverts the development and growth of the eye away from normal. In principle, therefore, on the basis of this finding alone, no child should ever be given glasses as left alone, the vision should normalise through the process of growth. In practice it will not be quite that simple: children are not chickens and, in particular, are more subject to the emotional disruption of vision so that the various benign interventions discussed throughout this book may be necessary to allow the process to normalise fully."

Do not assume that if you have defective sight you are limited by what may have occurred in the past to your own eyes. We already know about the work of Erismann and Kohler referred to earlier. The comment about this research also concluded that emotional influence was a factor and that even with people who had suffered over the long term, improvement could happen over a relatively short time. In other words, cellular activity is not the complete story. Other factors are also at work.

One final conclusion was that 'small corrections' can influence the growth of the eye and this knowledge could be used in a positive way. This is via the practice of using 'transitional' glasses and gradually weakening the glasses lenses in small steps so that the eyes can gradually adapt and so correct defective vision. I have already mentioned the point earlier, that when glasses were prescribed in the distant past, the idea was to give the patient one set of glasses to wear for about three days and then a weaker pair for another three days. This process continued until the eyes regained normal vision.

So to recap we now know the way the eyes *should* physically and actually move and we have looked at recent research into the micro-processes at work as our eyes grow and adapt to different seeing situations. A fuller understanding of your perception of movement and how you process it now involves a little further exploration. As you continue to explore the workings of your perception, remember that information creates understanding and knowledge. **Success arrives by using what you know!**

Your perception of movement

A summary of what we know will now be in order. When the eye is stationary the image of a moving object passes across the receptive fields of many cortical cells. Movement can then be coded by the passage of 'excitation' or 'stimulus' from one cell to another and also by those cells in the cortex and superior colliculus, which are responsive to movement in particular directions across their receptive fields.

The detection of movement is however, even more involved than this and is a quite remarkable achievement. What about the situation where your eye follows a moving object? The images on the retinas will remain more or less stationary, so no 'stimulus' of movement is produced. This does not, however, stop you registering a movement of the object. Maybe the object is viewed against a fixed background. This would provide information of speed. The signals still sweep across the retina as the eyes follow the moving object. The fact is though that you can still determine movement where there is no visible background. You must have been in the situation where someone has lit a cigarette in a darkened room. You were still able to see and perceive movement, although there is no image moving across the retina. The answer as to how you still perceive movement lies in the rotation of the eyes in the head. This will continue to provide information of movement and speed, even in the absence of movement signals from the retinas[14]. The brain is not fooled!

The reason for this seems to be that, as information is passed from the brain to the eye muscles, information is also passed to the 'movement perception system', so that when the brain commands the eyes to move, this also counteracts the effects of images passing across the receptive fields. How does this happen? The brain perceives the object as stationary if it moves in the opposite direction to the eye at a similar speed to that of the eye. An image that remains on the same spot of the retina as the eyes move is perceived as moving and so we can follow an object with our eyes and perceive it as moving in relation to its background.

Remarkably, the brain is also able to comprehend images moving across the retina and compensate for the fact that the whole human body is moving as well. Consider driving which is an activity in which the whole body experiences momentum. You still perceive the road as stationary while moving. Have you ever had the experience of looking out of a train window at a station and finding it difficult to determine if it is your train or one adjacent that has started to move? The brain is confused by the apparently contradictory data as its normal points of reference are mixed up.

The size of objects

It is known that the brain uses more than just the eye and image movement systems to perceive movement. The relative 'size of an object' can also have an effect. In another experiment carried out by K Dunked in 1938 he shone a light onto a large screen and moved the screen to the right. Most observers reported that they saw the screen as stationary and the spot of light moving to the left. The brain and the perceptual system *assume* that smaller objects are more likely to move. This clear example shows how it is possible for your perception of movement to contradict the evidence of your eye, image movement systems and probably the movement detectors in the visual cortex. What all this shows is that it can be quite easy for your visual system to become confused under certain circumstances. Poor vision can be rectified by what are in reality re-calibration exercises that work upon your perception.

What else do we need to understand about our perception of objects in the real world?

Our brains are able to enhance and enrich the raw information received from the eye. We see the word in depth, in 3-D. In reality the world could be represented in the same way as a painting. The canvas has no 'depth' as we assess it, yet our 'perception' is not of a flat picture. The images given by the senses are *interpreted* by the brain. It carefully assesses certain known 'clues' and the actual process of creating a 3-D picture by 'blowing it out', happens automatically. The brain receives information about the distances of the various parts of a picture. These can be explained by dividing the information sources into two types:

a) Monocular - these are accessible to the single eye and include decreasing size, height in the horizontal plain, gradient of texture, clarity, light, shadow, movement and perspective.
b) Binocular - these depend upon the interaction between the two eyes.

You have probably in the past seen a painting that depicts a building as you would see it if looking directly at it. Such paintings are two-dimensional yet a three-dimensional image is created. We all know that this is perspective. Let's also consider decreasing size, which we know is not always consistent. Remember a time when you have been watching a person walking away. It is known that as the distance of the figure doubles so the image in the retina halves. At a distance of three metres the retinal image is twice that at six metres. Your perception compensates for this and the figure is perceived as being the same size, irrespective of distance and not as alternatively growing and shrinking in size as the figure walks around. Your brain is able to provide an effect called 'size constancy' [15]

Do you see in a two-dimensional way?

Research has shown that a large number of people only see the world in a very two-dimensional way. One way you can test the quality of your own vision is through a 'stereoscope'. If pictures or films viewed in this way seem 'realer than real' then it is very likely this applies to you. You may still have normal binocular vision and yet still see in a very flat way. Once you have the opportunity of making a comparison you will be able to begin correcting this element of your sight.

Reading again plays a part in encouraging two-dimensional vision. As you know, reading is based upon the interpretation of a symbolic code that is meaningful to your brain because of past association and learning. Objects as presented to our senses in the real world have their own inherent characteristics. As we have already seen, reading requires a clear focus but causes 'staring' and 'fixation' of the eye. Unless reading is done properly, with a knowledge of the eye's requirement for movement, it provides little stimulation for your eye. The stimulation that is provided, is information that is presented in a two-dimensional way. Like any other habit, it is easy to transfer the habit across into other life situations and begin looking at everything in the same way. In other words your eye is not able to continually change its focus because it is focused upon print against a plain background that does not vary.

It will be obvious that using both your eyes and other senses in a way that allows you a real connection with the world is important. It is easy to become detached from the real world in a way that you are not aware. Logic and reason become the primary areas of experience. It can sound silly to say that exploring the world 'as a child does' will bring benefits but it certainly can. As a child you explored the world using all your senses and with a special type of curiosity. Once you stop exploring and examining in this way the process of *generalisation deletion and distortion* takes over. You have seen it all before. There is nothing new to learn. I always like to remind myself of how many colours or shades of green I can see when I look out into the world, particularly when I am in the countryside. It is easy to look and generalise these shades away. Simply classifying everything as 'green'. Once you start looking again for things that are available for you see, you will find that you begin reconnecting with your world in new ways.

Touch and sight

Use your sense of touch. When was the last time you took a common everyday object and explored exactly how it felt and corresponded with what you saw? There is a correlation between how well you see and how well you use your other senses. How do things look and how do they feel? How do you feel, what are your own kinaesthetic sensations within your body as you look at different objects? Once you begin using all your senses again you can then begin to use reading in new ways that reconnects you to the real quality of an experience represented by the words. The quality of your perception will change and improve as you do so.

A powerful discovery about movement and sight

As you consider your own eyesight and perception and the way in which you see the world, there is a very interesting discovery that you can bear in mind. David Hubel and Torstin Wiesel are two American physiologists. They carried out investigations into the *area striata* or 'visual projection area' of the brain. Using a cat's brain, they presented its eyes with simple visual shapes. They generally used light as the stimulus and this was presented at different angles of illumination. What they found was that, at certain angles, brain cells would fire with long bursts of activity. Others at the same angle were 'silent'. What they also found was that different cells would fire and respond to different angles. It is already known that the brain also has cells far deeper within it that respond to more 'general' characteristics, no matter which part of the retina is stimulated by light.

What is also extremely interesting was the discovery that **certain other cells *only* respond to movement.** Indeed, certain other cells were found *only to respond* to movement in a single direction. As you begin to consider the implications of this discovery for yourself, ask yourself what will happen if your way of seeing the world does not involve the stimulation of these cells necessary to stimulate those certain parts of your brain that control key elements of your visual process? The answer is obviously that you will experience defective eyesight.

What this research shows is that there are specific processes and particular mechanisms within your brain for selecting and choosing 'how' to select *certain features* of particular objects. Your perception and so your sight is built upon patterns and combinations of these selected objects. If you are simply not engaging and powering up certain circuits within your visual process, you will never have good vision. Habitual ways of incorrectly using your visual process can therefore be explored down to the micro level of cell stimulation that in turn determines brain response and visual acuity.

Dr Bates made a great point of emphasising the beneficial experience to be gained of movement in spatial relationships and the correspondence between sight and touch. There is a sound basis for doing so because the visual representation corresponds with the brain's representation of touch. **Touch and vision are very closely related**.

Binocular cues

Binocular cues are the data made available to the brain by the interaction between the two eyes. Retinal disparity has a specific effect with this overall system of operation. The eyes lie in different sockets in the head and so do not receive exactly the same view of any object. The closer the object, the greater the retinal disparity between the two images. Research has shown that a large number of people actually 'see' only through one eye. This leads to squints, suppression and anisometropia. Where this is the case, the solution lies in expanding the use of the side that is currently under used.

Convergence

This is a cue from the muscles that turn and direct the eyes. For objects more than twenty- five metres, the lines of vision the two eyes are parallel.

Objects which are closer than this mean that the eyes must converge, and the closer the object, the greater the convergence. Have you ever tried the game when you were a child of watching one finger as you bring it closer and closer to your face or the face of someone else? Watch the eyes cross as they converge to their fullest extent. This *convergence cue* is a signal to the responsible eye muscles about the extent to which the eye muscles and the eyes have to converge to focus upon an object. In accordance with Dr Bates' interpretation of the role of the eye muscles, as convergence takes places it means that the eyes also change shape or should change shape, if the muscles are in good condition.

It is due to your ability to use all the monocular and binocular cues referred to so far, that a flat retinal image can be translated into a more useful and functional 3-D perception of the world.

It is not difficult to understand how with such a complex process the function of sight often deteriorates. Calibration may change on the back of a strong emotional response to a situation, anxiety, trauma or new belief or association. The Snellen test is a good example. Understanding the factors that make sight and perception possible, being a combination of physiological and psychological mechanisms, it becomes possible to understand how faulty or imperfect vision can be rectified through the use of specific new technologies. The exciting part is that improving your vision will not cost you hundreds of pounds. It simply involves using the technologies in this book with the benefit of the overall background understanding.

Selective attention

We are predominantly visual in our interpretation of the world and it has been estimated that 'well over ninety per cent' of the information we receive about the world is received through the visual sense. There is however no guarantee that an image projected onto the retina will be perceived in its entirety. Indeed large parts of the visual images falling on the retina are coded by the retinal receptive fields and then transmitted along the optic nerve to the brain but do not seem to be processed any further. The brain is able to 'direct its attention' to any part of the visual image, which is then processed in great detail.

The brain therefore has the ability to concentrate your attention upon particular parts of the visual field. Experiments in this area have shown when looking with a glance, that we can take in only surprisingly small amounts of information out of the potential information that is available. Even so, the amount of information we do take in is far larger than we have a conscious appreciation for. There are certain things that are known to have a greater chance of being an accepted stimuli by the brain. These 'rules' apply to all the senses, not just vision.

So what are the types of stimulus that are more likely to make us pay attention?

Intensity. The more intense a stimulus (the brighter the light, the louder the sound), the more we will attend to it.

Contrast. Sudden changes in the intensity of a stimulus will gain attention. A change in light colour is one example. Another example in the auditory system is that a loud noise after a while becomes less noticeable. If the noise suddenly stops, attention is focused on the absence of noise. We hear a 'deafening' silence!

Repetition. The more a stimulus is repeated, the more likely it is to gain attention.

Movement. We are generally very sensitive to movement, particularly within our field of vision. This is connected to the survival mechanism.

So overall, all these factors cause us to pay *attention*. **Perception is adjusted to meet specific needs**. If you think about it, in order to move safely through the world it is far better for us to see 'physical objects' than it is to see 'sensations'. This is a feature of our human development that has evolved over time. Emotion and motivation do play a crucially important role in your perception and are also an important element in perfect vision.

One feature of the way in which our vision works that I found most surprising is that as we look at any object, we see a colour, the texture and the character. It's just as though you are looking 'out' through your eyes and into the world around you. It turns out that the reality is very different.

We do not see 'out' into the real world!

Light comes *in* to us and we do not see out! The interpretation our brains provide us with is that we are united with the world. We look out upon the world that is all around us. We can experience pictures that we see inside our heads. The reality is that there are no pictures inside our heads! We know that in order to see a picture there must be light. Light is the stimulus that creates the picture for us. We know that there is no light inside our brains (nor are there any sounds). If this is the case, how do we experience the things that happen within our brains? How do we make sense of the world? It seems that our brains represent these things in 'symbols'. Computer science has shown us that symbols themselves can be very different from the real things they represent. It is an illusion in the best sense of the word. Nearly everyone has seen illustrations and photographs showing the composition of our brains. The matter of the brain is dark and silent. The fabulous illusion is created for us that we 'see' pictures and 'hear' sounds.

Vision

The visual cortex of the human brain interprets the electrical impulses sent to it by the retina and reinterprets them into *the illusion* of pictures and images. So, in reality, perception and consequently vision use the medium of electricity and not colour to function. **When working fully and properly, normal sight is an *element* of perception.**

Explaining defective sight in terms of perception means that the perception we are receiving is not an 'accurate measure' of the physical world. The thing to remember is that perception is by its very nature an *active and interpretative ability* and not merely a receptive process of accepting information and reproducing it inside our heads. The discerning reader will see this is part of the answer to defective sight. Which category best describes you? Are you merely receiving and processing information or are you active and interpreting in your quest for information?

Simply receiving and processing information usually means disconnecting from the real world in some specific way or ways. The more 'disconnected' you are, the worse the problem. **Now** is the time to take back your right to be **active and interactive** within the world and this means **stimulating all your senses**.

Diagram 2 Examples of different types of reasons.

The observation of teachers of natural eyesight methods over the years has been that deteriorating vision is often directly connected to some form of trauma. Poor vision results because of the reaction to a specific event. In other words, you may react to one specific event in a way that affects your visual process. Other events of a similar nature do not affect your vision because you react to them in a different way.

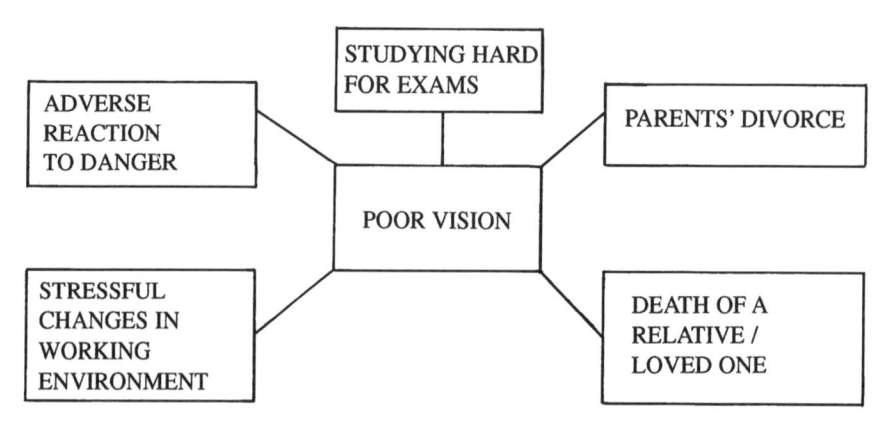

```
        ┌──────────────────┐
        │ STUDYING HARD    │
        │ FOR EXAMS        │
        └──────────────────┘
┌──────────┐      │       ┌──────────────────┐
│ ADVERSE  │      │       │ PARENTS' DIVORCE │
│ REACTION │──────┤       └──────────────────┘
│ TO DANGER│      │              │
└──────────┘      │              │
              ┌───────────┐
              │ POOR VISION│
              └───────────┘
┌────────────┐    │              │
│ STRESSFUL  │    │       ┌──────────────┐
│ CHANGES IN │────┤       │ DEATH OF A   │
│ WORKING    │            │ RELATIVE /   │
│ ENVIRONMENT│            │ LOVED ONE    │
└────────────┘            └──────────────┘
```

You see what you want to see!

You see what you want to see or indeed what you expect to see! When a person has experienced defective vision for some time, the way in which the brain operates means that you come to *expect* a defective image or picture of the world. The reason for the deterioration in your sight in the first instance is for other reasons but it is 'maintained' in part by the very system of perception and interpretation that makes sight possible.

To explore this situation a little further you may consciously want to have good vision, yet subconsciously for some reason you do not want to see clearly or you may be ambivalent toward seeing. Research shows that this type of situation manifests itself most frequently when eyesight is progressively getting worse and yet glasses do little to decrease the speed of deterioration. I introduced the idea earlier that causes and reasons for behaviour can become totally lost in our subconscious memories. Can you cure such a situation on your own? Soul searching is not needed and the exact reason for the problem is not needed once you identify that this is or *could* be the cause of your problem. This is provided that you fully align yourself with your objective of normal vision. If you find that anything is stopping you from achieving the results you want it is likely to such a subconscious objection. If you realise what it is, you can focus upon alignment of your whole self, with instruction and re instruction as necessary to achieve your objective.

The situation you are aiming for is:

1) achieve total relaxation for your visual process
2) break your old habit of poor vision by forming a new habit of central alignment[16].

The result will be perfect vision[17].

Provided that nothing from your subconscious mind is holding you back, based upon some long-forgotten reason and continuing 'misinterpretation' of information by your brain, you will find that your sight will recover. The experiments with perception show exactly what is possible.

If you find along the way that you are experiencing failures or setbacks, apply this understanding to them. Do not punish yourself, with self-talk such as:

"Why won't it work…Why can't I…It does not work…Maybe they can but I can't…"

These are all 'signals' or messages from your brain that identify this cause. Once you understand this you can begin to do something about it. Remember that **'practice and repetition are the masters of all ability'**. The main point is for you is to have 'decided' upon your objective, which means that *you will accept no other outcome.*

It is part of the assessment of how successful we are in interpreting our perception of the world. Under normal conditions the brain can sometimes mistakenly interpret information leading to a misperception of the object. As already indicated there are many reasons why this can occur. We have all heard the saying 'love is blind' and of people who look at the world through 'rose coloured spectacles'. These are the effects of emotion and motivation upon **the interpretation of information** from the actual sense organs. This is a very important distinction to be aware of as the process happens unconsciously and without our awareness. What happens when an emotion of a negative nature is attached to an experience of poor vision?

The examples given are perhaps the more obvious examples to illustrate the point. Errors in sight due to emotion and motivation are crucially important in the visual process and the reasons for defective vision. The brain learns quickly and the old maxim of alignment of mind, body and spirit is extremely apt.

It is a simple process that occurs. For those of us that have had perfect vision, which becomes defective, faulty vision does not tend to 'happen' overnight. We do not wake up one day and know we have defective vision. It tends to happen over a period of time. We come to experience over time the fact that our eyesight is less than perfect. What this means is that we begin to give our brains instructions at the subconscious level that we cannot see as well as we could. Gradually in consciousness we come to realise our sight is defective. We have in fact already been giving our brains this same message subconsciously for some time prior to our becoming consciously aware of our defective vision.

Your perception of your self-image

This is where you can begin to view the meaning of perception from a different angle. Your perception of your own self-image. You will recall that perception is defined as the brains interpretation of data. Self-image is nothing more than the brain's *interpretation* of the total data it holds, as it relates to you. With defective vision your perception comes to be that your vision is less than perfect. What this means is that your perceptions support the fact that sight has become defective (often for other reasons, as we saw above), thus reinforcing the fact of defective vision. A loop is made which becomes totally self-supporting. It all happens within your perception of your self-image and there is no force within you more powerful than your self-image.

The power of your self-image can also make it extremely difficult to accept that glasses are bad for you and that your eyesight can be corrected naturally and quickly. If it took a major adjustment within your personal

Knowing Our Perceptions Is Knowing How To See!

life, over time, to adjust to glasses and accept them, your own self-image has come to accept and incorporate them within your life. Resistance to change is understandable when considered against this background. If glasses have permeated your persona to such a degree, your whole outlook supports glasses and your beliefs are aligned behind them. Very deep-rooted psychological moulds may take time to change if the position is not stimulated by a massive personal desire for change.

One thing that we do know about the brain is that it learns quickly. It can quickly learn to perceive or *misperceive* information that it is receiving as 'normal'. What this means is that the brain forgets what normal vision is like, it learns a new defective way of seeing and perceiving. This is one of the reasons glasses do not cure poor vision and only re-enforce it or often make it worse over time. This may sound as though it runs contrary to common sense and that no one would voluntarily continue to have defective vision. The reason for this was dealt with above. The brain functions using conscious and subconscious operating procedures and it is subconsciously that so much happens.

The fact is that this process takes place subconsciously and so we are generally unaware of it. Our de-motivation of being unable to see clearly and resulting emotional stimulus supports this state of defective vision, as we begin to reinforce the state of defective vision by telling ourselves 'that we cannot see as well as we could'. This is not an instruction that we deliberately give to our brains, it is more a comment upon a state of fact as we perceive it. Unfortunately the brain does not accept it this way, it takes it as a command to reach a particular goal. Much is now known about the workings of the brain and it is essentially a goal-seeking organism. What this means is that we have to be very careful about the instructions that we give it. Many of these instructions are often generated in response to events but they are acted upon in the same way, as *'instructions to be carried out.'*

There is much work and research which has been carried out in recent years in this area and I can confirm from my own personal experience that these are indeed the essential operating principles of the brain. **These are the principles that got me results.** I became aware of these distinctions and used them. If something was not working for me I did not give up. I remained positive. I knew I would succeed and I continued to look for the distinction that would make what I wanted work. It may occur to you that quite apart from defective vision, this basic principle shows the crucial importance of being aware of *how* you are instructing your brain. It is a life skill. If it works for eyesight, where else will it work for you? This is not a skill that we are taught at school and the situation has been accurately defined by the describing the situation as *'being like having a computer without having an operating manual'*. The real implications of this statement are in fact far greater than they seem.

There is a definition of perception that acknowledges its interpretative role, (Gregory, 1966):

> "Perception is not determined simply by...stimulus patterns, rather it is a dynamic searching for the best interpretation of the available data...It seems clear that perception involves going beyond the immediately given evidence of the senses..."

> "Perception involves attempts to interpret data received from the senses that what is perceived is not data but the interpretation of it..."

This means that **your perception is an active system**, converting a world of sensations into a state of awareness of the world around you. The whole structure of your system is that it is *'active'*. An active system can always be altered. Begin to view yourself in a new way and realise you are not stuck in a mould. You are capable of adaptation and change and no where is this more true than in your visual process.

An exercise in perceptual awareness

Use the following exercise to make new distinctions. It is an exercise in internal 'awareness'. Things that are available to you, once you know *how* to look for them. It is exactly the same type of awareness that is needed for your visual process. The ability to be 'aware' is something you can always put to good use as you improve your seeing process. The exercise was originally devised for another purpose[18] but I find it useful to demonstrate the point, (for those not already familiar with it), that we can come to be aware of new things, in new contexts.

Wearing your glasses/lenses over time

Think back to a time five years ago. Did you wear glasses or lenses then? If so, fine. If not, think back to an earlier time, (in the more recent past, but before now) when you began wearing your glasses/lenses - the further back in time the better.

Next think of a time a week ago when you wore your glasses/lenses. The next stage is to think about wearing your glasses/lenses now. Pause for a moment and then think of a time one week from now when you will wear your glasses/lenses. Follow this on with five years from now, and a time you know you will wear your glasses/lenses.

This is an exercise in noticing the distinctions available to you within your inner perception. It does not matter about the content, which can be personal to you. Do keep the content the same for each event. What do you notice about *how* you represent each of these experiences to yourself? Have a sense of representing the experiences *all at the same time*.

Knowing Our Perceptions Is Knowing How To See!

What are the differences you notice that there are in the same event but represented over different times? You may notice that you are in a different location, e.g. a house or wherever. How else do you know that one experience is in the past and one is in the future? How do you know one happened a long time ago and another only last week?

You may well judge by memories of the event, however what else is available for you to notice? The memory would be a content difference. As you begin to notice other differences in your representation of the events, where do you hold *'spatially'* the representation of each event? Is each event held in a 'different location' or a different place? This may be in front of you? A typical representation is that the past events are held to your left and the future events to the right? What do you notice? Is five years to the future held further away than one week into the future?

What other differences do you notice? Is the future as detailed as the past? What about the size of each representation that you hold? Are they all the same size? Is the brightness of each image the same? What happens as you represent each experience at one time?

This is a simple introduction to some of things it is possible to become aware of within your own internal perception. The way in which you internally represent events through time. The aim is only to demonstrate that whatever way you currently perceive things, **there are always other things available for you to notice**. The way in which you perceive the world and your recollection and future projection of it can have a massive influence on how and what you do or will attempt to do.

---

[1] See Chapter 2.
[2] Fisher and Pogo
[3] We shall be looking later at the work of David Marr.
[4] The visual element of perception can be broadly generalised and described as consisting of a three way perceptual system. 1) The Visual Spherule –Band Fine –Area 4 system where information on colours and shades of grey is processed. The system is not good at detecting sharpness. 2) The Parvi-Intraspherular Pale-Bands route. This deals with static forms and detects boundaries made up of colour contrasts. It is a high resolution perception of static forms. 3) The Magno 4B Wide –Band –MT system. Here movement and stereoscopic effect are interpreted. The nuerons have a particularly fast response time but stimulus falls of immediately even when the stimulus itself is maintained. It does not distinguish boundaries containing only chromatic contrast.
[5] See diagram 6, Chapter 1.
[6] This should also be distinguished from excessive variation in refraction, where the eyes change focus continually and randomly, without stability and without focus.
[7] R Pritchard devised a method of achieving exactly this under test conditions and demonstrating that this is true.
[8] See Chapter 9.
[9] See also Chapter 1.
[10] Defined as lack of movement.
[11] Nickla, Wildsoet, Wallman 1997

[12] Changes in the synthesis of glycosaminoglycans in the choroid are correlated with changes in choroidal thickness.
[13] *Cellular Learning: A new look at the theory of Emmetropia.*
[14] There are two movement signalling systems a) the retina/image system and b) the eye/head system.
[15] First referred to by Gregory 1966.
[16] This is dealt with in Chapter 9.
[17] Research has shown that it only takes twenty-one days to form a new habit.
[18] Timelines – a specific area of perceptual exercises.

CHAPTER 7

GETTING STARTED - THE MAGIC EYE!

Have you ever seen a 'Magic Eye'? These are the strange and wonderful patterns that look like a piece of over patterned wallpaper. At first sight it is a bright, colourful and complex pattern but nothing else? If you have successfully seen the image which appears out of the pattern, when the brain, 'through the eye', re-focuses its perception, the transformation really is remarkable!

If you have never tried 'Magic Eye' go to the illustration at the centre of the book.[1] The first thing to do is relax in a quiet place. The way in which to see the image is to hold the image so that it touches your nose. Let your eyes relax and stare off vacantly into space, as if looking through the image. Relax and become comfortable with the idea of observing the image, without looking at it. When you are relaxed and not crossing your eyes, move the page slowly away from your face, perhaps an inch or two every two or three seconds. Keep looking through the page. Stop at a comfortable reading distance and keep staring. The most discipline is needed when something starts to 'come in'. This is the moment you'll instinctively try to look at the page rather than looking through it. If you look at it, start again.

A second method involves looking at the illustration in such a way that you identify the reflection. For example, hold it under an overhead lamp so that it catches its light. Simply look at the object you see reflected, and continue to stare at it with a fixed gaze. After several seconds, you'll perceive depth, followed by the 3D image, which will develop almost like an instant photo!

Persist until you 'see' the 3D image within the pattern. It is 'deep vision' and in order to see it you must firstly have one eye look at a point in the image while the other eye looks at the same point in the next pattern. After you hold your eyes in this way long enough your brain will decode the 3D information. The two methods involve either crossing your eyes or diverging your eyes. Crossing your eyes occurs when you aim your eyes at a point between your eyes and an image. Diverging your eyes occurs when your eyes are aimed at a point beyond the image. This is the recommended method[2]. It is even possible to purchase books full of these patterns[3].

You may be saying to yourself that these are just fancy optical illusions. How can they be an aid to correcting faulty vision? What these magic eyes *prove* is that you do have power over your own eyesight and perception. It is just a matter of re-training your visual capabilities. Thousands of people worldwide have enjoyed the effects created by the 'magic eye'. In addition some of the techniques necessary for good vision are needed in order to see the magic eye pattern. In particular seeing the image means you must 'let the image come to you', which is a habit of good sight.

What else do 'Magic eyes' show us? That *'what we see is not always what we get!'* Sometimes we all need to use our ability to use deeper vision. In re-training our perceptions, it is a little like riding a bike. Once you can do it, you wonder why you ever had a problem. More practice leads to further accomplishment.

If you cannot see the pattern immediately do not worry. Leave it for a little while and come back to it. Eventually, if you keep trying you will see the image contained within the pattern. You do not have to be able to see the pattern before being able to start correcting your eyesight. It is however worth the effort of finding out how to do it, to demonstrate to yourself that you are approaching the matter of your sight correction in a flexible and open-minded way. In other words, that you are prepared to see things in new ways, and that you will allow yourself to do so.

It also proves that no matter what you think you 'can' or 'cannot' see, the magic eye shows you what else is possible! In order for you to understand and 'see' the image within the 'magic eye', your eye and brain had to learn to 'see' in a new way. The way in which your brain does this has already been looked at in Chapter 6.

If you know that your eyes and brain, working in conjunction, are more than capable of learning to see *'new things'* in *'new ways'*, it will help to convince you of the relative ease with which your visual process can be restored to normal. All you are doing now is making adjustments to get back to normal. If you can learn to see things such as the magic eye in new ways, then you can certainly learn to make the natural adjustments to restore your visual process.

Again it helps to quote Dr Bates:[4]

> "It has been demonstrated in thousands of cases that all abnormal action of the external muscles of the eyeball is accompanied by a strain or effort to see, and that with the relief of this strain the action of the muscles becomes normal and all errors of refraction disappear...The eye may be blind, it may be suffering from atrophy of the optic nerve, from cataract, or from disease of the retina, but so long as it does not try to see, the external muscles act normally and there is no error of refraction. **This fact furnishes us with the means by which all these conditions so long held to be incurable may be corrected.**
>
> It has also been demonstrated that for every error of refraction there is a different kind of strain..." (Author's bold)

GETTING STARTED - THE MAGIC EYE!

How to start improving your vision now!

The process of proving to yourself that you do have control over your visual process is easy! I proved it to myself after I had decided to take action and start correcting my eyesight. I did this by finding a sign to read. It turned out to be a 'no smoking' sign. It had a white background and a red circular symbol with a red 'bar' going across the circle. It's a fairly common type of sign and I am sure you have probably seen a similar one. The actual lettering underneath the symbol was white, being reversed out of a red square box. It said, "SMOKING AND NAKED FLAMES PROHIBITED". I remember the sign because of the colouring and the fact it was the first sign I began experimenting with. I was about twelve feet from the sign as I viewed it straight on. I remember that the letters were not clear. The effect was a blur, the white and red colours had no distinct edges as I looked at them. They were in fact that blurred that I remember I could not initially make out what the sign said! I then decided to look at the sign from a sideways view. What I mean by this is that I turned my head immediately left and looked at the sign with my right eye. The left eye got a view of the shape of my nose. As I moved my head up and down and sideways I noticed that there were 'small changes' in the quality of my vision.

It is important that when you carry out this or a similar exercise to **you look for small changes.** No matter how small and insignificant the changes may be, become aware of them. If you are long sighted, practise the same exercise at a distance from which you do not have clear vision. The same applies to other types of visual defect. It is the guiding principle that is important. Look for and *extract* the small changes in the quality of your vision.

The next thing I did was to stop and begin exercising my eyes. I looked immediately up and did so until I could feel a slight strain upon my eye muscles. I then did the same exercise moving my eyes just right, and then the same again looking immediately right. If you can imagine a circular clock face, the last three positions would start at 12 o'clock, 7 1/2 minutes past and quarter past. (*see Diagram 1*)

Diagram 1

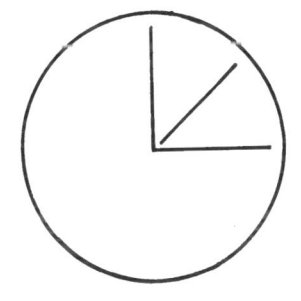

I continued with the exercise until I had completed a full circle in this manner. I did this a couple of times and then repeated my peripheral vision test. **I noticed that there had been a definite improvement in the quality of what I could see**. The boundaries between the different colours had become much clearer and the shape of the outlines had become much more distinct. There was also an improvement in my sight as I looked straight on at the sign.

The aim of the exercise is to become aware of your focusing process. If you know that one eye is weaker than the other, e.g. if the left eye is weaker than the right, try moving that eye slightly to the right. Stop and concentrate upon doing it. The only thing you are trying to do is obtain a change of focus. This may amount to only a change in blurring or definition. This is the change you want.

Blinking

You may notice that as you do this exercise you start blinking more than normally. Plenty of blinking at this stage is good for the eye. Blinking clears and lubricates the eye. An interesting thing to become aware of is that as you blink, there is for a quick moment a change in vision. The focus or image you are looking at changes. You may notice some improvement in definition. Do not expect to be able to see perfectly and automatically. This is very unlikely to happen. These changes are small and you must train yourself to look for them, feel them and become aware of them. The sooner you find yourself becoming aware of these small changes, the quicker you will make progress.

The exercise should be repeated, focusing and re-focusing and becoming more aware of the feeling in your eye as you do this. The muscle contraction as it operates upon your lens and eyeball. As soon as a change of focus occurs you will 'feel' the difference at the back of your eye. These are feelings and sensations that you will not normally be aware of so pay particular attention to them.

There is no doubt that the process can be a slow one to start with. This is only because you may not be used to paying such attention to these areas of your conscious thought. The thing to do is simply 'play around', without unduly straining your eyes. Make a decision that you will move forward and achieve these slight adjustments in your vision.

An interesting thing that you may notice, is that as you play around, specifically begin noticing and looking for the colour black. As the quality of your focus improves, you will notice that the colour 'black' is actually not 'black' as you normally view it. As soon as you start to notice the colour 'black' beginning to look deeper, darker and 'blacker', you will know yourself that you have made an improvement.

You will also realise that what you have until now accepted as the colour black is more of a washed out greyish colour. Its what you have generalised over a period of time to represent the colour black. Your brain has generalised this wishy-washy colour you think is black, as a substitution of what 'real dark deep black' actually looks like.

This may all sound a little nonsensical. That is because you actually need to experience and see the difference for yourself now! Reading about it may make intellectual sense but because it is a visual phenomenon, to understand it fully you must do it rather than read about it.

What we have just talked about is 'part' of what is known as the modelling process that all human beings use to make sense of the world. No two human beings actually experience the world in exactly the same way. This is because we all have nervous systems, which interpret incoming information from our senses in a way that is unique to each individual, although everybody's nervous system functions in the same way. There has been much discovery in the modelling process used by human beings in recent years. It is in part an understanding of these principles that makes improvements in your eyesight possible.

When I first did this exercise I was able to detect adjustments the eye was making in its focusing and the 'distance' of this new focus. The next thing I did was to try and get a continuous fixed focus. As I began to do this, I noticed the colours in the signs I was looking at and experimenting with were sharpening up and becoming more vivid. I became much more aware of signs that had black letting in them. The black definitely became blacker and clearer and generally better defined. At first I experienced a slight double vision as my eye was being forced to make re-adjustments. As this situation corrected itself the images almost looked as though they had become closer. It was a slight difference in magnification - very slight, yet at the same time large enough to make a real difference.

As I remember these exercises, I was aware that as I broke my gaze temporarily and then reverted back to look at the sign, the definition immediately became much sharper. What I did notice was a change in tone, the black becoming 'blacker', although it may not have been immediately fully focused.

The difference that these exercises make is quite remarkable. As I recall, in one instance, at ten feet, as I continued to look and see what appeared to be a thick black line on a piece of paper, it appeared only as a 'blur'. It did not even look like words! Suddenly and almost miraculously definition began to form, to sharpen and the colour became more vivid. Almost at the same time the whole thing came into focus. It really is a wonderful feeling to know that without drugs, without artificial aids and completely naturally, control over your eyesight has been regained.

The remarkable part is that you can control a part of your brains functioning that most people are taught to believe is beyond their control. It's exciting to know that you can have control over the power of your vision. It is even more exciting to know that you can have control over the power of your own brain!

How does it feel to know what is possible and to achieve such an improvement? My own personal feeling was one of elevation - a great sense of personal achievement, success and wonder at the power of what is locked within my own brain. It was the excitement of the other possibilities that I knew I could achieve which really began to stimulate me. I now knew I could break out of the restricting disability I had been experiencing. I immediately felt that my sense of awareness, of colour, form, shape, contrast, vividness, brightness and tone in the world around me had changed. These things had been lost in a 'blur' and I had not been able to appreciate it.

This was more than enough to convince me that I did have control over my visual process and that all it needed was a little time and some dedication to improve the quality of my vision. I reasoned that as it had taken some time for my eyes to get into this current state of being unable to see clearly, it would take a little time to rectify them.

Start a regular daily eye workout!

I knew at that moment that the answer lay in gradually exercising my eye muscles. Just like a normal muscle, my eye muscles needed building up again, gradually! I was extremely excited by the prospects and decided that I would make this one of my ***regular daily eye workouts.***

So to get yourself started you can either find a similar type of sign or use the visual correction eye chart[5]. Anything really to test the current state of your eyesight. This needs to be a subjective test. Something you can assess for yourself. You need to know what you are currently capable of seeing naturally. You also must know how it feels as the changes in your eyesight happen, as small adjustments become noticeable. It is the small changes that are your building blocks and your foundation for improvement.

Be clear that before you start you must assess what can see. It does not matter how good or how bad the state of your vision currently is. You have the ability to change it! To improve it to a degree you would not have thought possible. **Remember that no matter how poor your eyesight, others have already achieved the type of improvements you want by using these techniques.**

Keep a journal of your progress

As you make your initial assessment make a note of what you see. You will need a journal and this will be your first entry. I can't over-stress the importance of keeping a journal. This is your record from the point where you are commencing your journey. It is your evidence of the improvements

Getting Started - The Magic Eye!

you will make. The time may come when you feel you are not making any progress or that the progress is not fast enough. It is during these times that referring to your journal will show you how far you have progressed and push you forward into your next success.

It is all too easy to fail to notice the daily improvements that take place. I can say that my own journal was an invaluable source of inspiration and a record of my achievements and successes. You should record your success for your own personal benefit. The personal power you acquire through regularly completing your journal will show you that you do possess control over this essential function. This is something to be proud of. Something **you will achieve.** *Record all your successes no matter how small.*

There are other reasons for keeping a journal as well. Vision in a majority of cases simply deteriorates over time without you noticing when exactly it happens. Keeping a journal will ensure you notice the improvements that you make. It will also show you that **improvement is inevitable**. You do not have to believe what I say or what anyone else has written. You will have the evidence of change and improvement in your own journal.

One of the first things you *must* do is *decide* that you will follow through and take regular and consistent action to achieve your goal of normal vision. Again I cannot over emphasise the importance of your deciding that you absolutely must and will achieve your goal. That you will cut off any other possibility. You must make it clear to yourself and your brain that nothing less will do. *Decide to commit now.*

Write out your decision now in your journal. Why have you decided that you want normal vision? What will it mean to you? How do you see yourself in the future with perfect eyesight? What other benefits will having normal eyesight bring to you?

* Saving £100s of pounds per annum on lenses or glasses?

* The benefits of knowing your eyes will be healthy?

* Comfort in knowing that you are not continuing to damage your eyes?

* Convenience? How do you feel looking at a future where you are freed from poor vision?

* Which area of your life would be effected and benefit most?

* The knowledge that you are mastering real thinking power and learning how to use your brain and mind to gain a positive result!

No doubt you have many more personal reasons that you will add to this list.

FIVE STAR VISION

A useful way to perceive the ideas here and one that everyone can follow when doing these exercises is simply to 'imagine' what it would be like to improve your eyesight in the way described so far. Think first about how you will do it. How will it be as you alter the tension of the muscle in your eye that is responsible for focusing your lens? How will it be as you change the tension in the muscles of your eye that control the shape of your eyeball? Even if you don't think you can do that, *imagine how it would be if you could do that!* Stop and think about these things for a moment. Get a sense of how it will be to have greater control over your eye muscle. How will you feel as you obtain the change in your vision and focus?

It will pay you the dividends you want if you take the time now to consider the impact such changes will make for you.

There is an essential ingredient that forms the basis of all good habits of sight. Once you achieve it normal sight follows on naturally. We shall examine this ingredient of perfect sight in the next chapter.

---

[1] Reproduced with permission. © 1997 Magic Eye Inc.
[2] The technique is safe but do not strain your eyes. Relax and let the image come to you.
[3] *Magic Eye II 3-D illusions*, N E Thing Enterprises, published by the Penguin Group
[4] Dr Bates, *Better Eyesight Without Glasses* (Souvenir Press)
[5] If you have not already done so please apply for the **free** visual correction chart by referring to the note under the List of Illustrations and Acknowledgements.

CHAPTER 8

THE ESSENCE OF RELAXATION

"...enjoy a stressless hour of peace and quiet..."

As we move through an understanding of the visual process you will come to appreciate for yourself why the eye and the brain 'create' defective vision. For the body to carry out any task well it must be in its most natural state - a state of relaxation.

There are two types of relaxation: the type that leaves you completely limp and almost flaccid, where you do not think of doing or even attempting to do anything. The second includes the ability to maintain an *ease* or relaxation of the mind and whole body while carrying out some task. This is the type of relaxation required to carry out any skill and one that is given great emphasis in the martial arts. It is this second type of relaxation that underpins good sight and indeed is the true secret of any skill. So how do you know when you have got the form of relaxation required and how do you achieve it? Before examining how to obtain this state, it will be beneficial to examine the opposite state to relaxation, which is stress.

Stress

If we consider what we know already about stress it becomes easy to understand the correlation between stress and poor sight. If we look at the parallels in other areas of the body and assess the known effects of stress, it becomes obvious that stress plays a major role in poor sight. The specific types of *visual strain* that emanate from this stress is the cause of defective sight.

Research has shown that for every effort of the eye to focus correctly, there is a different type of *'strain'* associated to the problem. Myopia is always associated with a strain to see at distance and hypermetropia is always associated with strain to see a near point. An eye which otherwise has normal vision will still strain to see near objects, when temporarily focused on a far point and while still tying to see at a near point at the same time. The eye in such circumstances is trying to do the impossible. The changes that take place usually occur with evidence of increased strain and a lowering of vision.

When the eye strains to see at a near point it becomes flatter than it was before. If it was originally elongated it may well pass from this condition to a spherical condition and then through to a condition where it is flattened. An eye straining to see at a far distance does the opposite. It becomes rounder that it was before and may well pass from a flattened condition through to the elongated condition. In both cases if the changes occur asymmetrically the resulting astigmatism is explained.

As we go back and consider Dr Bates' work, he was able to conclude that when a strain to see is produced, it is *a strain of the mind*. Although this strain is automatic and subconscious in its nature, it can be controlled and corrected.

It has already been independently confirmed that stress is a major factor in many diseases with a significant psychosomatic component. In other words, diseases where physical symptoms are induced or even aggravated by mental or emotional disturbances. Impaired eyesight is obviously not a disease, but the connections and relationship between certain physical symptoms and stress has already been established. Stress related disorders account for between fifty and eighty per cent of all illness. Stress may not be the only factor but it often plays a significant role.

Stress is actually the body's response to a threat or demand made upon it. If you think about it, any demand made upon the body in a new or challenging situation can result in a stress level being generated. The condition of stress is produced as part of out evolutionary 'fight or flight' defence mechanism. Although we do not directly use the mechanism as much today it is still operating, often in ways that we are unaware. Under stress the body is able to make lightening fast physiological changes or adaptive responses.

Problems arise with the stress mechanism where activity commences to deal with a stressful situation but the full response does not take place. Maybe being caught in a traffic jam. It can cause all types of physical reactions and the body prepares for 'fight or flight' but is unable to carry out the action. It is recognised that over time repeated experiences of a frustrating nature can cause high blood pressure and similar conditions. There is a major list of stress related conditions many of which are not directly detectable. Stress can therefore have both a physical and psychological cause.

When we begin to draw the parallels of known conditions relating from stress and the cause of defective vision, the similarities become convincing. A lot more is known today about stress than it was when Dr Bates originally put forward the basis for eyesight correction treatment. At that time Dr Bates was still able to conclude, after thorough research, that poor sight was a direct result of 'strain'.

What is the definition of stress? Stress or strain results when an applied force or system of forces strains or deforms a body. If we apply this definition to the structure of the eye, it makes perfect sense. When the shape of the eyeball is altered into an incorrect shape because of incorrect functioning of the muscles that control the eye, strain results. Defective sight follows on.

Today our minds are under a tremendous amount of strain and stresses that we are unaware of. It just becomes natural. We wear the strain the same way we wear our clothes. We do not notice it. We have adjusted to it. The good news is that there is a remedy. All you have to do is apply it!

To commence a program to rid yourself of this strain or stress means firstly recognising the role strain has played in giving you defective eyesight. This strain has become part of your everyday life. No doubt you can also accept that ridding yourself of unnecessary stress will produce big results in other areas of your life. So the cause of imperfect vision is actually mental strain and this underlies the incorrect functioning of the visual process for both far and near vision. Dr Bates confirmed that the point had been convincingly demonstrated in thousands of cases. It is up to you to take charge of your visual process and **decide that you will rectify it.**

Have you ever considered how much stress and strain it actually takes to drive a car? You may not even think twice about it now but driving a car is a stressful activity. Think back to the very first time you ever got into a car to drive one. You probably felt apprehensive, some anxiety and some stress. It would not be natural if you did not. As you think back to that time you may remember feeling hot and sweaty as you began to perspire more at the thought of driving and the concentration that it required. Steering, accelerating, indicating, looking in the mirror, watching the road, being ready to break, pressing the clutch to change gear. Do you remember what it was actually like, what you saw, how you felt and what you physically experienced, the first time you attempted to drive a car?

You probably now do all the things required for driving naturally, without effort and without thinking about them. They have become subconscious and so has the original memory of the stress you experienced the first time you drove a car. If you normally wear glasses and you need them to drive, have you tried driving for any distance without your glasses on? How does that feel? Is it the same as driving with your glasses on or is it a lot more stressful? Do you feel a nagging doubt or worry in the back of your mind about driving without your glasses? Can you see properly to drive? What if you have a crash?

This is only one small example to demonstrate the point. We are subjected to many numerous types of stress and strain every day. The original reasons as to why you find an activity stressful will have long faded into your distant memories, being nothing more than a subconscious trace at the current time. The same thing applies to jobs, housework, looking after children. **All activities produce their own special forms of stress and we will very rarely be aware of the stress that accompanies them**. The point has already been made that when the eye is under a strain its ability to see is markedly decreased in certain circumstances. As previously pointed out sleep itself does not rest the eye.

There are in fact an infinite number of ways in which people generally (and you in particular) cause yourself stress. Luckily there are numerous ways to cure it.

The discipline of relaxation

What is true relaxation? Sitting in front of the television with a glass of wine or a beer? Watching your favourite program? Does this really rest your mind and provide it with the **relaxation it must have?** When was the last time you really experienced true deep relaxation? Have you ever experienced it? Do you really know the qualities of deep relaxation?

True deep relaxation

What is 'true deep relaxation'? What do I mean by relaxation? Certainly not the activities that you may have come to associate with relaxation in your own mind. The fact is that very few of us actually know how to truly relax today because of the culture we live in. Relaxation and leisure are not the same thing. Many people say they know how to relax but cannot maintain a relaxed state for more than a few moments before becoming distracted with worrying thoughts and concerns.

Once you experience a state of deep relaxation it is a 'state of being' that you will use as a standard or measure against which to practise your visual correction exercises. You will begin to use your power to enter into a relaxed state as you go about your everyday activities. This relaxed state is one that you can contrast to your normal state of activity. You will find the differences very significant and your vision will automatically show improvement, the better you become at accessing this state. There are specific exercises to help you. Once the exercise has been carried out a number of times, the whole process will fall back into your subconscious control and you will hardly ever think about it again, except perhaps to check your maintenance of the desired level of relaxation.

The answer is in reality quite simple. Trying to achieve it is a little more difficult only because it initially takes a little discipline to form a new habit of learning to be relaxed. It seems silly to say that we need to **'learn' how to be relaxed**. Ridding yourself of mental strain, which is the cause of the problem, will relieve the imperfect functioning of the eye at both near and long distances.

How long does it take to obtain permanent improvement? The answer lies with you. How long will it take you until you allow yourself to become free from strain? To gain the ability to access a relaxed a state whenever you need one and no matter what the circumstances? As you notice the improvements in your vision, grab them as evidence of what you will achieve. You may need to continue to practise for a few minutes every day to prevent your eyes relapsing but once improvement is complete it is always permanent.

It is actually impossible to place a limit upon the visual ability of the eye and a sure way to continue the improvements you make is to push yourself for ever increased powers of vision rather than placing arbitrary limits upon yourself.[1] Daily practice, like anything else makes the act a natural process and will reduce the cause of the problem, being the tendency to strain when disturbing circumstances arise.

How to approach your practice

The emphasis while practising any of these exercises is not upon the fact that you are 'practising', i.e. do this and this will happen. The point of importance is *the quality of what you achieve as* you practise. Thinking that because you are practising you must be correcting your vision is the wrong approach and the wrong emphasis.

Dr Bates actually recommended that glasses themselves should be discarded at the beginning of the visual re-education process. This is because their use delays improvements. If you can arrange conditions where doing without your glasses will not be a problem for you, this is ideal. This may not always be practical, particularly for activities such as driving or when the condition is so severe that sight is not initially possible without glasses. My own belief is that if you are to benefit from the knowledge of how to correct your sight, immediately discarding your glasses could have a negative effect. Unless **you are a very strong-willed character** and know that once you have **set your goal nothing will deter you from it,** you may not have the confidence to **make the progress you want**. Re-training your eyesight can initially seem to be a large task unless you chunk down each element and deal one at a time with each chunk. If you have a bad impairment, simply removing your glasses for all situations may result in a lack of confidence. This would delay your progress. The best way will be to approach the task in small chunks. Setting yourself small targets and goals in your program until you **feel confident** about your progress. Taking action is power but action is only powerful if it is the right type of action.

Practise in conditions without strains of this type until your vision is improved to a degree where **you are confident** about your own improvements in vision. Again do not think about the length of time or the number of times you practise but rather the 'quality' you achieve each time you do practise. You may then decide to visit an optician, (probably one who is unaware of your previous impairments), in order to confirm your improvements. Your own optician is bound to be influenced by his prior knowledge of your case and it can be better to for these reasons to see a new optician. Regular reading and practise with the visual re-training card was one of the main recommendations made by Bates and one which can be recommended for **producing results quickly.**

Where does strain come from?

Where does strain come from? It seems strain is created purely by a thought, which then develops and becomes a habit. Strain can be triggered automatically by what are known as 'anchors' in the everyday environment. Strain is also the 'effort' to try and do something well. The eye with normal sight never *tries to see*. The normal vision process is that, if for any reason, such as distance or poor lighting, an object cannot be seen, the normal eye will shift its point of vision. The reason for doing this will be clear from what was said in Chapter 6 about our perceptions. Do not try to bring out a point of vision by staring at it. This is the sign of an eye with imperfect vision. Trying to see and the 'effort' it creates is the cause of the imperfect vision. Once you have mastered this distinction and made the initial improvements in your sight this fact will become self-evident.

If you are unable to see at a distance you have strain. The eye at rest is adjusted for distant vision. Think back to Chapter 1 and the way in which the eye works. The shape of the eyeball cannot be adjusted during distant vision without strain. The same principles of strain and effort are true for vision at the near point. Although near vision is accompanied by a muscular act, this is no more a strain than distant vision, which is accomplished without the intervention of the muscles. The only difference is the use of the muscles but the use of the muscles themselves does not necessarily produce strain. This will be clear from any activity you carry out where you are able to use your muscles without strain.

Blurring

If you have ever noticed blurring of objects in your field of vision this is due to the fact that 'perfect' vision is only possible when the eye is absolutely at rest. Movements either in the eyeball or object of vision produce errors of refraction, (errors in the way light is bent as it enters the eyeball). Some movement of the eyeball is normally necessary (as we have already seen) but it is impossible to see a moving object 'perfectly'. The natural movements of the eyeball are inappreciable when the movement of the object seen is slow enough. When objects move very rapidly they can only be seen as a blur. It was for this reason that motion pictures were originally arranged for viewing in such a way that each picture was halted for one sixteenth of a second and screened while it was moving into place.

The actual act of seeing is therefore best described as being 'passive' and requiring no effort. Objects and print are waiting, perfectly black and perfectly distinct in terms of shape and outline. Imperfect vision is characterised by the effort in 'seeking out and chasing'.[2] The eyes are

THE ESSENCE OF RELAXATION

making the effort to go after the object sought to be seen. The mind itself when generating thoughts of effort, of whatever sort, transmits an energy impulse to the eye. It is the degree or strength of the impulse which effects the normal shape of the eyeball and so influences the ability to see clearly.

The way to **perfect sight** is to **avoid 'effort'** and the consequent strain produced in the mind, which then manifests itself in the malfunctioning of the eye muscles. Unfamiliar objects produce eyestrain and consequent errors of refraction because they firstly produce a strain in the mind. You may be wondering how you will achieve this state of **'effortlessness'** but the first point is actually being aware that this is what is happening. The exercises **you will perfect** will show you how.

A point, which it is worth bearing in mind, was made well by Dr Bates:

> "Mental strain may produce many different kinds of eye strain. According to the statement of most authorities there is only one kind of eyestrain, an indefinite thing resulting from so-called over-use of the eyes, or an effort to overcome a wrong shape of the eyeball. It can be demonstrated, however, that there is not only a different strain for each error of refraction but a different strain for most abnormal conditions of the eye."[3]

In other words there are different strains which account for different conditions. There is one cure for all of these conditions and that is **relaxation**[4]. You will be learning shortly how to control your thought processes and obtain the state of relaxation that will improve your vision.

Again it will be helpful to quote directly from Dr Bates himself.

> "The origin of any error of refraction, of a squint, or of any other functional disturbance of the eye, is simply a thought, - a wrong thought- and its disappearance is as quick as the thought that relaxes. In a fraction of a second the highest degree of refractive error may be corrected, a squint may disappear or the blindness or amblyopia may be relieved. If the relaxation is momentary, the correction is momentary. When it becomes permanent, the correction is permanent.

> "The relaxation cannot, however, be obtained by any sort of effort. It is fundamental that a person should understand this..."

Understanding the cause of the basic problem with your visual process will often lead you to **find** your own solutions to your particular problems. **Relaxation** of the mind and how to achieve and maintain it is your constant theme. To achieve actual physical relaxation of the eye organ itself there is a **special** exercise you can practise. The ideal state and your objective, is to achieve both forms of **relaxation** at the same time.

Palming

This was a term first phrased by Dr Bates. A passive relaxation process, its aim is the same. To reduce and eliminate errors of refraction. Many people find it easier to relax with their eyes shut. There may well be good scientific reason for this. Dr Les Kirkup has shown that with the eyes closed we can 'think harder' and so in a more concentrated fashion. The brain produces more of a certain type of 'unique electrical impulse' when the eyes are closed. The reason why this is so is not clear yet but research into mind controlled electrical appliances is already underway. It seems that palming may have an effect upon the electrical impulses discharged which results in relaxing and indirectly soothing the mind.

We already know that movement is represented in different neural channels[5] and these different channels point to different directions of movement. It has been suggested that prolonged stimulation can lead to these channels becoming fatigued or 'adapted'. This happens with other neural channels and so there is every possibility the same thing happens with the visual channels. Palming would obviously have a sound basis to explain its relaxing effects. Blocking off the light and so the source of stimulation rests and relieves these neural channels.

Closing the eyes is actually shown to relax strain. In palming, the eyes are closed and *covered* by the palms of the hands. It is important that you do not exert any pressure on the eyeball. Simply rest the lower part of the palm on the cheekbone and fingers on the forehead. The effect is to stop light entering the eye without touching the eye. Even with the eyelids closed some light still enters the eye. Excluding the light however gives a greater degree of relaxation for the reasons outlined above.

Are you manufacturing illusions?

What is interesting is what you see when you close your eyes and palm in this way? Do you see total blackness? Total blackness is what you should see because there is no light entering the eye. If you try this and still find you see light do it under the covers of your bed at night in a darkened room when you can be sure that you are not seeing any light at all. If what you actually see is an array of different lights and colours, your mind is actually *manufacturing* illusions of light for you. In a later chapter that examines memory we shall look at how we know that being able to see true black means that you will achieve total relaxation.

When I first tried this I found I had lots of little star-like dots that penetrated the blackness in a constant stream ever coming toward me. At the time I wondered how it would be possible for me to achieve this state of total blackness, as no matter how I thought about it, the lights remained. This was however just a reflection of my own mental stress and strain at

The Essence Of Relaxation

that time. Over time and with a little concentration upon the right things I was able to achieve this state of total blackness when closing my eyes and palming in this way.

Investigation has shown that these illusions of light can range all the way from grey- black swirling clouds to multicoloured fanfares. Sometimes the appearances are vivid enough that they seem to be actually seen with the eyes. As a general rule, the worse the condition of the visual process, the more different types of illusions are created. Test your own condition now and make a note of what you see. Enter it in your journal.

It is not possible to see perfect black unless your eyesight is faultless. This will only happen when your inner mind is at rest and relaxed. One thing you should avoid in your desire to see total blackness is a new 'strain and effort' to produce mentally complete 'blackness'. This will only make things worse. This may sound a little strange but it shows just how easily you can unconsciously produce strain of a different type, even while trying to achieve mental relaxation!

What I found useful was to first find some object or colouring that was totally black and really study it. Study the nature of the shade of blackness, the depth and richness of the colour. Give your mind an example of what true black actually looks like. If you don't do this you are relying upon your memory of black. As I point out later, although you may think that you are seeing true black, it may in fact be a 'greyish' black that you are seeing. Some people I have spoken to even see yellow, brown or red. It is not until they become conscious of the difference that they realise this. Obviously it makes it impossible to remember black perfectly if it is not *seen* perfectly.

It helps to use your imagination. Imagine what it would be like to be totally immersed in that colour, so that it is all that surrounds you. No light, just the total blackness that you would experience in the middle of that colour. Think of other things you know are black and have that 'black' quality. Coal is one example. Black paint is another. Look out for things that are **deep black** so that your mind has a reference point when you are palming and doing this exercise. In effect what you are doing is giving yourself a memory image of the real quality of blackness. As you view the blackness, test your memory image of it by closing your eyes, palming and recalling the nature of the blackness - the shade that is total black, its deep richness and depth. The memory image in your mind's eye should be the same as that which you see with your eyes open. Keep repeating this until the memory is of perfect black, including the whole background.

This is an exercise you may need to do on a few occasions, depending upon the quality of the memory image you are able to recall. If you still have difficulty, a recommended exercise is to take one of the letters on the visual correction chart and find the distance at which the shade of black is 'seen best by you'. Next, while palming remember the black letter you saw. If the white background is remembered as well, just gradually remember *only* the blackness of the letter. Focus upon the blackness and after a few moments the background will fade away to allow the whole memory image to become black. You will know if you are being successful. If a relaxed state is produced, you will be able to imagine a deeper shade of black than you actually saw. You will then use this as a contrast point for your brain to remember 'this deeper black' when you look at the letter again. You should see it blacker than it first looked. Repeat the same process again, imagining a still deeper colour black and again transferring it to the visual chart. It is possible to obtain a perfect perception of true black using this process of engaging the imagination and superimposing it onto the real world. As your perception of true black improves then so does your vision.

If you find that your vision is not showing signs of improvement after palming in this way and you think that you can see and remember true black perfectly, have a second look. Move closer to the black object you are observing and notice what its true qualities are in terms of shade and depth. You will find that your mental recall is not of perfect true black.

Watch for changes in the quality of the perceived blackness as you progress with these exercises over time. As soon as you can approximate blackness in your mind while palming, you will find that your vision has improved. Monitor what happens. Keep your journal updated. As your eyesight does improve, watch the quality and richness of this blackness begin to increase. It is an ideal way to test and monitor the current state of your visual ability and the relaxation of your mind.

As I said above it is far easier to imagine black without any stress or strain if you have a good memory image of what *true black* looks like. Other ways of achieving relaxation are also possible if you find that you cannot see true black under these circumstances. When palming, relax in a comfortable place and begin to recall a pleasant memory from your past. You may find that unless you practise deep relaxation on a regular basis, it may be difficult to totally absorb yourself in the memory. To be really effective you must be able to recall the memory in all its detail and atmosphere. Just as though you were living it again.

A self-induced state relaxer

If you have difficulty doing this then there is a transcript for a self-induced state relaxer in Appendix C. It is easy to prepare your own audio tape for the purpose of taking you into a deeply relaxed state of mind. There are different levels of relaxation and as soon as you experience a deep state of relaxation, you will be able to make a comparison with your normal state. Your mind again has a reference point for achieving true relaxation. As you learn to relax and maintain that state of mental relaxation your mental image of true uniform black will improve. This is exactly what I found as I made progress in this area.

Moving on, we find it is possible then to achieve the same objective by more than one route. Weather you use one of your own pleasant memories or the self-induced state relaxer, remember that in your imagination you should not direct your mental attention to only one part of the memory. This is the equivalent of staring. If you do it subconsciously, then you will also do it during your normal visual process. This is a distinction that can make a major impact. To begin taking advantage if it now, start remembering objects or images that are moving and that allow you to **direct your focus of attention to different parts of the image.** This amounts to practising in the imagination what the physical eye *should* be doing during the normal visual process.

If you find that you can see perfect black but only for a short time you can apply the principles of *central alignment* [6]. Focus your attention upon 'one part of the black', (i.e. take one area of the colour black you are looking at and focus only on that one area.) As it forms in your vision you will notice a part becomes 'darker' than the rest. You will come to see a smaller area of black for a longer period of time. Gradually the time period during which you can maintain continuous black will increase.

Try the results of palming for yourself. You may find a **rapid relief of eyestrain** and when you uncover your eyes do you **notice an improvement** in your visual acuity? Notice these small advances which are the building blocks of your larger **success**. Again, ensure you record your results in your journal.

What is the key ingredient to successful palming? Remembering not to strain. Some people may find the longer they practise palming, the greater the degree of relaxation and the more 'depth' in darkness for the black. Some people find they can only palm for a short time before beginning to strain, which defeats the aim of the exercise. The other key is to be sure that it is a memory of true black that you are recalling. If you open your eyes and compare your memory to the real colour black and you can perceive differences, then you have not remembered black perfectly.

One of the great things about palming is that once you familiarise yourself with the technique, it is something that can be done during spare moments of your day. The more frequently you do it, the better the results. It will pay you dividends to set aside a special time or times and to practise it when you can feel your eyes under strain. Perfect relaxation is your goal, which is reflected in your ability to see perfect black. The objective, however, is to transfer this relaxation, achieved through palming, into the real world. If you only allow yourself to relax partially during palming, then as soon as your eyes are opened the benefit will only last for a short time. The better you palm, the better you relax. This means much more of the benefit is transferred when you open your eyes. Even a few moments improvement is a success, as it again provides you with a contrast point so that you know what is possible and what the goal is that you are aiming for. Look to extend the time for which you receive an improvement upon each occasion.

It is important to remind yourself to be alert to how the rest of your body feels when you palm successfully, as **relaxation is a state that effects the whole body**.

Eyestrain and computers

If you work with a computer then your risk of injury to the eye through overstraining the eye can be increased. Injuries among office workers have been increasing at a faster than average rate and some people **feel** that computers are to blame. If you work with a computer then you should pay extra attention to **the benefits** that can be obtained **by palming**.

Musco-skeletal damage accounts for vast majority of reported injuries. It is accepted that prolonged use of the computer monitor has the potential to cause eyestrain and all the resulting muscular strains. Some optometrists have compared the situation to 'staring' at the tip of a pencil for an hour while it's held twenty inches from your face. What does this do to the muscle physiology of your eyes? If you work with a computer watch out for known factors which can aggravate eyestrain such as the brightness of the monitor, abnormal contrast settings and screen glare.

If you find glare on a computer screen caused by artificial lighting, the best course of action is to remove the source of the problem. Changing the lighting angle will usually clarify the screen and remove the reflection. The other option is obviously adjusting brightness and contrast settings but this does not deal with the cause of the problem. Approach the problem from the viewpoint that whatever puts your eyes in the most natural viewing environment is to be preferred. Avoid strains wherever possible.

What about the different colours used in different programs? Think about all the times your eyes will be called upon to adjust and re-adjust their focus as you look at a screen. Different colour combinations can lead to a fixating of the muscles that allow focusing to take place.

Keep your visual acuity alert and flexible. Counteract these effects by reducing background lighting and using desk lamps where possible. Resting your eyes every fifteen minutes is recommended and palming as often as possible. The same principles apply and you should ensure that you do not reinforce a habit of 'staring' because of the close work with the computer screen. Keep the eyes moving using the principles of central alignment and shifting[7]. Where possible break your gaze and focus in on a distant object. The recommended distance for monitor range is sitting at least fifty centimetres from the screen to minimise eyestrain.

Exercises you can do to massage the muscles around the eyes

Try the following exercises (see picture section). If you feel any pain or discomfort then obviously stop the exercises.

1   Gently press your thumb and forefinger on either side of the bridge of your nose, massaging up and down three times.
2   Locate the area just under both eyebrows with your thumbs. Press and hold for between three and five seconds.
3   With your index fingers on top of your cheekbones begin massaging in light circular motion seven or eight times.
4   With the index finger and thumb apply a light pressure above the eyebrows and around the eye.

Practised together with palming, these exercises are very effective at relieving strain. If you find that circumstances do not allow you to palm openly, you can still obtain a measure of relaxation by practising mentally. Close your eyes and imagine a palming exercise while at the same time relaxing any feeling of tension in the eyes. Even doing this for a few seconds helps to break down the elements that combine to cause strain. Some of the mental exercises that follow later can also be usefully applied while working with computers.

Remember that being relaxed is a form of refreshment for the body and the mind. It's the time your body should be in a natural state of equilibrium with all parts perfectly balanced. It creates the **conditions you need** in order to achieve good sight. Once you have acquired this state of equilibrium you then need to add one further very important ingredient in the total visual process and we shall look at this in the next chapter.

---

[1] We will examine this further in Chapter 20 - CAPE
[2] Which description of the process best describes you? If you are unsure, stop for a moment and assess how you approach this aspect of "seeing".
[3] Dr Bates, *Better Eyesight Without Glasses* (Souvenir Press), 52
[4] This refers to relaxation directed and focused with the visual process as its purpose.
[5] Hubel and Wiesel referred to earlier.
[6] This is dealt with in detail in Chapter 9. You may need to return here after reading that chapter.
[7] Shifting is an exercise dealt with in Chapter 14.

CHAPTER 9

THE ALIGNED EYE AND THE RECTIFYING FORCE OF CENTRAL ALIGNMENT

> "The eye with normal vision...sees one part of everything it looks at best, and all other parts worse, in proportion to their distance from the point of maximum vision."
>
> **Dr W H Bates**

The aim in re-training the eye is to encourage mobility of perception. What does this mean? It means that we ordinarily make sense of the world through 'a sense of movement'[1]. Orthodox treatments do not take this into account when prescribing remedies for poor sight. This is where an appreciation of the effect that glasses can have becomes meaningful[2].

Our attention is naturally mobile and generally shifts in a continuous fashion from one part of an object to another part. In a similar way, our thoughts move from one aspect of an idea to another continuously. We have 'a continuous shifting of the mind'. This is our natural state, that is also ordinarily mirrored as a process in sight, by a continuous shifting of the point of attention.

As we have already seen, the retina of the eye has a point of maximum sensitivity, where perfectly clear images are recorded. This point of sharpest precision is known as the 'fovea centralis' or central pit. You will recall in Chapter 1 that we looked in detail at the structure and make-up of the eye. The centre of the retina contains the small circular elevation known as the yellow spot. This area takes on a yellow colour when we die and so the reason for the name. It is in the centre of this spot that the fovea is contained, recognisable as a deep depression of darker colour. Here there are no rods and the cones are elongated and pressed very closely together. The other layers become extremely thin here or disappear, so the cones are covered very barely with these other layers at this point.

We have already explored the precise function of these rods and cones and we already know that the centre of the fovea is the place of the most acute vision[3]. As withdrawal from this spot occurs, the acuteness of the visual perceptions rapidly decreases.

What at first sight seems to be a slightly confusing scenario arises at this point. The eye with normal vision sees *one* part of everything it looks at 'best' and all other parts 'worst'. This is in proportion to distance from the point of maximum vision. What does this mean exactly? It means that we should look and *'see best'*, where we are looking. You may ask yourself how you could possibly manage to do anything other than *'see best'*, where you are looking? It does not seem to make sense.

The fact is that research carried out has shown that people with defective vision ***never*** see best at the point they are looking at. This will require a little further exploration and explanation.

We normally are aware of and see *'best'*, the part of our visible environment that has light (and so an image), thrown from the object and onto our fovea, (being the point of sharpest vision). The images we see using the outer areas of the retina are consequently less distinct in all major respects of shape, colour and form.

When impairment of sight occurs for any reason, it is because the sensitivity of the fovea has generally *decreased*. The eyes are using the other less efficient parts of the retina to see with. The ability to use the process of central fixation or 'central alignment' has been lost. The cause can be any form of mental strain or stress. This starts acting as a catalyst and begins working its way through to the visual process, so making it operate incorrectly.

Explaining this further in practical and understandable terms, this means that when vision at the centre of sight has been effected in this way, a person can no longer see 'best', the point at which he is looking. He sees objects *not looked at directly* with better vision. It may seem illogical at first but this is because **the sensitivity of the retina has changed.** If you have defective sight, you become unable to see 'best' where you are looking. The other point that should be clear is that this all happens subconsciously and generally over a period of time.

The effect of glasses can now be considered and we already know how they work, by holding the physiology of the muscles in a fixed condition. This creates its own type of strain with the result that the central part of the retina becomes less sensitive than the surrounding areas. If you think about this, it is because more of the surrounding areas are effectively being engaged as a result of the optical aids. As soon as glasses are removed, sight is better through the peripheral areas or the sides of the eye, rather than through the centre. A crucial objective in attaining correction and restoring vision to normal is re-establishing this ability of central fixation or 'central alignment'.

What does central alignment mean?

I consider that the original term used to describe this situation, i.e. 'central fixation', is an unfortunate term. The word 'fixation' implies and refers subconsciously to the very thing you are trying to avoid, which is the habit of 'staring'. The objective is *image alignment* upon the most sensitive portion of the retina, being the fovea. So although we have a principle of constant movement of attention, **it is a natural and continual process of 'alignment' upon this one key spot in the eye that produces normal vision.**

So to recap quickly, we see only a small area at which we are looking directly, out of the centre of sight. When the eye is not functioning properly this point of central alignment has been lost. A simple test can demonstrate this. Look at a sign with lettering on it, first directly and then by moving your head to the side and looking immediately left. Can you see the difference?

The problem of loss of central alignment arises from trying to see every part of an area at the same time. This is an unconscious 'habitual' strain. When the eye has central alignment, it has perfect sight and is perfectly at rest without muscular strain. (The condition shows itself normally by the eyeball moving at irregular intervals from side to side, vertically or in other directions. Sometimes nervous movements of the eyelids accompany the condition.)

Start using and benefiting from central alignment now!

As part of your program of noticing what works, this strain will be reduced just as soon as **you relieve the strain** that causes it. Check for yourself now and see if you actually do see 'best' where you are looking? Can you see 'worse' when you look some distance away from an object rather than when you look at it directly? As you do this, you will **give yourself a new subconscious measure** and be able to reduce the distance at which you have to look in order to see 'worse'. Eventually you will be able to look at the bottom of a letter and see the top worse and vice versa. The smaller the distance you have to look in order to see the opposite part of a letter indistinctly, the greater your relaxation and the better you sight will be. This means being able to do this with a single letter. It will be possible to see the letter perfectly clearly and black. Such vision may come only in flashes at first, the letter appearing clearly and distinctly only for a moment before disappearing again. This is the sign you are looking for. You have made the improvements you need! By committing yourself to the improvement and continuing to practise, the **improvements will become permanent**.

The guiding principle of perfect vision

The fact that this area of clearer attention and focus exists becomes a guiding principle upon which to establish your visual correction program. We know that our normal perception is directed by attention toward mobility. Mobility of the eyes themselves follows on as a necessity. The mind automatically and subconsciously shifts its attention when viewing any object. The part being paid the attention is that which is most clearly sensed. The rays of light entering the eye are then reflected directly to the fovea. When this happens you are seeing with central alignment.

It is probably clear that in order to view every part of an object clearly, the eye, from moment to moment, must make an enormous number of changes and rapid shifts in the point of focus. It is when the eye fails to shift and fails to see all parts of an object with central alignment that it fails to see with maximum clarity.

We have already looked at the way in which we make up our perceptions. As already said mobility is the normal and natural condition of the mind's perception. Mobility is also the normal condition of sensing for the eye. **So how do you learn again to re-establish this natural condition?** This is something we will now look at.

Re-establishing mobility

During infancy most people learn **unconsciously** to keep their minds and their eyes in a state of 'mobility'. Consequently 'seeing' is done with central alignment. There are numerous reasons, all related to stress and the acquisition over time of poor visual habits, which lead to this natural state being lost. You will recall that we looked at reading earlier. There is a natural way to read, in which we keep our attention and visual focus mobile. There is also the developed habit of 'lazy reading', involving a fixated gaze at what is being read.

When your attention becomes fixed directly, when the eyes cease to shift and when continuous easy movement from point to point is not present, you develop a state in which you 'stare'. This should not be confused with the normal expression and meaning of the word. It is a subconscious 'stare'. **The inability to move your *internal* focus of attention from point to point.**

So knowing this what are you now going to do about it? Are you going to say to yourself, "well yes, that's great but it takes too much effort to think about it and what can I do about it anyway?" or are you going to **decide to commit now** to taking action and start doing whatever is necessary to **begin getting your vision back to normal**? Don't you owe it to yourself to do what you know you must and show yourself you do have what it takes to succeed in overcoming your limiting subconscious habits? **The only person that can decide to do that is you.**

Be aware that it is this habitual way in which you have learned to do things that causes the resulting mental and physical stress. Stress produces more malfunctioning of the body and mind and over time a vicious circle is established. The visual process suffers distortion and errors of refraction result. Your vision deteriorates and glasses themselves reinforce these bad habits. No one will confirm that glasses are good for you or that they will cure your condition. It is common knowledge that over time your condition will become worse. Not attacking the cause of the problem simply leads to the cause of the problem becoming harder and harder to resolve.

Think about it now. When you 'stare' aren't you trying to achieve the impossible? Aren't you trying to see every part of a large area as clearly as every other part? Yet the structure and make-up of the eye is such that it is not possible for it to see every part of the whole simultaneously. This means that your mind cannot do the job it is designed to do for you, unless its attention is continually shifting from point to point of an object being viewed.

Another feature of the subconscious habit of trying to see an object equally clearly with all parts of the retina leads to an over-stimulation of other areas of the retina in an effort to compensate. Some people have been known to develop a secondary area of sensitivity on the outer edges of the retina. The result is that these people get their clearest vision not when looking straight in front of them but when on object is viewed from an angle! This sideways vision is nothing like as clear as normal vision and is generally known as *eccentric fixation*.

Staring

So what causes us to develop these subconscious 'stares'? It is probably anxiety in wanting to achieve the greatest amount of quality vision in the shortest possible time. We are continually under pressure to do things quickly. As the habit of staring develops, it is the visual process trying to do the impossible, with resulting strain, errors of refraction and poor vision. Like anything else, there is a build up in different small ways of doing things incorrectly. By the time all these deficiencies are added together, the result has grown out of all proportion from the individual significance and effect of the original failure.

Do we all have central alignment?

It is apparently rare for the habit of central alignment never to be acquired. When this is the case it is usually due to disease of the eye at an early age. The majority of cases of loss of central alignment are simply due to the fact that the habit is lost, generally as a result of other indirectly associated fears and worries[4], which affect the proper functioning of the mind and thought process. Luckily eccentric fixation is rare and in the case of the person who develops the habit of 'staring', who looks straight ahead and tries to see everything equally well, the reported cases show the fixation tends to be defused over the whole retina.

It may be becoming clear that if this way of perceiving the world happens without our awareness and affects the eyes in this way, the mind is also affected in other consciously unknown, unappreciated ways. Examine yourself and your thinking. Only then will the ways in which you are restricting your personal potential begin to reveal themselves. The state is one known as 'unconscious incompetence'. The first stage in dealing with it is being aware that **this is something that effects you**. The second stage is deciding to do something about it. You have then reached a stage of 'conscious incompetence'. By a process of self-examination and evaluation you will aim to move through to the stages of 'conscious competence' and into 'unconscious competence' in the area of your life that requires re-evaluation and change for correction of your visual process.

If your life is unsatisfactory in any area, for any reason and you are unable to make the changes you need and desire, it will be because of a 'mirror situation' in your perception of the world. In other words, a parallel form of thinking in the type of forces and habits, creating effects in other areas of your life, similar to those that restrict and affect your vision. You may be effected in many ways that you are currently unaware of. The self-realisation and examination of the forces that hold you down, that restrict you and prevent you from getting what you want is one of the most liberating and exhilarating personal experiences possible.

The main point to understand with regard to your visual process is that you become aware of exactly what it means when you do not see 'best' where you are looking. In order to do this, you can help yourself see an object 'worse' when you look away from it, than when you look directly at it. Do the following exercise. Use a strong light as a point of reference. Look away from the light and you will be able to see it less brightly and more easily. Next use a black letter that you can also see worse when you look away from it. Following these steps, it will then be easier for you to see the letter worse when you look away from it. The objective for this exercise is actually to *decrease* your visual ability in the first instance. Doing it this way, you will then gradually and constantly improve it again. Ultimately you do wish to see best at the place you are looking. These are simply the steps that help you achieve this.

Myopia is the defect in the eye where you can only see clearly those objects that are close up. Where this is the case, you will assist yourself by practising 'seeing worst' at this point, i.e. the point where you normally see best. The distance is gradually extended until it becomes possible to do the same thing at twenty feet. Do this simple test. Look at an electric light bulb. Does it 'appear' and can you see it better the further you look away from it? By alternatively looking at the light at the near point and looking away from it, you will soon see it brighter when you look at it directly than when you look away from it. You may also notice a great feeling of relaxation in your body as every nerve begins to relax and a feeling of comfort and quiet calm permeates your whole body. Once you reach this stage your progress will be rapid and self-evident.

There is a principle known and used with success in many areas. The basis of the principle as applied to vision is this. Once you know and are aware of the reasons *'why'* your sight is defective and you have yourself actually demonstrated that you can make your sight worse, you will unconsciously avoid the strain that causes the problems. This is something that I did.

Sometimes you need to know that you are really in control of your body and those functions that you may otherwise believe are outside your control. (People who wish to lose weight can find this an equally powerful demonstration. Actually deciding to put on weight first, perhaps half a stone, shows that you have the ability to alter your body weight. If you can increase it under your control, you can decrease it with similar ease and control.)

The process at work is actually bringing back into conscious awareness the fact that you can actually make your sight worse! When you consciously do this, you will be able to correct the unconscious effort of the eye in trying to see all parts of a small area, equally well at one time.

What is the best tip to bear in mind when re-learning to see 'best' where you are looking? Simply remember that you will always see one part of an object 'best', when your mind is contented to see the remaining and greater part indistinctly. The best way to achieve this is to change your focus of attention around. Do this by thinking of the points not directly seen as being less distinct. Make these the area of awareness rather than directing your thoughts toward the point that is seen 'best'. If you take a line of type out of a book, concentrate upon one particular word in the line. Close your eyes and imagine seeing the line with one word that you have chosen as more clearly defined, sharper, and with more depth than the rest of the line. Do this however by noticing the rest of the line is blurred, undefined and unclear. Open your eyes and repeat the same exercise. Keep doing this until the line becomes a total blur and the word in question becomes clearer and clearer. It must do this because of the poor quality of the rest of the words in the line. It is the poor quality of the rest of the words that makes the word you have chosen stand out and it will do so without any effort on your part. As this happens you will find the word itself does actually become clearer. Note the improvement and how you did it. **Notice how you feel** at the exact moment the word becomes clearer. **Improved clarity is a definite sign of better vision.**

The same process is used to further improve your sight by decreasing the size of the area focused upon. Take a part of a word and do the same thing. Next move on to individual letters and then to parts of the letters themselves. When you can see one part of an individual letter better than the rest of the letter, **your vision** will by that time have shown **massive improvement.**

Remember that ordinarily this process takes place at extremely rapid speed. The skill of central alignment and the mobility of perception work in perfect unison. Consciously practising it will eventually ensure the directions filter through to your subconscious. And also remember that **repetition and practice are the masters of all ability**.

The limits of your vision

The principle of central alignment is an important one. Have you ever had the experience of being able to read a sign from a great distance when you see all the letters are alike? When you master the principle of seeing one letter best you will be able to read smaller letters you did not know were there! This is one of the first signs of your improving vision. If your vision is currently at the stage of being unable to recognise the fact that there letters on signs, perhaps all you see is a blur of two colours. As your skill in this area increases you will come to see for yourself the remarkable improvements that are possible.

Attaining a higher degree of central alignment than you currently have will provide you with superior vision. Remember though that this will be impossible without mental control, and relaxation of the mind. The aim is central alignment of the mind and mobility of perception. Normally-sighted people should also be aware of the ways in which their own visual process can be preserved. **It is common sense that everybody should be made aware of the principles of good sight.** It is something that must be taught at school. It is a problem that eventually effects eighty-five per cent of people at some stage in their lives. Being aware of the tell-tale signs and identifying and knowing the feedback being received would ensure that people's sight is maintained in the best possible condition. Consequently people will then be able to take the best course of action for their health. The need for optical aids could then be avoided in most cases, simply by using consciously the good habits that are foundation of normal sight.

Without delay let's move forward into the simple but effective techniques by which central alignment can be attained, but before we do that let's look at building some mental momentum to really get you moving in the direction you want to go.

---

[1] See Chapter 6.
[2] See Chapter 4.
[3] See Chapter 1, diagram 2.
[4] We examined this in Chapter 6.

CHAPTER 10

BUILDING YOUR MOMENTUM

"The impetus of simply contrasting an idea, or a thought, can in a moment put in motion an unstoppable force..."
Thomas Platt, artist

You now know enough to start really moving yourself in the right direction. You are now going to learn how to begin a generative change in the direction you wish to go. Regaining perfect vision!

We are going to look at a simple version of what is called "The Swish Pattern". Some of you may already be familiar with this technique, although not applied directly to the visual process. The Swish Pattern is a special program for your brain - a way of training it to go in a new direction. It is particularly appropriate for habit control. The effect is to create a special type of energy, a vigorous internal energy that works at moving you quickly toward your chosen objective.

Credit for the pattern goes to Richard Bandler.[1] There are three elements that comprise a good swish technique.

1) choosing a cue to swish from
2) building a desirable attractive and motivating self image
3) using the differences in submodality[2] shifts to link two images together.

If you have not heard of submodalities before do not worry. These are dealt with later. The information detailed here is sufficient for you to begin with.

"You can imagine your future."

Henry J Kaiser

For this pattern to work you must know *'what you are like'* as you move through the world with imperfect vision. How do you see the world? Can you think of a time that you have just begun to look at something before realising that you could not see it clearly? You know you would like to see clearly but you don't. It's a split second thing, but if you concentrate you will know the experience I am referring to. Identify what you actually see in that situation, *just before* you realise you can't see clearly. Everything you know and are aware is wrong with your vision.

Building Your Momentum

This is where real attention to the micro-elements of your behaviour will pay dividends. Think what it is that is unpleasant for you, as you realise what this situation means to you; how it restricts you, what it 'means' about you as a person.

It is important that you don't see yourself in this first picture as you make it and form it in your mind. In other words, it's a picture of you viewing the world through your own eyes. Just **hold that image,** as you will use that picture shortly.

The next thing you need to do is *see yourself, as you will be,* if you can see the world with perfect vision. Use the distinctions you know about and how exactly and specifically your sense of sight 'should' be, how things would look if it were perfect. How would you see yourself as being different? What would it really mean to you? What would be the value of your making this change? What difference would it make to you as a person? What would it mean about you? What would you have achieved? Create a picture of this you, the you that has achieved the change, that has perfect vision! What effects will it have on your life? What are the qualities you would now be experiencing? How will your energy level feel? Achievement and accomplishment always create their own unique form of propulsive and explosive energy. Take your time and really experience what the change will mean to you! Now for this picture, it is important that you do see yourself in this picture.

The first picture is an *associated* image of what you see out of your own eyes, the second picture is *disassociated,* how you will see yourself as you look at yourself with the changes having been made. How you see yourself differently! That is the key! What new qualities will you have? What new possibilities will be available to you?

Keep adjusting the quality of this second picture until it is an image that is really attractive to you. An image that draws you strongly toward it. Something that makes you glow with pleasure!

The next step is to take the first picture of how you are and make it big and bright. In the lower right hand corner of that picture, put a small, dark image of how you will see yourself differently, if you no longer had this major problem of defective eyesight.

The next thing is to do the "swish". You make the small dark image that you placed in the lower right-hand corner quickly get bigger and brighter until it covers the whole of the old picture of the old you, which simultaneously gets dimmer darker and shrinks. The knack is to do this really fast in less than a second. At the same time it helps to make a "swishing noise" and then as soon as you have "swished", open your eyes and look around.

Go back inside and do the same thing again, start with the first picture, and the smaller dark picture in the bottom right hand corner. Do this a least five times and be sure to blank the internal screen and to open your eyes at the end of each time you do it.

Once you have done this, test it and see what happens. Think of the old you, the first picture and what happens? Do you notice that the first picture is hard to hold? The new picture appears as the old one fades out?

You will see improvements sooner than you think! The swish pattern directionalises your brain and starts it going in the right direction. What it is telling your brain to do is head in a particular direction. Your behaviour will begin to follow suit and go in the same direction. You will start becoming who you want to be, a person with normal vision. The aim is to 'directionalise' your thoughts towards what you want.

What you will now begin to notice is that the small improvements in your sight become much easier to become aware of. This is certainly what happened with me. You are going in a new direction. I found the technique a very effective way of focusing my attention. You will find the same thing because this pattern employs one of the key principles upon which your brain works, which is contrast.

Do not be afraid of repeating this exercise just as often as you wish, the more times the better, the more frequently the better. If the exercise seems a little strange or unfamiliar at first, familiarise yourself with it. This may be a new way of thinking for some. Like anything it takes a little practice. Don't forget this is not hard physical labour, it is all using your mind! Commit to rigorously set up the direction you wish to follow. The other thing is to experiment and find what has the most powerful impact for you.

Normally a swish pattern is set up to deal with a specific habit - one that has specific cues, e.g. biting nails. Before a person starts to bite their nails they will often be able to identify particular circumstances that repeat themselves whenever the habit occurs. Defective sight is slightly more complex in that it is a generalised state, even though it is still a subconscious habit. The way around this is to choose a specific instance in the first place, where you know you can not see what you want and should be able to see. Make it a familiar situation. Do the swish for this specific time, (being a cue) and notice what happens the next time you encounter that environment. **You will find that your mind begins pushing you to improve the quality of your sight.** If you are not familiar with these types of exercises, be very alert to any changes or stimuli you experience the next time you encounter the environment in question. Being aware and learning to notice even small changes is the real building block of larger success.

This is exactly the way that I adapted the swish to work for me and I found it very effective. You can receive exactly the same results.

Another variation on this swish referred to above is to form the two pictures in exactly the same way. This time visualise a giant slingshot. Put the first picture in the centre of the slingshot and imagine stretching the second picture right back in between the two pieces of elastic. Stretch it so far back it is barely visible. To swish, simply let go and watch the new picture smash through the old picture totally replacing it. Make the same swish noise at the same time. The effect may be more powerful. Test it and see.

We shall be examining submodalities in more detail in Chapter 16 and it will pay you to return to this chapter after you have more knowledge about submodalities. Brightness and size are usually two critical submodalities for most people so play around and find out what works best for you.

Relaxation

Bear in mind that all the methods you will use to eradicate your errors of refraction, that cause your problem, are simply different ways of obtaining relaxation. Can you imagine creating a swish for yourself, one in which you are experiencing all the affects of stress and strain as it effects your visual process, (although until now you may have been unaware of it?). Now create an image in which you have found the power of true relaxation and applied it to your everyday environment as you move through the world?

This is really an introduction into the ways in which you can exert more choice over the effects of your own internal neurology and a way of responding differently to circumstances by improving and enhancing your visual process and removing the subconsciously imposed limitations that affect your visual process.

---

1 Richard Bandler, *Using Your Brain for a Change* (Real People Press, Utah,1985), 131

2 See Chapter 16

CHAPTER 11

YOUR BELIEF AND YOUR VISION

"How many things served us but yesterday as articles of faith, which today we deem but fable."?
Michel de Montaigne (1533-92), French essayist

Before we move into the techniques for achieving central alignment, let's look briefly at the power of your belief and how it controls your vision. If you previously held the view that your vision could not be rectified by natural methods then that belief has, I trust, been challenged and changed. As such an important part of your visual process rests with the power of your mind and how you perceive the world, total belief in your own abilities and what it is possible for you to achieve is crucial.

Some people have a fear in their subconscious based upon the fact that they have had defective sight. It is a fear of not seeing clearly. It is part of a perpetuating cycle. For some reason in the past vision has become defective. As this condition has developed over time the mind comes to expect it as the normal state of things. In addition the memory images of what you perceive become less efficient, less reliable. Expectation becomes a subconscious command to your brain to see what you expect. As you know, your brain works to carry out the instructions you give it. In addition, you have the powerful influence of how you feel, working as part of the overall equation. You may not be conscious of any type of feeling but if you stop and really become aware of the emotions you experience, they will gradually become apparent. This is where an appreciation of the difference between your conscious and subconscious functions becomes useful. With this knowledge you can **break the cycle of expectation and restrictive belief.**

If you stop and examine this for a moment, has there ever been a time when you have felt apprehensive and uncertain? There is probably one occasion that readily jumps to mind as you think about it. What was it that made you feel that way and what is it that you notice, as you think about it now? If you can re-access the experience you will be able to feel what you felt then. Some people are able to feel shivers down their backs, others react in different ways as they recollect such memories.

The next thing to do is recall a specific time when you felt totally and absolutely confident about something. It can be anything at all. Even the

YOUR BELIEF AND YOUR VISION

fact that you are totally and absolutely confident you know your name. If someone contradicted you and said you were not who you knew you were, how would you react? What feeling would you have as you expressed yourself, totally confident in the knowledge that what you were saying was 100 per cent correct?

How does it feel to be that sure and that confident? To be absolutely certain!

Follow on by comparing these two experiences. What's the difference between how you felt when you were confident and certain and how you felt when you were apprehensive and uncertain? If you have done the exercises you will appreciate that they are two totally different feelings. ***These feelings support your actions*** - the things you will be prepared to do in pursuit of some objective, what you will do and what you won't do. The way you feel can support or hinder you. Your feeling about something can support your belief or destroy it.

As you progress with the re-education of your visual process provide yourself with feelings that will support your goals and beliefs. **Be aware of the feelings you are generating.**

> "...with most people disbelief in a thing is founded on a blind belief in some other thing..."

G C Lichtenberg, German physicist (1742-99)

The thing to appreciate is that coming to this conscious realisation is stage one. You can feel confident that the next time you look at an object you will see it clearly. If for whatever reason you fail, your confidence is attacked and it simply increases your previous expectation of defective vision. The way forward is to progress in small stages. Be alert to small improvements as they happen and build up your **new expectation of improving visual acuity** over a longer period of time.

If you are doing the daily eye workout exercises you must **notice**, at some time, some form of **improvement**. When frustration occurs this is because your brain knows you have set it a goal that it is aiming for, but not yet achieving. Interpret any feelings of frustration not as failure but as vital feedback for your brain, information which tells you the difference between where you are now and the goal your brain is working towards. Provide your brain with details of the improvements and progress you have made, so that a measure of what is needed next can be assessed. You will find that your next improvement will come quickly. Invest in the idea and proposition that you will accomplish your objective, say it to yourself, do it and consider it to be true.

As we have already seen and which should now be more clear, there can often be a conflict between what you want consciously and what happens subconsciously. The subconscious is the most powerful director of the brain in achieving objectives set for it. Consciousness accounts for only a small proportion of the functions that we carry out in our daily lives. Although we are so used to directing our lives through our conscious thoughts that we believe it to be our main driving force, a number of philosophers have questioned why we need our conscious. Many of the functions it performs could be carried out better by the subconscious.

I am not asking you to believe that improving your eyesight is possible only because I say it is. I have improved the quality of my vision to a degree that I would not have thought possible when I first started. Thousands of others have achieved similar results over the years using natural eyesight correction technologies and management. With a good understanding of how your visual process works and the understanding of the mental process that forms such a crucial ingredient in the mechanism that makes up sight, your belief is now built upon a solid basis.

What you believe is very important because you should realise that any behaviour you carry out is built around your beliefs. Believe you can and you will, believe you can't and you won't. Such is the guiding influence of your belief. If you **decide to follow the exercises in this book** and **practise doing your daily eye workouts**, it will be because you believe that you will improve your vision. Simply reading about what to do without ever trying it or without practice and persistence will not get you the results that you want. If you believe in yourself and the power of what is possible, you can harness that power of your belief to propel you forward along your directed pathway of visual re-education.

> "At eighteen our convictions are hills from which we look; at forty-five they are caves in which we hide."
>
> **F Scott Fitzgerald, author**

Belief in yourself is really the key to succeeding. The mind and body work as a single unit. As your visual acuity increases and improves again, this needs to be supported by your own beliefs. If you hold any reservation at all about your ability to succeed with these exercises, now is the time to re-evaluate yourself and really decide that you will not let your own preconceived personal limitations stop you. Other people have already achieved what you want - normal vision. If you think that something could hold you back, think again. Have you ever believed you could not do something in the past, only to find that when you tried it and gave it the attention it deserved from you, that you achieved it quite easily?

If you have ever had that type of experience what was the difference between believing that you could not carry out a task and then finding out that you could? What changed for you? If you hold a belief that something is too hard or complicated or that you can't do it, what would it be like to **hold a belief that it is easy, uncomplicated and that you can do it?**

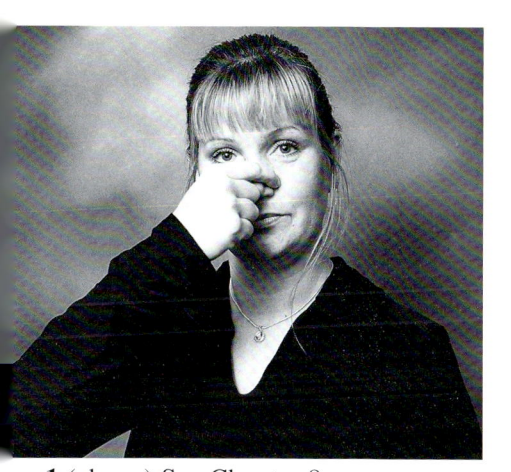

1 (above) See Chapter 8
3 (below) See Chapter 8

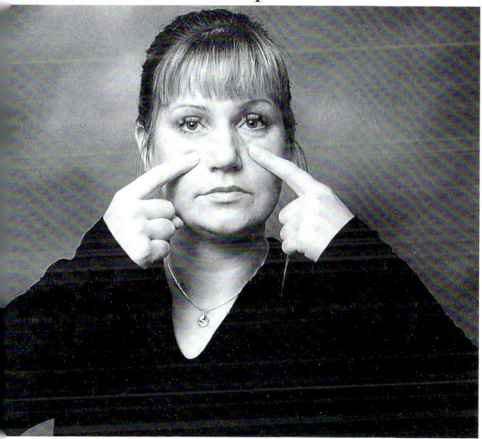

2 (above) See Chapter 8
4 (below) See Chapter 8

5 (below right) View of retina through an Opthalmoscope

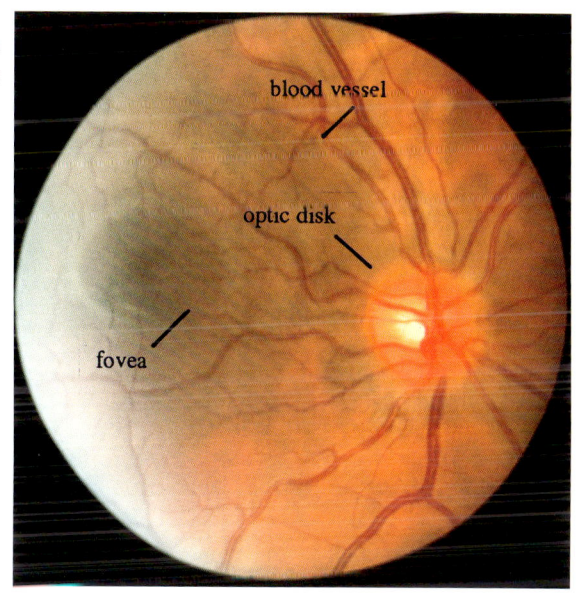

blood vessel

optic disk

fovea

6 (left) **Short sight** Short-sighted people cannot focus far away because the eyeball is too long and the rays of light converge in front of the retina. Convex lenses alter the angle of the rays as they converge on the retina.

7 (left) **Astigmatism** Vision is out of focus on either the horizontal or vertical plane because the eyeball is irregular. Astigmatism is traditionally treated with lenses shaped like a lengthways slice from a tube.

8 (right) **Long sight** Vision is clear at distances but not close up because the eyeball is too short from front to back and light rays have not converged when they reach the retina. Convex lenses shorten the focal length.

9 (right) **Normal** A person with normal sight can focus on an eye chart at 20ft (6m) and closer. The eyeball is the right shape for light rays to converge exactly on the retina. It also reacts fast to changes in light.

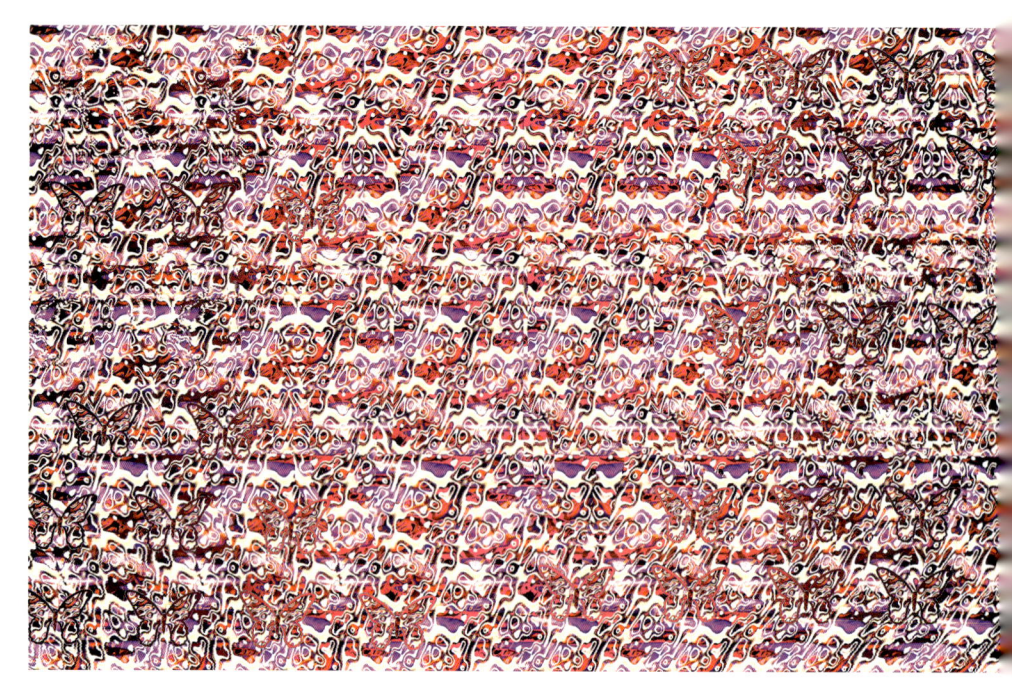

10 (above) The Magic Eye

11 (below) The image encapsulated in the Magic Eye

Have the belief that you can learn! As you follow the exercises in this book notice the results you are achieving. Let the improvements provide you with evidence of feedback that what you are doing is working and build your belief. As you build your belief you will find that improvement is happening constantly and often easily. Make these changes work for you by expanding their driving forces, through the power of your own belief in your own achievements. Belief creates a powerful dynamic that allows you to achieve things that you would otherwise find impossible.

What you do to improve your own eyesight and the actions you decide to take for yourself will maintain and reinforce your belief. Think of your belief about what you will achieve and how you will achieve it as a blueprint for your future actions in correcting your visual process.

Expectation

It is important to remember that with any new skill (or in this case consciously re-learning an old skill) it takes practice[1]. It is during the time that you are practising and perhaps not reaching the level of expectations that you must maintain belief in yourself. Improvement will come but practise is a necessity. If you stick to the task your performance will rise to meet your expectations. This is part of the brain's natural working mechanism as a goal-seeking organism. So maintain and build your belief in yourself and avoid becoming discouraged. Remember that any task you have ever achieved has always required persistence. You have a strategy for achieving your visual goals so continue to follow it.

Without change nothing happens!

Have you ever considered just what you have had to do in order to maintain your current state of vision? However good or bad it may be, you do things on a consistent basis to maintain it as it is. If you need your glasses to see only a few feet in front of you, what is the first thing you do when you wake up in the morning and go to the bathroom? Put on your glasses? Before you do that you may start the whole process by thinking, "I can't see, where are my glasses?" Or if you need your glasses or lenses to see at a distance have you ever attempted to do anything different to try and change things? Perhaps until reading this book you did not realise there was anything you could do.

Whatever your circumstances, as far as your visual process is concerned, you must decide to take some form of different action to change doing what you have always done out of habit. Once you believe in yourself and your ability to reach your target you will find yourself creating the new visual habits that you need. Be committed to your end objective and decide now that minor frustrations along the way will not deter you!

When first commencing the task of correcting you eyesight it can seem like a formidable task. You will probably bombard yourself with all manner of questions as you progress along the pathway of re-training your eyesight. Some questions will have a positive influence upon you, others will be entirely negative. Each individual is different in that the length of time required to complete their objective may differ. We are all the same, however, in the fact that we can all approach the task in a way that is **guaranteed to produce results.** Breaking down your goal into small, achievable and manageable steps is the recommended way to progress. It is the way I achieved my result. Some people may read one thing in this book and find their **eyesight correction takes place very quickly** because they immediately stop doing what they have been doing wrong.

There is no point setting yourself a goal that cannot be achieved. Yet you should always feel 'stretched' in order to make real progress. Along the way towards accomplishing any objective any person will experience set-backs. It is how you respond to these set-backs that is important. Will you simply give up or will you push yourself forward into the next stage? By being aware and learning from what is not working for you, you will advance. Sometimes by failing a little and not getting what we want immediately, we appreciate all the more, the value of what we are trying to achieve. Make what you want out of your visual re-education program really significant to *YOU*. Give it the primary importance it deserves in your life.

The major quality I found that pushed me through my sight correction program was faith. I simply adopted an attitude that involved having total faith in what I was doing and that I would achieve what I wanted. I had to trust myself and have the conviction that this approach would produce the results, provided I showed myself I was determined. You will achieve the same results, only much quicker, because you have the benefit of not having to make the mistakes I made along the way. You will **follow the path of least resistance toward your outcome.** Avoid confronting yourself with an impossible situation where you want to remain faithful to certain outdated beliefs, while at the same time trying to release yourself from these same beliefs. It is an impossibility and you will find you begin producing all types of inconsistent excuses to yourself.

Belief in yourself and your ability to overcome any limitation that has been holding you back is the platform from which to launch yourself into sight correction. So let's now look at how you can attain central alignment and correct your vision.

---

[1] I would emphasise again that 'quality' as you practise is vital.

CHAPTER 12

ACCEPT THE BENEFITS OF CENTRAL ALIGNMENT!

"Man is always more than he can know of himself, consequently, his accomplishments, time and again, will come as a surprise to him."

Golo Mann, historian

A quick recap is in order because of the importance of central alignment. You will recall that central alignment is the ability of the eye to sense every part of an object with maximum clarity. In order to do this the eye must make an enormous number of minute and rapid shifts from point to point. Problems with your vision arise when the eye fails to make the shifts required and to see all parts of an object with central alignment.

You can teach your mind to move again

In teaching your mind to move again you can escape from the inertia that has come to characterise your visual process. The benefits will be twofold, as you will also teach your pupil to move again. Your pupil must come to experience the fact that it cannot see every part of a large area with equal clarity. This can be achieved either directly or indirectly. Whichever course is adopted the aim is to build up a habit of mobility to force the mind to shift its areas of attention. The result is that the eyes' viewing of their area of greatest sensitivity, (from point to point on the object being surveyed), will be achieved.

Research has shown that when an eye with normal vision looks at a letter either from a near or far point, the letter may appear to pulsate or to move in various directions, from side to side, up and down or obliquely. Also when the eye looks from one side of the letter to another or along the whole line of letters, the letter itself, or indeed the whole line appears to move from side to side. This movement is due apparently to the shifting of the eye and is always in a direction contrary to the eye's movement.

This is normally shown if a person is looking to the top of a letter. The letter is below the line of vision and therefore *appears* to move downward. On looking at the bottom of a letter, the letter is below the line of vision and so *appears* to move upwards. Looking to the left of a letter it *appears* to move right because it is to the right of the line of vision and vice versa.

Again this is something that a person with normal vision will not be conscious of because it is in fact *an illusion of sight*. It may be difficult to detect but professional observation has shown that subjects always become able to appreciate these phenomena.

When sight is impaired the letters may remain stationary or move in the same direction as the eye. As you already know, it is in fact impossible for the eye to view a fixed point longer than for a fraction of a second. Trying to do so results in strain and a lowering of visual ability. A simple exercise will demonstrate the point if you have never experienced it. Try holding your vision on one part of a letter for a prolonged period of time. No matter how good your sight it will eventually begin to blur or even to disappear and an effort to maintain it can result in pain. Even when some people seem to be able to hold a point of sight for some time, this is because the eyes shift unconsciously. This is measurable with the appropriate instrument, although it is normally not visible to the naked eye.

The rapidity with which the eye normally operates is extremely quick. It has been shown that a normal eye can read fourteen letters on a Snellen test card[1] at a distance of ten to fifteen feet in dim lighting conditions so rapidly that the letters *seem* to be viewed all at once. Considering the practical requirements of this, in order for our eyes to achieve this they must make roughly four point shifts to each letter. So we can understand how, in order to see at a distance, it is impossible to see such letters unless one is able to shift from top to bottom and from side to side. In reality this is necessitating about seventy shifts in a fraction of a second!

What is even more amazing is that in order to view a movie it requires *thousands* of shifts per second to be able to see all the detail contained in an average screen. Consider that we actually see twenty-four frames to a second when viewing a movie and you will appreciate for yourself the rapidity with which the actual shifting of the eye is carried out. The human eye needs 0.25 of a second to receive an image and transmit the information to the brain for recognition and interpretation. The overlapping of picture information every $1/_{24}$ of a second easily exceeds the persistence of vision requirements. This means that images portrayed on screen seem to blend into one, with photographs showing successive positions of a person or object in motion, giving the illusion of a continuously moving picture.

The operation of the human eye and mind is amazing

When you stop and think about it, the rapidity with which the eye and mind are able to recognise such phenomena is absolutely amazing. Tests with artificial intelligence and attempts to give computers the ability to see, in the same way as the human eye and brain do, have so far proved fruitless. The human brain achieves the task of viewing movies without

Accept The Benefits of Central Alignment!

any strain or effort and indeed it is only when the eye is able to shift with this degree of rapidity that the eye and the mind are 'at rest', in a relaxed state and working with maximum efficiency.

In effect what we can come to understand from this, is that the more unconscious the shifting of the eye, the better your vision will be. If you do, however, try too consciously to make a shift too rapidly a strain will be produced. The remedy for this is to follow the exercises provided and to gradually **improve the quality of your vision without straining.**

Achieve total mental control

The prime ingredient of good sight is the training of the mind in the continual shifting of the visual process. This requires the subconscious to carry out the task of thinking of thousands of pieces of information in a fraction of a second. Each point of individual visual alignment has to be thought of separately. This is beyond the capability of the conscious mind but through the correct training, the subconscious mind can be directed to produce the required result. We know it is impossible to think of two things at once or two parts of one idea perfectly at the same time. The eye with imperfect sight is however trying to accomplish the impossible by looking at only one point for a length of time or 'staring'. If you already have poor eyesight, have you ever tried looking 'consistently' at a strange object? Your aim was of 'seeing it better', but the result was probably that you failed to see it as well as you could have done. This is because of the way in which you subconsciously approached the task. Defective sight is produced and this is one of the key causes of poor vision.

Shifting and swinging

Once we start asking ourselves the right questions, enquiry into the best techniques of rectifying defective vision have shown us that one of the **best methods** of improving sight is to imitate consciously the **unconscious shifting** of normal vision. You can start now to realise for yourself the **benefits** of the apparent motion produced by such shifting. Dr Bates first named these procedures for exercising the eyes. They are primarily designed to make you aware of the 'apparent' **movement** of external objects. By using this exercise you will aim at increasing the **mobility** of your visual process and re-training the elements of your mind necessary for achieving normal vision.

What happens when this exercise is successful? When mobility re-establishes itself the unconscious tensions present in your mind and visual process are **relaxed**. Staring is replaced by **rapidly shifting central alignment**, with a consequent and marked improvement in your vision.

Normal sight can also be improved in this way. Shifting allows the eye to rest, and lessens and corrects errors of refraction. So why does shifting work? The eye with normal vision never tries to hold a fixed point for more than a fraction of a second and when it shifts it will see the point of previous alignment worse.[2] When your eye stops shifting rapidly, it is 'mixing it all up together'. It stops seeing the point it has just shifted from 'worse'. The point it is currently viewing must always be seen 'best'. As I have already said, once this specific chain of ordered transactions is varied or breaks down, sight ceases to be normal. It is this understanding which lies at the heart of successfully improving sight by the exercise of shifting. It is therefore well worth while grasping a complete understanding of what is involved.

As you now have a basic understanding of the principles involved when carrying out the exercises, remember that the best way to achieve central alignment is not to try and see one small area at a time **'better'** than all the others. Concentrate upon the **mobility** of the visual process, which is necessary to **see successive small areas** of an object with maximum clarity.

First increase the mobility of your eyes and mind

The recommended way to progress is first to increase the mobility of your eyes and mind - to teach yourself to keep your eyes and your attention in a **constant easy movement**. Only when you have achieved this do you **move** on to other exercises aimed directly at making the pupil of **your eye** more conscious of central alignment. You begin by regenerating the visual process through movement and then it will be time to advance and consciously appreciate the unmistakable benefits of central alignment by being able to identify these benefits and consequently increase their power and intensity.

What swinging is and how to do it

Whenever you are moving and you view objects in the environment they appear to move in the opposite direction to the motion of your movement. Our visual perception means we can see those objects that are closest to us moving most quickly. This rate of movement decreases the further the distance of the object from us. Objects at a great distance can appear stationary when viewed from a speeding train or car.

You will now become more aware of this apparent movement of objects in your external environment as you view them. Why are you not currently paying attention to these phenomena? We all make sense of our own particular worlds through modelling processes known as 'generalisation, deletion and distortion'. These processes determine exactly what elements in our environments we pay attention to. The fact is that your brain has *learnt not to pay attention* to the apparent movement of external objects as they are viewed. In other words the cells that require stimulation in order to be activated and do their job are not receiving the input they need[3]. The process is totally subconscious and you are now going to start taking control over your own visual process again.

Short swing

The short swing is an exercise to be done so that you can stand and look at a distant object while also viewing some near-by object. One way is to try standing in a doorway or in front of a window. If a window is selected the side bar or top bar of the window frame will serve as a near object while a lamp post or part of a house will serve as a distant object. Chose one that is on the other side of the street. Other options if inside a room could be a lamp or a hanging electrical wire, while a painting, ornament or something similar can represent the more distant object.

Position yourself so that you are standing with your feet approximately eighteen inches apart. Next swing your whole body regularly and gently from side to side. Move the weight from one foot to the other as you do so. Alternate the weight onto each foot. The actual swing should be just less than a foot and the head should be kept in position and not turned in relation to the shoulders. Remain looking straight ahead and move yourself in unison with your trunk.

What is the effect you are looking for? Well, as you swing to the right, the near object, e.g. the window frame bar, will appear to move to the left across the distant object. As you swing to the left it will appear to move to the right. Accustom yourself to this created movement and be aware during a number of swings *how* you represent this movement to yourself. Next close your eyes but continue swinging from side to side. Visualise how the movement looked of the window frame bar across the lamppost. Open your eyes again and watch the real objects that you have chosen, as they move back and forth. Again close and visualise and continue the exercise for two or three minutes.

A testimony of success!

These exercises have a number of intrinsic benefits and the writer, Aldous Huxley (1894–1963), was a great proponent of using them. Huxley himself benefited greatly from the Bates' method of visual correction. In 1910 he contracted an eye infection which made him almost blind for some eighteen months. He had only one eye just capable of light perception and the other eye had a capability of vision to read the two-hundred-foot Snellen chart letter at ten feet. Poor vision indeed. The condition became far worse for Huxley and his sight began to fail badly in 1939. Huxley by this time found that glasses were of no use to him. He was left with no choices but he did not give up. It was at this time that he came across Dr Bates' method of visual re-education. Quite remarkably Huxley found himself reading without glasses after two months and found that strain and fatigue, which had always accompanied his efforts at reading, disappeared. In addition Huxley had suffered with opacity in the cornea which had been a persistent condition for twenty-five years. This condition began to clear up with the continued practice of the visual exercises. Huxley was able to testify that the opacity cleared to such a degree that his worse eye, which for years could do no more than distinguish light from darkness, was able to recognise the ten-foot line on the Snellen chart at one foot.

Independent proof that this method of visual re-education of the seeing process works. All it takes is the will and determination to succeed. To follow through with what you know works. As Huxley said about the *Art of Seeing*:

> "My own case is in no way unique; thousands of other sufferers from defects of vision have benefited by following the simple rules of that *Art of Seeing* which we owe to Bates and his followers."

Let's return directly back to the swing. To receive the proper benefits from the exercise, ensure that you practise it regularly. Make your own mind aware of the *quality of movement* and familiarise yourself with it. Breaking free from your eye's bad habit of staring will gradually lead you to shift your focus of attention and achieve central alignment. Indirectly you are learning to relax again while also being actively engaged in the visual process. The rhythmic movement of the swing also produces a kinaesthetic sensation in the body, which has an effect upon the mind in creating a soothing and calming sensation. It is important to be aware of your body sensations because over time you will come to experience for yourself that good vision involves much more than just your sight.

The long swing

A variation of the swing is the 'long swing'. This exercise involves standing with your feet apart, as previously but this time you will swing in a wider arc. Now swing the hips so that your whole trunk moves together with the head in unison with the trunk. When swinging to the left your weight will be thrown onto your left foot with the heel of your right foot lifting slightly. It is the same process in reverse as you swing to the right. Most importantly as far as your eyes are concerned, the motion created will mean that they cover an arc of one hundred and eighty degrees or more as you swing. The external environment has the impression of vacillating backwards and forwards in a wide sweep. Do not pay attention to anything within your field of vision, simply **relax and accept** the incoming information into your senses in an almost peaceful and unconcerned way. Let your mind rest without any effort to perceive your environment.

Remember that your objective is breaking your eyes' habit of 'staring'. Bear in mind that when doing and returning to the 'swish' pattern, referred to in Chapter 10, you can visualise yourself as you will be, having controlled your subconscious habit of staring and how you will be when your sight has improved as a result of acquiring this control.

In addition to the swish, the swing is a physical aid to this mental practice program. It temporarily inhibits the established patterns of incorrect use of your visual process and starts the task of building new, regenerative habits that will aid your visual process. Breaking the pattern of subconsciously, yet consistently, 'staring' allows the mind to begin functioning in the type of environment it must have - one of free and non-strained mobility, in an atmosphere of total relaxation.

The forefinger swing

A nice easy exercise that compliments the exercises that we have looked at is the forefinger swing. One of its appeals is the ease with which you can use it. The near object for your eye to focus upon is your forefinger. Hold it about six inches in front of your nose. Now move your head from side to side while at the same time being aware of the apparent movement of your forefinger across the more distant objects within your view. On a regular basis close your eyes and allow your mind's eye to replicate this movement. After a short while open your eyes and focus alternatively upon your forefinger and then upon the more distant objects that you can see your forefinger passing across.

Create favourable conditions for better vision

By now you should be a lot more involved in the attention that you are paying to your own vision. As this involvement increases give particular attention to the micro-elements of your visual process. The things that would normally pass you by because they have been deleted, generalised or distorted away. Whenever you are moving and as you view the world, become aware of its passing by and *'how'* it is passing by. In particular, as you walk or drive in your car note the approach of trees, house's, other cars and people. Notice when you turn your head how objects which are close by, move across objects that have a more distant point of vision. A key principle in re-educating your sight is being aware of the mobility of the world and environment around you. Increasing the mobility of your eyes and mind creates the conditions for better vision. It is a first vital step of becoming conscious of the ability, before the skill is reassigned to the subconscious after re-training.

Daily practice makes perfect

Incorporate these *daily swing exercises* into your 'daily eye workout'. Perfect vision is not possible without the ability of the eye to achieve continuous movement over an object and a constant changing of the focus of attention in relation to the parts of the object being viewed. Cultivate for yourself the necessary awareness of the apparent movements of objects, even as you go about your daily life. Apply the principal of the swing to varied circumstances and the benefits will soon begin to **_provide you with your desired reward._**

Further exercises

An example of an exercise borrowed from the martial arts also helps to aid the mobility process of mind and eyes, so aiding central alignment. In the martial arts this exercise is used to speed up reflexes in the visual process and train the eyes and mind to respond quickly to new situations and information.

Take three dice and throw them on a table. Look quickly at all three dice, one to another. After one second, turn away or close your eyes and name the numbers appearing on the face-up side of the dice. The exercise supports the process of a rapid shifting of attention of both the mind and the eyes. It also develops the mind's powers of perception.

If you prefer, the same thing can be achieved using the letters from a scrabble game. It is the principle that is important.

Continue to score points and progress remembering that these exercises are attacking the bad habits in your visual process. As they are broken down and you gradually re-train your sight, **so the improvements you notice will become permanent.**

---

[1] See Chapter 15.
[2] You will recall in Chapter 9 the earlier distinction explaining points of 'best' and 'worst' vision.
[3] Chapter 6 on perception dealt with this process.

CHAPTER 13

CREATING BETTER MOBILITY AND INCREASING YOUR POWER OF PERCEPTION

"...no two people see the external world in exactly the same way. To every separate person a thing is what he thinks it is - in other words, not a thing but a think."
P Fitzgerald, author

We can now move into the area that will begin to re-train your visual capabilities and begin improving your natural powers of central alignment.

Flashing

In aiming to create mobility and to increase your own powers of perception and alertness a technique known as *'flashing'* was devised by Dr Bates. Nothing to do with other definitions of the word that may spring to mind, this exercise is complementary to the exercises that have already been described. Flashing is an additional method of breaking the staring habit.

Glance quickly at an object now, then close your eyes and remember what you perceived in the instant that you observed the object. Cultivating a sense of alertness is what flashing is all about. You do not fix your gaze by immobilising your mind and eyes, and straining to see all parts of an object at once, and trying to see them equally well at the same time. It is an extension of the principles that have already been referred to.

You will find that as you practise 'flashing', you actually perceive a great deal more than you are initially aware of. There is an interesting psychological experiment that was carried out by Postman and Bruner. Before looking at that experiment it will be of benefit to explore in greater detail the processes of 'generalisation, deletion and distortion' You will recall that all human beings make sense of the world in which we live, through these three modelling processes.

Basically we act and direct all our behaviour in the world through these three processes. It is likely that we form our visual models in much the same way as our other behavioural models. What we can understand from this can be explained by taking a not uncommon example from a therapy situation. A common case history is a person who has been 'rejected' at some point in their life. Case histories show that it is quite possible for such a person to react in a very specific way in response to what is perceived by them as 'rejection'. It has been found in numerous circumstances that such a person may form a *generalisation* that he is "not worth caring for". In many cases what this generalisation can then mean is that he *deletes* messages or communications that give a contrary indication. Alternatively, messages and communications are 'reinterpreted' to correspond with his generalisation.

In such cases a person remains unaware of messages contrary to his generalisation, "that he is not worth caring about". This is a description in psychology of the classical positive feedback loop. Also known as the self-fulfilling prophesy or forward feedback. **A person's generalisations or expectations filter out and distort his experience to make it consistent with his 'expectations'.**

If this is accepted as a view of the modelling process, all human modelling processes are built in a similar way. The key point is of course that these modelling processes are subconscious. It is easy to see how the same principles can be mirrored in the visual process. When our personal visual experience of the world for some reason shows us that we can no longer see as well as we did, we come to form subconscious *generalisations* about what we *are* able to see. Remember that Dr Bates' research showed that when the eye views an unfamiliar object an error of refraction is *always* produced. Dr Bates even said:

> "During 30 years devoted to the study of refraction, I have found few people who could maintain perfect sight - that is, with no refractive error - for more than a few minutes at a time, even under the most favourable conditions; and often I have seen the refraction change half a dozen times or more in a second, the variations ranging all the way from twenty diopters of myopia to normal."[1]

Consider this now against the background of what is known about the human modelling process and a number of personal experiences which support the subconscious idea of defective vision will soon form into 'generalisations' in the subconscious mind. Generalisation as a modelling process works in such a way that expectations filter out and distort experience to make it consistent with those expectations. The classical positive feedback loop is formed as there are no contrary experiences to challenge those generalisations and so expectations are confirmed. The cycle continues in this way until it is interrupted. This is a very important understanding.

Generalisation and the habit that forms out of it are closely linked. That this process accurately reflects how we model our visual process is supported by the fact that as soon as we start to provide ourselves with visual re-education, through the exercises provided, we provide the exceptions to the generalisation process that let us start forming a new visual model. From this it will be clear that practising the eye workout exercises on a regular basis will help **prevent relapse.**

Further support is provided for this interpretation when the effects of hypnosis upon the visual process are considered. We shall look at this in more detail shortly. Before we do let's return now to the 'expectancy experiment' by Postman and Bruner.

"In this psychological experiment experimental subjects were asked to identify on short and controlled exposure a series of playing cards. Numerous cards were normal but some were made anomalous, e.g. red six of spades and black four of hearts. Each experimental run was constituted by the display of a single card to a single subject in a series of exposures. After each exposure the subject was asked what he had seen and the run was terminated by two successive correct identifications.

"Even on the shortest exposures many subjects identified most of the cards and after a small increase all the subjects identified them all. For the normal cards these identifications were usually correct but the anomalous cards were almost always identified, without apparent hesitation or puzzlement as normal. The black four of hearts might, for example, be identified as the four of either spades or hearts. Without any awareness of trouble, it was immediately fitted to one of the conceptual categories prepared by prior experience. One would not even like to say that the subjects had seen something different from what they identified. With a further exposure to the anomalous cards, subjects did begin to hesitate and to display awareness of anomaly. Exposed, for example to, the red six of spades, some would say: that's the six of spades, but there's something wrong with it – the black has a red border. Further increase of exposure resulted in still more hesitation and confusion until finally, and sometimes quite suddenly, most subjects would produce the correct identification without hesitation. Moreover, after doing this with two or three of the anomalous cards, they would have little further difficulty with the others. A few subjects, however, were unable to make the requisite adjustment of their categories. Even at forty times the average exposure required to recognise normal cards for what they were, more than ten per cent of the anomalous cards were not correctly identified. And the subjects who then failed often exclaimed; "I can't make a suit out, whatever it is. It didn't even look like a card that time. I don't know what colour it is now or whether it's a spade or a heart. I'm not even sure now what a spade looks like. My God!..."

"Either as a metaphor or because it reflects the nature of the mind, that psychological experiment provides wonderfully simple and cogent schema for the process of scientific discovery. In science, as in the playing of the card experiment, novelty emerges only with difficulty, manifested by resistance, against a background provided by expectation. Initially, only the anticipated and usual are experienced even under circumstances where anomaly is later to be observed[2]."

This is an interesting experiment from a number of perspectives. It illustrates the modelling process of generalisation. It shows that the subjects made a generalisation that the colour and shaping options would be *the same as they had always experienced.* Black with clubs and spades and red with hearts or diamonds. **Expectation played a major role in their assessments.** They supported their generalisation by distorting either the shape or colour dimensions in the anomalous cards.

As far as our sight is concerned it is easy to see how the same modelling processes are often brought into action. Once the expectation of poor vision is established subconsciously, then the modelling process reinforces it. The process of distortion in this experiment *prevented people from seeing what it was possible for them to see.*[3]

Support for the view that this modelling process is at work arises when the effect of hypnosis is considered upon eyesight. There have been reported cases of people under hypnosis being age regressed to an earlier age and time when they first had to wear glasses. The hypnotist has the subject 'keep the quality of the eyes that the person had at that time, as a child' and then has the subject 'grow up' retaining those qualities. The method has proven successful with myopia.

Hypnosis as a way of treating defective vision can work and the results can last, provided the subject is not getting what is known as "secondary gain" from the condition of defective vision. If that is the case, the benefits of the secondary gain have to be established and interrupted with different ways of dealing with the secondary gain found.[4] One example taken from a reported case history would be of a person who had 'blurry vision' but *only* during times of stress. This may be in response to the desire to avoid having unpleasant feelings *'in response'* to something seen.

Applying the modelling process to our visual process, we are always able to sense at any given moment many more parts of our visual field than we actually select and are aware of. Consciousness ensures that we filter the wealth of available information to prevent overload of our nervous system, so that, at any one moment, we only pay attention to a small number of stimuli. This is the human modelling process in action.

A person's model of the world is a description of how a process works (but not the possible reasons for how it can work). A person's model of the world is built up of internal processes, beliefs, and behaviour that allow him to function in a particular way. A model is a way of organising experience and is a 'description' that applies to your own experience.

In the branch of psychology known as NLP, or Neuro Linguistic Programming, the process called modelling is the discovery of the sequence of internal representations and behaviours that allows someone to accomplish any task. Once the components of the task have been detailed, the skill can be passed on much more easily. This is in effect a more precise explanation and description that encompasses the work and methods propounded by Dr Bates. Effectively he created, through his years of research, a model that is now available to rectify defective eyesight. At the time of Dr Bates' initial discoveries little was known of the functioning of the mind and much of what he initially found now has sound principles to support his work.

We do not always consciously remember what we see

Sometimes we look but we do not see because for one of the reasons mentioned, the mind is incapable of making itself aware of what the eyes are sensing. An error of refraction occurs.

It seems that when the eyes sense a stimulus through the visual process they leave a mnemonic trace or engram[5]. This is simply a way to describe the behaviour of large sets of interacting neurones. These traces can be subsequently revived giving rise to a memory image. It has been found that stimulating certain parts of the brain while under surgery, patients have been able to relive events long forgotten, in all their original detail. They are able to visualise fully the experience - evidence that your mind and brain do record far more information than you consciously have access to. The actual storage capacity of the brain is almost unlimited and it is believed we currently use only five per cent of our brains' actual capacity.

The experiences of those who have taken visual re-education courses in the past has shown that stimuli often left traces, which could be remembered under certain conditions. Under normal conditions the detail could not be remembered or accessed because of the limited capability of the conscious mind. People recalling forgotten events or details unknown to the conscious mind through the power of hypnosis are not uncommon. The point is that **your brain has actually recorded far more than you were aware of** or indeed more than you could see[6].

Flashing as an exercise

When people who suffer with defective vision have carried out the flashing exercise, making a flashing glance at some object, it has often been recorded that they do not see it all or see it only as a blur. It has been reported that it has often been the case that upon diverting their attention away and closing the eyes, they have a memory image of what was perceived. As soon as the person stops trying anxiously to recall what was seen and relaxes and leaves it to intuition, they frequently turn out to be able to recall what they actually saw in its totality.

The examples given from hypnosis also demonstrate this fact. **It is possible for us to recall what was perceived subconsciously although we did not see it**. Relaxing the mental tensions of the conscious process through training will yield the same results.

One way to view the effect of strain and stress is as part of the generalisation process. Once the habit of faulty vision is learnt, strain becomes a characteristic. As the effects of relaxation and so exceptions to the generalisation process are experienced, there is a gradual improvement in the ability to perceive. When you close your eyes, practise recalling the memory image of an object in as much detail as possible. It is a part of the skill of increasing aspects of your sensory acuity.

Sensory acuity

Sensory acuity is the process of refining your ability to make distinctions in your visual, auditory, kinaesthetic, olfactory and gustatory systems. In this particular case you are concentrating upon visual acuity. Give yourself a fuller, richer sensory experience and the ability to create detailed visually sensitive interactions with your external world.

Imagination plays an important part in the visual process, as we shall see. Allow yourself to become more adventurous in your perceptions of the world. For example, try this exercise. Have a friend show you a domino from a distance which is just beyond what you could normally see. Take a flashing glance at it, then close your eyes and "reach out into the air for it". Literally do it - as it would be if you did this with a real domino. Raise your hand, close it around the emptiness where the imaginary domino is, lower your hand, open it and look into your palm. What could you see? What does your intuition tell you? Does your answer correspond with the real domino?

It is important to realise that this is an exercise in increasing your power of perception as recorded by your subconscious mind. It is based upon the principles outlined above. Your own attitude to this exercise is reflective of the state and power of your perception.

The aim is to lower the mental barrier that exists between what can be sensed and what is actually seen. Persons with defective vision frequently demonstrate this block. In reality it simply means such persons always activate the same 'neural patterns' in response to a certain set of circumstances. Lowering the barrier, so that accessing through revival of the memory traces left by the act of sensing, gives rise to fully conscious vision. In other words, *seeing and perceiving what is sensed*, in the same moment it is sensed. You will begin activating new neural patterns of behaviour that will give you the results you want.

As you practise in the early stages there may be an interval of several seconds between the act of seeing or sensing and the act of recalling what was sensed. As the psychological block between the function of the eyes and the brain is lowered so the interval will become shorter until you are able to sense and immediately relate in your mind what has been seen. The performance will then occur almost simultaneously.

You are increasing the power and capability of your senses, in particular your visual sense. It is already clear that we actually see through a complex series of active perceptual filters. The world you perceive is not the real world but a 'map' made by your own neurology. **What you pay attention to is the key.** Expanding and re-training your attention points is the answer. The ability to notice more and to make finer distinctions is a theme that runs throughout this book. You will be concentrating upon your visual sense but the principle is one to apply across the whole spectrum of your life. Reactivating your visual sense and re-empowering it is only the start.

Like a painter, become sensitive to the nuances of colour and shape. Re-educating your visual process is seeing more but also **becoming aware** of what to look for. Learning to perceive the difference that makes a difference for you**, in your visual process**. You can change the way you see the world, but you must have the determination to develop a rich awareness in your visual sense. To build upon it remembering all the reasons why **you want to do it** and all the things it will mean to you once you achieve your objective. How many people do you know who are even aware that they can rectify their defective vision? How many people do you know who are doing something about it? You are taking the action required to **make the improvements now.** You will look back in a short time and feel proud of your achievement in re-educating yourself and **giving yourself** the ability to see clearly again. The development of a **rich awareness in your visual sense** increases your sensory acuity.

When the time difference between your seeing or sensing and perceiving or recalling is almost simultaneous, you will have increased the power of the visual element of your sensory acuity.

Practising flashing

Do the exercise of **flashing** as part of your 'daily eye workout'. Flashing can, however, be practised anywhere which means you can do extra work with this exercise. You will remember that the objective is to avoid staring and this is an exercise that will help you break that habit. **Acquire the habit** of taking quick glances at objects and then redirecting your gaze or momentarily closing your eyes and remembering what was seen.

This is also a useful test of your ability to visualise consciously. What do you see in your mind's eye when you recall the image of an object you have just looked at? Do you see the object fully and clearly just as though you were looking at it with your eyes open? Many people find they have a poor ability to make visual images consciously when they think about it. Everyone can make visual images, it's just that they do not always realise how they do it or when. The process may still be unconscious for you and with practice you will be able to improve and remember far more of what you see.

Some people find that when they first start to do these exercises consciously they remember very little detail or do not recall in full colour. Your mind is like a video camera and is capable of recording everything you see, hear and sense. Continue practising until your powers of recollection become almost perfect. If you cannot do this at the moment it simply reflects an area of your mind which you have not yet developed to its full potential. **Practice will pay you dividends.** I found that when I first began doing this my ability to access visual images in my mind was very poor. I have now improved this ability tremendously.

As you practise, try looking first at nature, perhaps a hornet hovering over a flower. Recall the event in your mind. Do you achieve the full movie, details of the colours and movements? If not first try billboards and other advertisements. Also car registrations are always a very useful practice point for flashing exercises.

It is better if you *practise while in a relaxed state* rather than under conditions demanding full concentration. Being a passenger in a car or while riding on a bus when there are no demands upon you are the type of conditions to aim for. Remember that strain or stress will prevent you from seeing with the quality and richness that is available to you when *you are relaxed.*

Again avoid the over-anxious desire to see. Be content with glancing at the world and then recalling the inner mind's eye's memory of the object. It is almost true to say that when you stop trying to see you will begin to see naturally.

More specific exercises

Simple dominoes have been used very effectively in the past to help achieve results. Pick any domino, hold it out at arms' length and then quickly view the domino by a quick glance across it. Close your hand around it. Close your eyes and remember what was on the upper half of the domino and then the lower half. Open your eyes and confirm the results. If you were correct, your powers of perception are improving. If wrong, simply continue on with the next one and keep practising.

A further exercise using the dominoes is the same procedure but with more dominoes. Take twelve dominoes and stand them along the edge of a table in a row. Sitting in front of them at the boundary of your normal viewing limit, begin to swing your eyes from left to right along the row. The dominoes should be counted a quickly as possible. The objective is to have the stationary eyes and your attention set into motion at unaccustomed speed. Next re-focus upon the first domino again and close your eyes and name the numbers in the upper and lower halves of the dominoes. Check your accuracy by comparing with the real dominoes. Next count the whole row again and then glance back to the second domino. Flash again, close your eyes and name the numbers. Continue with the exercise until you reach the end of the line.

The importance of actually doing the exercises in this book cannot be over-emphasised. It is fine reading about the exercises but unless you begin to take the action, to start working your eyes and your perceptual system, you will not experience any improvement. Things can improve quicker than you think, so make sure you commit to yourself to doing the exercises.

Referring back to the domino exercise, if you are short-sighted or 'myopic' and it is hard for you to see anything except at very short range, do the exercise initially within easy-seeing distance and gradually move slightly further back and repeat it. Familiarity increases and you will find that your distance gradually improves. Remember to stretch yourself always with new limits and new challenges. Increase your range of vision.

If distant vision is easy, (hypermetropia) and you have difficulty with short-range seeing, simply reverse the process. Again, start from some distance away and gradually move closer using the same basic exercise.

Also notice the differences as you perform all these exercises daily. What differences? - the difference you are alert to as you become increasingly aware of your visual function and exactly what you can and cannot see. What micro-changes can you become aware of? These are your building blocks. The really crucial thing, as I have said before, is to notice even the smallest of changes. These small changes really are your springboard for gradually and consistently improving your visual process. Persist, give yourself the chance you deserve and notice the difference between where you were when you started and the changes that occur even over a very short time. Note the changes in your journal. Keep a record of your achievement. Improvement happens quicker for some than for others but improvement will happen if you persist.

Once you begin noticing the improvements you make, you will feel the whole process taking on a momentum of its own. You will feel the thrill of knowing you have control over your own visual process and that **ultimately control is yours**. You will even begin making your own assessments and measurements of achievement based upon these principles.

[1] Dr Bates, *Better Eyesight Without Glasses* (Souvenir Press), 28-29
[2] See 3 below.
[3] For a full discussion of the modelling process, Grinder and Bander, *The Structure of Magic, Volumes 1 & 2* (Science and Behaviour Books, 1975).
[4] Secondary gain occurs when a person has a purpose for maintaining a certain condition, which may not be immediately obvious when a treatment is given, but which if present and not dealt with can lead to other problems arising. This may detract from the effectiveness of the original solution.
[5] This can be more readily explained as a special pattern of synaptic connections between neurones. When certain neurones fire a particular representation is activated. Think now of the 'Houses of Parliament'. Until mentioned this memory representation in your brain was inactive. Simply thinking about it stimulates the representation, which is **a combination of relevant neurones** in your brain firing in a particular pattern.
[6] To demonstrate the point your brain often fills in parts of a three dimensional representation. If you look at the rear of some ones head this is what is directly in front of you. Your brain will infer a face on the other side of the head. You would be shocked to see a head in a mirror that looked exactly the same in the mirror as it did at the back of the head you were seeing.

Chapter 14

SHIFTING

So far the exercises that you have been introduced too are aimed at encouraging you to attain the mobility of mind and eyes necessary for improving your vision. A point to be aware of is, that as you become more aware of your own visual process and begin to make improvements, each exercise on its own and also taken together, has a cumulative building effect, each working on its own, yet also as part of an overall strategy. Indirectly you will be increasing your ability in re-educating your point of central alignment.

Having practised keeping your focus of attention in constant movement, both visually and mentally you are now less prone to 'staring', which means that you can now progress to increasing your ability with central alignment.

How long will improvement take?

I touched earlier upon how long it would take you to correct your own vision and said that this depended upon how long it would be before you 'allowed' yourself to improve. We can now get a little more specific upon this. It is fair to say that the latest theories upon the functioning of the brain and mind consider that the brain works upon a 'computational' basis. The work of David Mar will be looked at later.[1] Ray Jackendoff has similarities in his thinking on the subject. If we take a very simplified approach to these ideas, it can be said that our brains use a type of 'standard' computation in arriving at certain conclusions of what things mean to us. It is a type of 'embedded knowledge' represented by a set pattern of neural activity that activates any time certain stimuli are presented.

The process of visual awareness is very complex because it utilises many different processing abilities of the brain. The key point is that the established computational patterns used by our brains, e.g. to recognise a face, mean that our brains use certain generalised patterns to identify a 'face' as a 'face'. Then our brains become more precise by specifically 'computing' the individual features of the face that make it unique.

A good analogy is a computer spreadsheet. The primary formulas that are put into the spreadsheet form the basis for all later and more complex calculations. Spreadsheets can provide a wonderful set of results when all the information is correct. If the primary formulas are wrong, all subsequent calculations dependent upon them will be wrong. The initial calculation in a spreadsheet is not re-performed each time, rather it is used as a platform from which to carry out further more complex calculations. Remember that numbers on a spreadsheet are only 'symbols' that represent things to us in our brains. In the same way our brains use a form of symbolic coding - the brain's language. We have already looked at this. The symbols are not necessarily the things they represent. Our brains interpret these symbols. You will remember that we looked earlier at exactly how our vision is produced and that we do not actually have pictures inside our brains. We have an 'interpretation' of the brain's symbolic code that represents the objects we see in the environment.

If we return for a moment to the spreadsheet analogy, let's assume that your visual process operates along similar lines. If your 'deep structure' basis for making the visual calculations necessary for sight is based upon faulty input or is being calculated wrongly by your brain's processing or computational activities, everything that flows from that, i.e. the subsequent visual process, will be faulty. The result is defective vision. In other words, you have a deeply embedded pattern of neural activity and processing of this code that is always used to begin your visual processing and the consequent resulting sight.

It is believed that an area of the brain known as the 'neocortex' probably acts in two ways. Our genes and embryonic processes produce a very crude form of 'wiring' that our brains adopt and use by drawing upon real life experience. The brain is able over time to establish features in the environment that it can place into its bank of established 'computations,' which then form the basis of further assessments of what things mean to us. In our visual process it means building a basic library, e.g. of shapes, which is subsequently used as part of greater or larger assessments of what an object may mean to us. i.e. what we see.

This is a very simple analysis of what is undoubtedly a very complex process. The point it leads to, however, is that bad sight has a functional basis on a micro level. While some of the exercises may seem very simple they are designed this way for a purpose. You are re-training your very basic visual processing. In other words, re-calibrating the basic measurements upon which you base your whole visual process. Going back to the spreadsheet analogy, you are re-checking and correcting the basic calculations upon which all other subsequent calculations are made. As you begin to draw upon your new visual experience, adding it to other experience, you are literally 'rewiring' your neural pathways so that new patterns of activity are fired in response to visual stimuli you receive. Mobility as a principle is all about stimulating these new neural patterns.

So how long does changing these patterns take?

The answer lies in the current state of your brains 'computational' ability. Let's be specific and we can relate it directly to the current quality of your vision. If your vision is very bad, your brain is making a number of incorrect computations. Let's take a very simple example. If in a spreadsheet a formula calculation is that '1+2+3+1=8', then the basic calculation is wrong. There may be two or three calculations like this in the whole spreadsheet that are also wrong. This throws out the whole spreadsheet. It is easy to correct them once we know that we need to look at them. It becomes obvious. We recalculate the sum and arrive at the answer '7'. Anyone can do that. All subsequent calculations which involve using that sum will then be correct. They are built upon a solid and accurate basis.

Your eyesight is very similar. If all the basics are correct than the adjustments needed to correct it will happen quickly. If not it will take a little longer while the basic matters upon which sight is built are put in good order.

One of the reasons that we do not correct our own sight automatically when it goes wrong is because of the speed at which the visual process functions. It is an extremely rapid process and your brain uses established patterns of neural activity that it has used in the past and which it believes is probably going to represent the object you are viewing in the environment. There is a certain level of 'expectancy' built into your visual process depending upon the *pattern of stimulus* you are receiving.

So the answer lies in the current state of your brain's functioning. If most basic elements are in place, doing something once will be enough to correct the defect. If the problem goes slightly deeper and adjustments to very basic elements are required, it will take longer. Once these basic elements are in place, they can then be used to build new correct ways of using your visual process. As I have already said the whole process is a marvellous dynamic. Once you understand the nature and basics of how the dynamic operates, correction comes easily and quickly. Let's now move forward into further exercises that will motivate this whole process.

Small scale shifting

You must now gradually become aware that it is the small micro movements and shifting of the eyes and mind with greater concentration and attention which are needed for ongoing improvements. Mastering these smaller scale shifts in the visual process is really just acquiring the natural incessant shifts that normal vision entails.

We have already seen the remarkable ability of the eye to make these shifts. The almost imperceptible small movements, from point to point on any object in view, are the objective. Building up consciously the habit of small scale shifting is the next goal. Most people learnt the habit when young; however, over the course of time, some people have acquired bad seeing habits.

Micro looking

Have you ever had the experience of looking at an object in real close-up detail? If you have a video camera with a very finely attuned zoom facility, it is able to capture some very fine detail that would ordinarily pass you by. It is only when **you stop to pay these things real attention** that you come to appreciate them again.

Paying such acute attention to an object does not however mean staring at it. The rule is not to see all parts of the object equally well at the same time but to deliberately divert your attention to seeing it almost 'piecemeal', seeing and perceiving one part of that which makes the whole, one piece at a time.

Increasing your visual acuity

You will remember that general sensory acuity is the process of learning to make finer and more useful distinctions about the sense information that you get from the world. Increasing your visual acuity is doing the same thing while concentrating upon your visual process.

Tony Robbins in his book, *Unlimited Power*[2], gives an excellent example of the differences we can become aware of, simply by paying attention to things through different representational systems. He describes a house using the auditory, visual and kinaesthetic representational systems. If you are unaware of the differences it is a useful reference and way to increase your sensory ability. You can begin to make a list yourself of visual words as a way of focusing your attention upon this representational system. For example:

> Picture, look, insight, focus, imagination, scene, blank, shine, clarify, examine, outlook, reveal, survey, hazy, illustrate.

There are probably many other words that you can think of and add to this list. The point to be aware of is that these words do not actually represent the process of seeing itself, they are merely descriptions of things that make sense to you as something connected to the visual process itself, i.e. 'seeing'. The words are only labels for particular experiences that make sense to you. The actual experiences represented by the words are much more then the label identifying the experience represented by the word.

For example you may look at a house and as you do so you see the number of windows, the position of the door, the colour of the bricks. You may find the house visually stunning or maybe just dowdy. It will create a sense impression in your mind - the outline and shapes particular to that house. It will have a relationship to other objects around it such as trees and lamp posts.

This may all sound elementary yet it is vital to **begin re-examining**

SHIFTING

and improving your powers of memory and concentration. It is part of the process of generalisation that causes some of us to stop noticing the detail in objects as we observe. This is because they are common and we have seen them hundreds of times before. Start to form clearer mental images and concepts of what you see. In this way you begin stimulating new neural patterns of activity or expanding those you already have. It is important to remember that this is something that you need to do until your visual process has been re-trained, after which the whole process will be given back to your subconscious.

At this time you can begin to compare your normal visual process. Do you just stare and form some vague image of an object you look at or are you able to recall a number of interesting and significant details about an object you see. What is your strategy for examining objects in your environment? Play around and see what else you can become aware of. Paying attention in this way will improve your vision because the next time you look at the same object you will have a detailed memory of it. As we saw above, the neural activity will 'rewire' itself so that you can begin to pay attention to new features, which means seeing things in new ways and your brain can then respond accordingly. As you will recall from the chapter on perception we see things most clearly when we are familiar with them and the ability to improve your conceptual and perceptual appreciation of an object will always help to broaden your sensory acuity of that object in the future.

This process therefore helps your vision there and then by training the eyes and mind to shift quickly and continuously from point to point. It also increases the power of your perception by providing the basis for improved vision at a later date. Making objects more familiar means paying attention to their detail and not 'generalising', as in the normal subconscious process. I can tell you that this way of viewing the world will produce some of your most memorable and satisfying achievements in increasing your visual powers. **Learn to love the small distinctions that you notice.**

When looking at letters or numbers on signs begin seeing the outlines, the shapes and the colours that make up the whole letter or number. How does it stand out from the background? If it is not clear, identify precisely what is unclear so you can start working on it. I particularly used to find that red lettering against a white background had a blur, a complete lack of definition and shape so that the boundary between the letters and the background was not clear and sharp, the way it should be.

By focusing upon the lines, shape and corners you begin paying attention to the micro-elements that require your eyes and mind to do a large range of small scale shifting, which is a basic building block to improving your sight. In many respects the more familiar an object, the better, as it gives you the opportunity to challenge your own generalisation process. It is **guaranteed** that as you become more alert to these areas of the visual process, your future ability to sense and perceive the same things will become **quicker and easier**.

It has been shown that the human eye scans the face of another in a particular pattern and in a particular way. This natural scanning pattern takes in thousands of different points in a matter of moments. Another's face is very important to us as a source of rich subconscious information about our communication with that person. We consciously and subconsciously respond to minute facial changes and expressions in other people and use this information to form our future communications with that person.

It has been found that people with defective vision tend to make strenuous efforts to see the faces of those with whom they are in contact. It re-enforces the habit of staring. The remedy is developing your sensory acuity so that you follow the principles already outlined. Do not expect to see immediately every part of another's face equally well at the same time. Instead cultivate the way of shifting rapidly over all parts of the face you are looking at. Use the usual and normal lines of vision, being the ideal way to see the face you look at. From eye to eye, ear to ear, then mouth to forehead. You will find that you will feel more relaxed and you will not give the impression that you are staring. The other person's subconscious will in fact pick up that your eyes are moving in natural, rapid, small scale shift patterns. This will make them feel at ease as well and so has indirect benefits for you as it improves the quality of your communication with that person.

Remember the chapter on how we read? Now is the time to make a note of a further conscious distinction. When reading a book or newspaper you can use the shifting principle to shift from one word to another or from one letter to another or even from one part of a letter to another, at the same time being aware of the eyes' natural reading patterns.

It will be clear that cultivating an attitude of deliberately making small scale shifting is one of your most important abilities. Do it wherever the opportunity arises and vary your distances for the objects that form the subject of your attentions. This will improve vision both at the near and far points.

Exercising with your calendar!

A well-established exercise for practising shifting is the calendar exercise. Find a calendar where the current month is printed in large type, with the previous month and the following month shown printed below in much smaller type. This offers the advantage of viewing type of different sizes on the same sheet. The principle is familiarity with what is being seen. Make this exercise part of your daily eye work out.

Hang the calendar on a wall which is well lit, preferably by natural daylight. Position yourself so you can see the large numerals easily. Make a note of what you see. Use all the subjective observations that you are able to distinguish. If the calendar has black numerals, consider the depth of the black that forms those numerals. Is it black or is it more of a grey? One interesting thing, which has been mentioned previously, is that you will notice the depth of black will gradually increase and become true black as your sight improves. **When you begin to notice the difference** your sight will be on the road to recovery. It is really a good example of how the process of generalisation works on our perception of the world over time. What you take as being 'black' now can have a much deeper, richer quality about it. As your eyes and mind begin to make the adjustments necessary to correct your visual process you too will notice the difference.

Returning to the exercise, you can if you wish use this as an opportunity to 'palm the eyes' before you begin, in order to relax them completely. Next, turn your head to the right, as though looking over your right shoulder. Slowly and smoothly begin to swing your head back until your eyes are able to rest upon the number one on the large type of the calendar. Make a mental note of the figure and how you perceive it. Close your eyes, and breathing easily but deeply and rhythmically, continue the movement of your head so that you end up looking over your right shoulder. Open your eyes again at this point and swing back until your eyes come to rest upon the number two on the calendar. Follow the same procedure, swinging back to the right and focusing upon the 'three'.

It will help you to remain focused upon the background colour, often white, which surrounds the numbers. A blank surface has no elements which will strain your vision. As you alternate your attention to this area there is nothing specific for the mind to interpret through the seeing process. It obviously requires specific concentration to achieve this and is part of the skill you will master with a little practice.

It should be clear that you are creating a contrast for your eyes. While viewing the background space the eye and mind is relaxed. As soon as it is called upon to see the numbers, your focus is upon the necessary, rapid, small scale shifting and movement to achieve quality vision.

The second part of this exercise actually demonstrates two things. As it will require greater visual acuity to see the smaller numbers, you may find yourself holding your breath as you focus in upon the smaller numbers. Unless you have an awareness of your kinaesthetic system, you may also find that as you hold your breath your body becomes tense. Try it and be aware of the sensations in your body as you do so. It is important to concentrate upon exactly what you do feel and what tensions may be present, because many of us find that we have done this for so long that it just seems natural. High degrees of focus can even lead to you breaking out into a nervous sweat. It is specifically at times like this when you need to be able to access your ability **to relax totally**.

Five Star Vision

If you find yourself doing these things, ensure that you take long, deep, regular breaths and stop for a moment and clearly imagine a quite, calm, peaceful place - somewhere you have visited that is tranquil. Think of it now and as you remember it, imagine feeling able to breathe in the essence of that atmosphere.

A pertinent observation, and something to remember, is that if you are doing this now, how many times does it happen during the course of a day when you are totally unaware of it?

Exercise progression

The next part of the exercise involves an alternation of attention between the figure 'one' in the large calendar type and then moving the eyes down to the figure 'one' on the small calendar type. Do not stare but look for a short moment, close your eyes and relax for three or four seconds. When you open your eyes revert to the large figure 'one' and then drop again to the small figure 'one'. It is important to maintain your breathing and to ensure your body remains in a state that is relaxed. Tension tends to creep up on you subconsciously and quite unexpectedly. Continue to monitor it. The advantages of having experienced the relaxation exercises will now become obvious to you.

Continue with the exercise this time focusing upon the large figure 'two'. Then drop to the small 'two'. Close your eyes, continuing your relaxed breathing and when you re-open your eyes focus upon the large 'three'. This exercise should be continued until you reach the end of the month. If your eyes become tired then go as far as you can and increase the numbers done on the next occasion.

The challenge may be the small type. If this is the case do not strain to see the figures. Avoid tension. Rely upon the gradual increase in the power of your perception and the flashing principle. When you close your eyes do you have a memory image of the small number? As you think about it, remember that it is exactly the same as the large number so you know what you should have seen. As you practise you will find that the images become stronger and clearer. Eventually the images will become simultaneous with the moment of sensing.

Rest your eyes for a few moments before proceeding. Close your eyes and think of a number on the large calendar, e.g. ten. Open your eyes and as quickly as possible locate the large 'ten' on the calendar and then on the small calendar. Close your eyes again and pay attention to your breathing and body tension. Are you still relaxed without any awareness of tension in your body? Be particularly vigilant of the neck and shoulders and areas running up to the eyes. Repeat the same exercise with the same numbers before moving on to think of another number and repeating the exercise. Build up to a dozen repetitions as part of your 'daily eye workout'.

Shifting and swinging

You will now progress to using the small-scale shift and a short swing. Again you will use the large numbers on the calendar. First, look at the large 'one'; this time focus your attention upon the smaller detail. Look at the top of the number and then the bottom. Then shift the eyes back to the top and again to the base. Repeat the process three or four times remaining relaxed and without tension. Keep your breathing regular and rhythmic. Close your eyes and relax. After a few moments do the same thing with the letter 'two'. Continue with each number of the large print until 'fourteen' and then re-divert your eyes to focus upon the small calendar and begin again. If you cannot see the small figures move closer.

It is recommended that you also make the same type of shifts 'horizontally'. What this means is to swing from one side of the figure to the other instead of up and down. Eventually shift your focus with movements of top to bottom, corner to corner and side to side. This is the way you will learn to see fully the numbers and other figures you look at. Consciously practising the way your eye regards such figures when viewing normally will soon lead you to build the natural vision process again automatically.

Your mind works by the use of contrast

It is a known fact that your mind works by the use of contrast. Use this fact to your own advantage. Use your mind to help you. As I said above, it is important to pay real attention to the small distinctions and improvements that you become aware of. The richness and quality of the colour 'black' is one example. As you work your eyes you will become alert to the ways in which your vision improves through the use of small scale shifting. 'Black', which may well have looked grey and even 'dim' when you first looked at it will blossom into deep, clear definition. 'Black' will suddenly begin to look black again! If your sight has been bad for some time you will find the contrast stark.

Once you become aware of these distinctions, other distinctions will occur that you are able to determine for yourself. Remember the differences as you improve. Each progression provides a new contrast point for comparison with the point where you started, the memory of the image of how bad your sight actually was. It is important, however, to focus finally always upon your progress and the new levels of achievement you have reached. Always look for the positive advances you have made, no matter how small they may appear. Your mind needs to be focused upon the contrast between these two places. Your subconscious then knows where to start from upon the next occasion. Your mind has a new measure to judge the difference between where you are and your ultimate goal, which is normal vision.

In other words, keep your goal in sight at all times, particularly after finishing an exercise session. It is about giving feedback to your brain, so that it is able to make the new adjustments it needs to build progress. This is one of the most important things you can do. Do not underestimate its importance.

There is a word of warning while you consider this point. Always analyse your progress positively. It is easy to begin assessing your progress in negative terms, without even realising it. What do I mean? Well, many people often assess their progress in negative terms by saying things such as — "well I can't see that letter", or "I'll never be able to see that", or "I've made some progress but I will always be short-sighted". These are just a few examples but if you stop and think about what you are "instructing your brain to do", you'll soon realise that you are telling your brain, in fact giving it a 'command', that you will not be able to do the thing envisaged. You should know that your brain works literally according to the instructions you give to it! How many times do you unintentionally give instructions to your brain during the course of a day, which are based on negative terms? Stop and think about it for a moment. Not only what you tell yourself about your vision but also what you tell yourself about daily tasks and targets you have for yourself. How does your self-talk progress as you proceed through a task?

Incorporate the power of contrast into the 'swish'

Chapter 10 shows you the swish pattern. When practising that pattern use the power of the distinctions you make here, as you establish contrast points and so speed up your progress.

Try this exercise:

Let's refer back to the swinging shift exercises above. You can use the same principle in your daily life whenever the opportunity arises. **Letters and numbers** surround us in our daily lives so there are plenty of opportunities available for your **improvement**. The advantage of your having practised in a relaxed environment is that when the same situation arises in your daily life, the circumstances are familiar and so the process of 'seeing' is easier. If you find yourself unable make out letters or numbers practise small scale shifting on them, doing what you have already previously done successfully on your own. You will notice a difference. **Improvement will come if you let it!**

You have now progressed along the pathway toward achieving central alignment. Next you can become fully conscious of what it means to 'see best' only a small part of what you are looking at, if the exercises you have done so far have not already given you this awareness. You will find that it becomes difficult not to be aware of central alignment as your practice with these exercises increases. Try this brief exercise. Hold up the

Shifting

forefingers of both hands approximately eighteen inches apart and about two feet in front of your face. Looking first at your right forefinger, what do you see? Is it more distinct than the left? You should also see the left forefinger at the very edge of your field of vision. As you turn your head and concentrate upon the left forefinger it immediately obtains better definition than the right.

Next begin bringing the fingers together in stages. Make them one foot apart, six inches, then three inches. What do you see? Next one inch apart and finally have them both actually touching. Have you noticed that the finger upon which you focus your primary attention, with both your mind and your eyes, is the one that is seen more distinctly than the other?

This is central alignment. If you have now overcome your habit of staring then you will notice differences as you read books and newspapers. For example if you look at the letter 'E', become aware of the top line of the letter. Is it clearer and a deeper black than the rest of the letter? Is it more defined? Next move to the bottom line of the letter. Is that now clear, a deeper black and more defined? You will remember earlier how I pointed out that as your vision improves the quality of 'black' improves. Once you can make the distinctions within the form of letters themselves you know you are succeeding. Don't stop there! The key to improving your vision is always to make finer distinctions. Once you feel you have nearly mastered the differences that are available to you on a large letter 'E', progress on to a small latter 'e'. After that go for a smaller typeface 'e' but look to achieve the same thing.

As you progress remember to keep a note in your journal of your daily improvements. Notice the differences in richness and distinction appropriate to each type size. As the power of your vision increases, so you will find the smaller the area you will be able to see with maximum distinction.

How to measure your progress

Test the principles involved for yourself. Reversing the effects of the exercises described above will show you consciously, what you were previously doing subconsciously. Now that you have experienced the difference go back to trying to see all parts of an object equally well at the same time. What happens? Does the quality of your vision become worse and do you feel that in-built tension as you attempt to do what is impossible for you to achieve?

Shifting and swinging are in fact aids toward achieving maintained relaxation and you will now see results simply by having shown yourself that staring lowers your visual ability, while shifting improves it. There have been reports of people who have mastered this distinction within only half an hour and had their vision improve so rapidly that it has almost become normal for the distance involved. Such is the power of an appreciation of the benefits to be obtained from shifting and swinging - a simple yet remarkably effective set of exercises.

---

[1]See Chapter 17.
[2]Tony Robbins, *Unlimited Power* (Simon and Schuster Ltd, 1986), 214-215

Chapter 15

THE SNELLEN CHART

> "The letters are **deliberately meant to confuse**...so that a patient's ability to distinguish between letters and gaps between them is really put to the test."
> **Comment on the purpose of the Snellen Chart,
> Anonymous, 1990**

The Snellen chart is over one hundred and twenty years old. It was introduced by a Dutch eye specialist, Dr Hermann Snellen. It has become a familiar 'test' chart to most people. We shall be examining its qualities shortly.

The chart is generally the starting point for an eye examination. Although a visual test is being carried out, the results are communicated by the patient to the optometrist, by the patient *telling* him, either what he can or cannot see with each eye. A stated objective of the 'test' is to confuse the patient. The reason for this is expressed to be so that an assessment can be made, to a fine degree, of *how well the eyes are working*. Some opticians also use certain objective testing techniques as well. Using this information, the optician is then able to prescribe 'corrective lenses', (where required). Let's look at an example. Two similar letters may be placed together, that have very similar shapes. Perhaps the letter 'P' and the letter 'F'. This makes it hard to distinguish between the letters and where the 'gaps' seem to be. Screwing up the eyelids, in an effort to reduce aperture and improve the depth of field is not allowed. It is said to be 'cheating'. We shall return to explore this viewpoint shortly. Before we do so, let's have a look at some of the other things said about eye tests.

The benefits of eye examination

One of the reasons often quoted for having an eye test is so that the optometrist can examine the general state of your health. It is important to have your eyes regularly tested as examination of the eye itself can reveal any degree of cataract or other symptoms such as glaucoma and other retinal changes. The signs may be present of disorders affecting other parts of the body and this can include brain tumour and diabetes. This is possible because blood vessels and the end of the optic nerve can be viewed clearly without the need for surgery. The eyes are the only place where this is possible. It is also possible to ascertain with fair accuracy, to within a couple of years, the age of a person.

"The eyes are the window to the soul..."

I believe it is possible and should become the normal practice, to distinguish between the two objectives of a sight 'test'. Lumping both objectives together blurs the benefits to be derived from each element of the test objective. The preventative health objectives are commendable and highly desirable. A detailed and careful inspection of the interior and exterior of the eye can ascertain ocular and general health. It is true that eye co-ordination can be tested and pupil reactions checked. General focusing ability can be assessed and other matters relating to visual acuity. The solutions to identified vision problems have a need to be separated from the general health advantages to be gained by having an eye examination. It is at this point that visual re-education, as an alternative to optical aids, becomes **the real alternative.**

The Snellen chart gives only an approximate guide to the sharpness of vision. It may be that the test is used in conjunction with 'trial frames'. If you have ever had an eye test, this is where the 'heavy spectacles' emerge. They are adjusted to the eye condition through the insertion of different lens types. It is equitable to say that exact weaknesses can be identified in this way. There are as many as two hundred different lens types, each serving a different function. This results in thousands of possible combinations.

Other tests can include following a moving object, to estimate the strength of the eye muscles themselves and testing for combined eye efficiency. Pupil reflexes are another area that can be looked at, in particular their light sensitivity. These checks are all extremely useful and can be quite effectively utilised in determining eye condition. Once the eye condition has been established, alternative methods of vision correction come into their own.

Exploring the optometrist's world

You have probably wondered exactly what it is that an optometrist looks at when he examines the back of your eye. Have you ever had the eye examination where a strange little device that looks like a torch shines a beam of light into your eye? This is the retinoscope. The light is shone through your pupil and onto the retina at the back of your eye. You will recall that the retina has the receptors that convert the light waves into nerve impulses. Well these receptors bounce back a pattern of light as the retinoscope surveys the eye. This provides an idea of the shape of the eyeball. Remember in Chapter 2 how we looked at the various eye conditions resulting from different optical conditions? This is where the different shapes of the eyeball are indicative of the visual condition. Examining the cornea will reveal whether it is 'squashed' in appearance, which means that images are distorted. This is called 'astigmatism'. Sometimes the beam of light does not reach the destination point (which is the retina). This will be due to some form of obstruction and in many cases, a milky film is identified, being a sign of cataract.

A second type of instrument used by the optometrist is the 'opthalmoscope'. Again, this is a hand-held instrument, which is distinguished by the small wheel at the side that houses a number of lenses. These lenses allow the focusing on different parts of the eye. Light is directed at the transparent centre and back of the eye through the pupil.

How does the optometrist tell if your eyes are healthy?

If the eye is healthy he will see a clear pink-orange circle, with a hierarchy of nerve tissues and blood vessels that are indicative of general health. It is at this time that any age-related changes to the visual system can be detected.[1]

One problem that affects older people is 'dry eye'.[1] The fluid that washes the eye can become blocked and this is tested by measuring the pressure build-up in the eyeball using a tonometer. The instrument is placed against the eye and pressure is measured in millimetres of mercury. Another variation is the 'air puff'. A puff of air is released against the eye and pressure is measured by the speed of air bounced back.

Characteristics of the Snellen chart

So now we know a little about what goes on during an eye examination, let's return to the Snellen chart and its characteristics. It is important to remember that it is only a tool. Like any other tool it is 'how' it is used that is important. The Snellen chart contains letters of various sizes. These normally decrease in size from top to bottom. The actual size of the letters on the chart is determined in accordance with certain geometrical principles.

Astronomy in fact has its part to play in the basis for the charts. It was found that the human eye could see two second-order stars but to be distinct from each other they had to be separated by a sixtieth part of one degree, (one minute) of arc. This became the measure of the human eye's power to distinguish very small objects. The Snellen chart uses the same assumptions.

The principle behind the Snellen chart is that each letter is of such a size that the whole letter has an angle of five minutes at defined distances. The norm is for charts to range letters from five minutes of arc at sixty metres, down to six or five metres. Vision is tested at six metres with the patient attempting to read the smallest letters he can see at that distance. This is then recorded as a fraction. How does this work?

FIVE STAR VISION

Diagram 1 How does a Snellen test chart work?

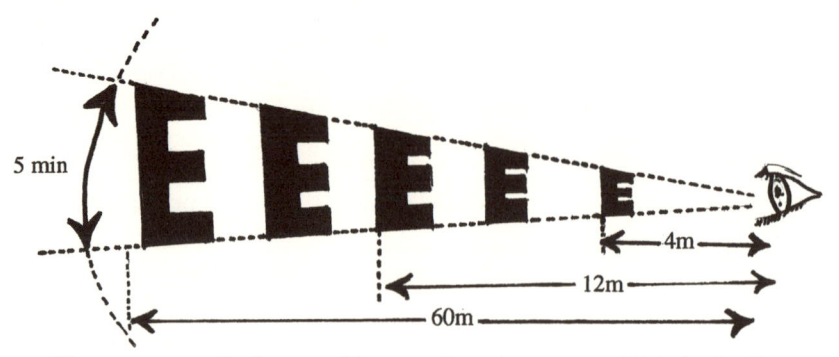

The numerator is the test distance, i.e. six metres. (This is the figure on the top line of the fraction). The denominator is the distance at which the letter can be correctly read, and subtends an angle of five minutes. So if the top letter is read, vision is 6/60. A person with normal sight could see the letter perfectly at sixty metres. The opticians then record sight as 6/6. The USA uses feet instead of metres and this is where the saying "20/20" vision comes from.

Visual acuity

When we talk about 'visual acuity' and relate it to the Snellen chart we can become more specific about what the term means. It is the ability to see the difference between two points of light and this is what gives us our 'sharpness' and the ability to see detail. There is no exact norm for visual acuity as each individual's acuity differs. The Snellen chart, however, gives a standard to measure each eye against.

Near vision

This is normally measured using reading types. Ordinarily, a number of different paragraphs are used containing sizes of Times Roman types. These 'reading types' are also measured by points. A point is $1/_{72}$ of an inch. Normal close vision is 'N5' point type.

Referring briefly to cataract symptoms, these are normally visual and result in a mistiness of sight. Often when exposed to bright sunlight, vision can become dazzled and opaque. Colour perception and vision can become a problem if cataracts develop as blues are subdued and reds are more vibrant. Rembrandt suffered from cataracts and it has been commented, (and it can be seen in his paintings), that as he got older, his paintings began to reflect more reds and oranges because his cataracts were developing. These absorbed more green and blue light with a resulting increase in the amount of red and orange reaching his retina. This is one example of the way in which it is possible for each of us to view the world differently, without necessarily being subjectively aware of the differences.

The Snellen Chart

Diagram 2 Snellen type test chart

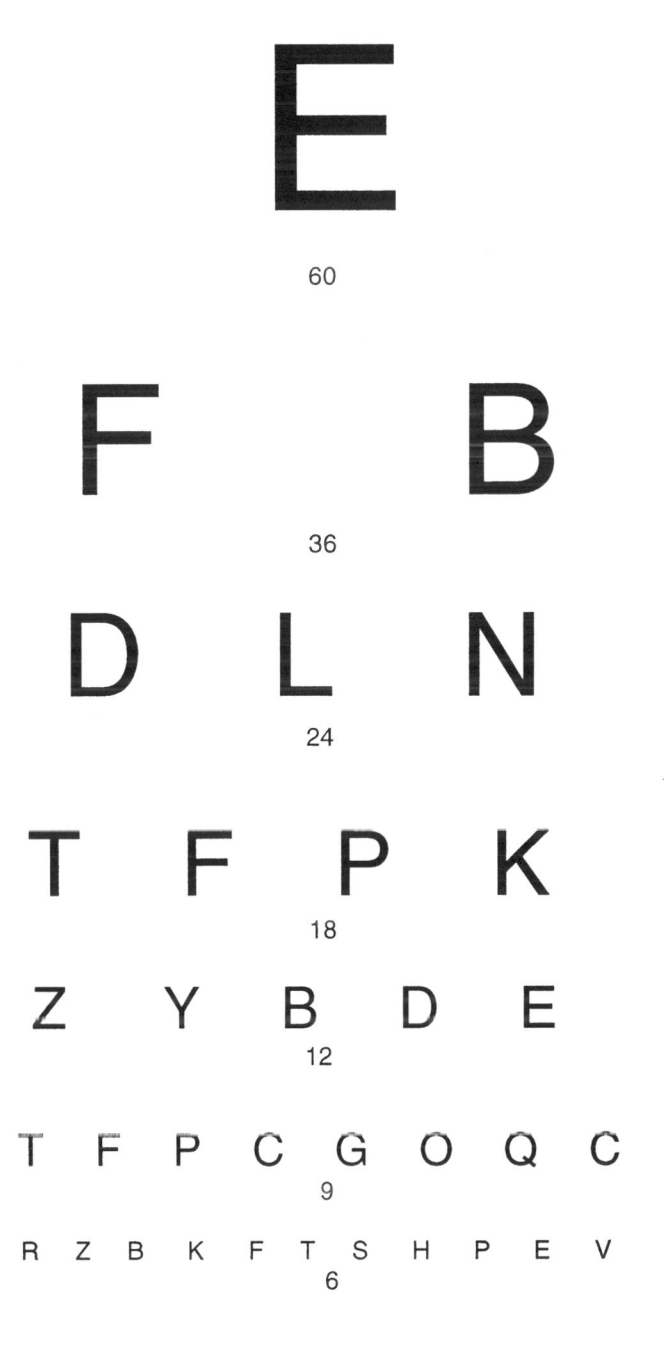

E
60

F B
36

D L N
24

T F P K
18

Z Y B D E
12

T F P C G O Q C
9

R Z B K F T S H P E V
6

Five Star Vision

Example

N5 –

N8 – Clarity, sharpness and the ability to perceive detail

N12 - Rest the eyes by closing or palming

N18 - Shifting can be done slowly or rapidly

N24 - Total visual control

N36 - Be aware

N48 - I HAVE NORMAL VISION

The lens of the eye is transparent and obtains its nourishment from the aqueous humour in which the lens itself lies[2]. To maintain its transparency the necessary nourishment passes through the outer capsular membrane in order to reach the cells within. The lens consists of a type of protein peculiar to the lens of the eye. Known as 'organ specificity', it means that animal lenses can not normally be used in humans for fear of allergic reaction. Apparently in 1952, a 'Dr Shropshire' claimed an injection of fish lens protein could eliminate cataracts. In humans, however, the body can become allergic to foreign proteins. In the cases where this treatment was offered it was found that not only can the body become allergic to foreign lenses, in this case fish, but that the body also then becomes allergic to its own lens. Some patients treated in this way apparently lost the eye itself as a result of severe inflammation.

What is even more remarkable is the transformation of a Greek myth into reality. So the myth portrays, people 'walked around with a tooth in their eye'. This very operation has been carried out! The problem of rejection of acrylic lenses by the eye's own tissue is circumvented by placing the lens in a tooth taken from the patient. The next stage is to drill a hole in the tooth, placing the lens into the tooth and then implant the tooth in the eye!

So how should an Eye Chart be used?

It is at this point that we arrive at a divergence of opinion upon how the benefits of the chart can be utilised. Traditional purposes[3] have been as a tool in assessing what glasses are required. Understanding the distinction made earlier about how the problem of defective sight is tackled leads to new conclusions about the uses of the chart. If the objective is to deal with the problems thrown out by defective sight, then the traditional uses of the chart is all well and good. If however the objective is to **defeat the cause of the defective vision**, by visual re-education, then the chart can be used much more productively and beneficially. How do we do this?

The aim of deliberately confusing the patient and employing the chart in that way is wrong if you wish to defeat the cause of defective vision. This may seem a highly controversial view that flies in the face of over one hundred years' traditional use of the chart, but **the evidence of visual re-education shows this view is correct.**

How to use a Visual Correction Chart effectively

There is an essential difference in using a visual correction chart. The first point is that you use it yourself as 'a visual training aid', rather than having it used 'on you', as a way of trying to confuse your visual sensory function. This old Snellen test, the traditional approach, flies directly in the face of all the principles outlined so far required for re-training your eyesight. The Snellen test is hardy conducive to creating a relaxed state, and, if anything, the Snellen test itself is responsible for creating a state of tension and anxiety. Do you automatically assume that you have to read the bottom line of one of these charts? This may not be physically possible. The effect, however, is that this immediately generates anxiety and stress with the result that your visual capability will be much worse than normal. Your visual process will never perform to its best under these conditions and the reason for this is now probably self-evident. You know now that so much of a normal visual process relies upon the subconscious functioning in the correct manner. The circumstances and aim of the old Snellen chart would therefore seem to nurture a set of circumstances where visual acuity is actually going to be *reduced*. Of course, the evidence of your own eyes normally means, in such circumstances, you will submissively accept the poor quality of your vision 'as a fact'. If you know your eyesight is starting to develop deficiencies and poorer quality, the very circumstances of the environment exacerbate the problem. Your subconscious is the most powerful controller of all your physical functions. This is an accepted fact. If you really think about it, the power of your own subconscious is working against you in these circumstances. This is because of the entire nature of the environment and the situation in which you find yourself.

You cannot fight and win against your own subconscious by applying conscious effort. Your visual process will fail you. Your sight will be recorded as 'defective'.

Diagram 3 Contrast shows how the chart must be used for visual re-education. A difference in underlying objectives reflects the different aims and goals of visual re-education.

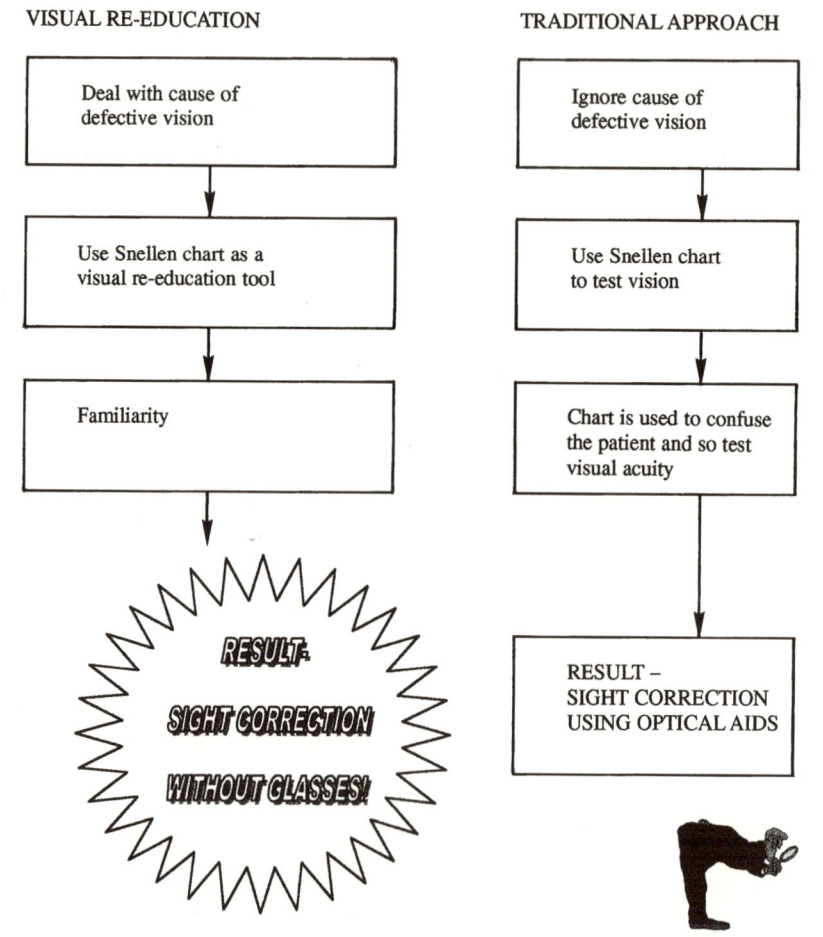

VISUAL RE-EDUCATION

- Deal with cause of defective vision
- Use Snellen chart as a visual re-education tool
- Familiarity
- RESULT: SIGHT CORRECTION WITHOUT GLASSES!

TRADITIONAL APPROACH

- Ignore cause of defective vision
- Use Snellen chart to test vision
- Chart is used to confuse the patient and so test visual acuity
- RESULT – SIGHT CORRECTION USING OPTICAL AIDS

Use the visual correction chart to secure familiarity and strengthen your power of perception

When used correctly, the speed with which a visual correction chart can improve your sight is remarkable. I can personally testify to this fact. It was a major tool for me in correcting my own eyesight. Use it and it will

The Snellen Chart

do the same for you. It will become clear why the visual correction chart works so well as we discuss how to use it.

This difference from the old Snellen test is based upon the principles already outlined, being the development of familiarity with the form and quality of common letters and numbers. You will recall that the reasoning for this was dealt with in Chapter 6 and involves not just physical vision but also your powers of perception and interpretation.

The advantage for you of using the visual correction chart is that it incorporates numerals and geometric shapes. Dr Bates first used this type of chart because the effect is to require greater powers of perception and acuity. Another version of the chart used in visual re-education methods is a black chart with white lettering, instead of the traditional black-on-white lettering. The reason for using this type of chart is because black letters tend to 'blur' at a distance. You have probably experienced this for yourself. White letters, however, on a black background remain visible, although they may look a little distorted. This is another great contrast point to be aware of while re-training your visual process. As I have already said your brain uses the power of contrast to learn, so using both types of chart in your re-training program can have excellent results.

What do these visual correction charts show you?

1) The first point as you begin to use the chart is to check your level of tension as you read. What do you find yourself doing?
2) Where is your sight variable? Find your current measures. Can you begin to notice any pattern in the way your eye performs?
3) Find the areas you can immediately identify that you need to work upon. Like any other task, it may need breaking down into its individual elements. There may be a number of parts in your visual process that are all working incorrectly at the same time. These problems stem out of the same basic cause, as we have already seen. The results you have are simply the symptoms. Check your ability to distinguish the following areas as a starting point.
   a) Form and definition
   b) Boundaries and edges
   c) Clarity – both at the near and far point

One of the easiest ways to use the correction chart is to place it on a wall at a distance of between ten and twenty feet and simply devote three minutes a day to reading the smallest letters you can see. Do this with each eye separately. Use your hand to cover the other eye without touching the eyeball. The more time you devote to the chart the quicker your improvements will be. You must of course apply the general principles of eyesight correction while practising. You can keep your own record of achievement in the same way as described above, using the fraction method.

If you use the visual correction chart that comes free with this book[4] and work in feet, the large 'C' should be read at two hundred feet. If you could only see it at ten feet, the fraction would be represented as 10/200.

It is quite possible to increase your visual acuity to a degree greater than normal, such as being able to read a letter at twenty feet that one would ordinarily only expect to read at ten feet. It is even possible to achieve what is known as telescopic and microscopic vision in some cases. What about setting these as your ultimate goals for your own visual process, now that you know what is possible?

It is usually the case that if you have worn glasses, you will have to devote a longer period to practising with the visual correction chart and some additional time with other exercises. For reasons of improving your perception and visual acuity, it can be very beneficial to have two charts. Place one at a near point, one where you can see it comfortably. Place the other between ten and twenty feet away. Once you have practised with the near chart switch to the far one. Using the principles of subconscious image memory recall[5], the letters seen at the near point will help to bring into your sight the letters seen at a distance.

Dr Bates himself was quite adamant about the advantages of using such a chart. As he said:

> "Parents who wish to preserve and improve the eyesight of their children should encourage them to read the test card every day. There should be a test card in every family, in fact, for when properly used it always prevents myopia and other errors of refraction, always improves the vision, even when this is already normal, and always benefits nervous troubles. Parents should improve their own eyesight to normal, so that their children may not imitate wrong methods of using the eyes and will not be subject to the influence of an atmosphere of strain. They should also learn the principles of central fixation in order that they may teach them to their children."[6]

Your posture can affect your vision!

Bad posture can also be a contributory cause of poor sight. It is fair to say that children can and do pick up habits of bodily posture from their parents. In fact certain branches of psychology provide classifications of "people types" based upon certain body posture characteristics[7]. It has also been found that in people who suffer from myopia, their general body posture tends to be one that is very poor. This may result from the fact of short sight or it may be the cause. The result is a slumped type of posture reflected in a stooping and hanging of the head. F M Alexander who invented the 'Alexander technique' found cases in which myopic children were able to

The Snellen Chart

regain normal vision simply after being taught the correct way of holding themselves in a proper posture, carrying the head and neck in a proper correlation with the trunk.

In adults the same posture rectification is not sufficient in itself to restore normal vision. This is probably due to the process of generalisation as represented by the body as a habit. The habit itself has worked in conjunction with the visual process for so much longer that correction of the posture does not influence the other learned habit of faulty vision. A correction of both elements will yield quicker results.

The visual correction chart on its own, as a visual aid, has brought about some remarkable results, particularly with children. Dr Bates reports examining the eyes of several hundred children at Grand Forks, North Dakota. He reports children who could not read all the letters of a test card on the first attempt but who could read them on a second or third attempt. The occurrences were so frequently repeated that **Dr Bates concluded that in some way vision was improved by first reading the test card.**

This is not as ridiculous as may first appear. The point is shown by the case of a boy whom he reports at first appeared myopic and whose teacher found him to be very short sighted. This boy was able, with encouragement, first to read all the letters on a test card. His teacher found the result hard to believe as Dr Bates had found his vision normal. The teacher at first rejected the findings because she knew the boy had had difficulty reading what was written on the blackboard and seeing maps and other charts. Apparently, he had also been unable to see people across the street. At her request, Dr Bates is reported to have re-tested the boy under the teacher's supervision. The errors the teacher had suggested had gone and the boy was able to read writing in figures and words written by the teacher on the board. The teacher is reported to have asked the boy to tell the hour by an hour clock some twenty-five feet away, which he did correctly.

The result was the teacher asked for a visual correction chart to be placed permanently in class so the children could **practise reading the smallest letters** they could see from their seats, at least once every day. This they did, first with both eyes, then each separately. This serves to illustrate something that will become familiar to you. You cannot see any object perfectly unless you have seen it before. It also means seeing the object *in the correct way* and using the correct visual process. So again, familiarity becomes the key together with a state of relaxed persona. Unfamiliar objects cause strain upon the eye and visual process, as the eye 'tries' to see. This is what Dr Bates observed in his examinations of school children. The whole basis of this principle is to **give yourself daily exercise in distant vision with a familiar object.** (If you are long-sighted, do the reverse and exercise the near vision with a familiar object).

Dr Bates' methods were so successful that they were in fact introduced into all schools of the city of Grand Forks at that time. Used for eight years, results showed myopia to be reduced among school children from six per cent to one per cent. The results speak for themselves and illustrate that the same basic information, (in this case the results from a visual chart) can be taken and used in a new way to achieve an improved result. Information itself is never inherently good or bad, only the way in which it is used.

One of the reasons for the success of the method is based upon the inspiration behind the method. Other approaches have assumed that it is excessive use of the eyes for near work that causes myopia.

I personally have used the principles that support this method with very good results. On my daily walks, I spotted a large number nine on the entrance to a field. It was a black number with a white background about nine inches high. I knew I could see this number from one of the buildings I often went in and out of. I decided to use this as a long distance 'trainer' for my eyes. At first, viewing the number from about two hundred feet away, it was blurred, out of focus and hardly distinguishable. The fact that the number was familiar meant that with a little dedication and persistence, I eventually began to notice the small improvements that are the foundation of improving your vision. The black began to look blacker and the shape of the number became more defined. The blur that occurred between the number and the background began to look the way it should. These changes did not happen all at once and on some occasions my sight initially did not seem to have improved. I persisted until one day, after about ten days, I glanced at the number (almost unconsciously, as I had my mind upon something else). I knew I was about to do my daily check but I was not concentrating upon it at that moment. To my surprise the number was perfectly clear and sharp. It actually took a moment or two for this fact to register, but as soon as it did I told my mind to **"hold that mental image"** as a future reference point. Remember the point about contrast earlier? This was a contrast point for my brain. One I was determined to record so that I knew what was possible. It was a remarkable moment for me because it showed me what determination and using the power of my own brain could achieve. The great point is that if I can achieve it, then so can you! All you have to do is decide that you will.

Dr Bates was also able to claim success with hypermetropia and astigmatism. He said that the method must also have prevented other errors of refraction because using a retinoscope he could demonstrate that both conditions are actually 'acquired' conditions. What this means is that no matter how astigmatic or hypermetropic the eyes may be, their vision can become normal when viewing a blank surface, without trying to see. He backed up his conclusions with examinations demonstrating that when children are learning to read, write, draw or do things requiring them to look at unfamiliar objects at the near point, hypermetropia or hypermetropic astigmatism is always produced. The same results are shown with adults.

The Snellen Chart

What these results have shown is that **visual education is crucial.** Familiarity avoids strain and progress is simply a matter of securing the technique that allows you to look at strange objects without strain. When distant vision has been appropriately trained and improved the eyes can be used without strain. The results also illustrate and confirm a point made earlier. These methods succeeded better where the teacher did not wear glasses and consequently demonstrate the 'nervous strain' produced by defective sight. It is easy for children to copy the visual habits of a teacher without knowing they are doing so. We all give out subconscious signals and messages that, as a form of communication, can be much more influential than our normal conscious communication. This is because the messages go directly to the subconscious without challenge. Their effect is therefore immediate. These ways of communicating are indeed the most influential available. The problem arises when we subconsciously send out the wrong messages and do not know that we are doing so. Dr David Lewis in his book, *The Secret Language of Success*, provides a thorough examination of how we can become aware of our subconscious communication and its effects.

Dr Bates was even able to conclude that children in classes of the same age, with the same lighting, whose teachers did not wear glasses, were always found to have better sight than those children whose teachers did wear glasses. There were even specific assessments done which supported these conclusions. So it has been shown that where children are able to relax and start using their correct visual process, they can often carry this relaxation over to situations where they are viewing unfamiliar objects. One of the most beneficial points about this method is that implementation is not expensive. It can also be seen how the practice falls in line with the known operating principles of the brain that we have already looked at.

---

[1] See Appendix B
[2] See colour photo section.
[3] See Chapter 1.
[4] Ophthalmic study is based upon 'facts' but it is the 'tradition' to interpret these facts in a particular 'fixed' way.
[5] See note at foot of List of Illustrations And Acknowledgements page
[6] This is dealt with in more detail in Chapter 17
[7] Dr Bates, *Better Eyesight Without Glasses* (Souvenir Press), 156.
[8] Satir category types are one example - Virginia Satir

CHAPTER 16

SUBMODALITIES

"The precise building blocks that make up the structure of human experience".

You may be familiar with submodalities already or you may be wondering exactly what submodalities are and why you need to know about them? You will remember earlier that we looked at your ability to form a mental image of an object, as a way of helping your inner world assist with your visual process in the outer world. What do we really mean by a mental image? An understanding of submodalities will help you to appreciate in greater detail how you personally make up your own experience and perception. You can use these new understandings as a direct way of improving your vision. Another way to view submodalities is as a 'descriptive language' for certain personal experiences, that you may not have been aware of before. Your mind and how it works for you is an integral part of the complete visual process and so it is important that you devote some extra attention to this area. Being in the right 'state' to see can be extremely important in achieving your objectives for sight correction.

What do you think the difference is between *how* you produce a state of despondency when you try to see something and fail to see it clearly and the state of exhilaration that results from making a leap forward in your visual progress? Some people may say that the cause is the result of the actual ability of seeing or not seeing. There are different ways of considering the matter. NLP[1] looks at the structure of human experience, not the content or results. This turns the circumstances around from many people's traditional way of thinking about such things. An appreciation of the principles involved will aid the mental side of your visual process, in ways that you will soon come to realise.

In many respects this chapter is following on from the earlier chapter on perception. Submodalities really examine the main differences in the way you structure your *internal* representations.

Internal representations

You structure your internal representations through your five senses: sound, touch, sight, taste and smell. Your total experience of the world is in a form that is stored in your mind as represented through these five senses - your 'memory' images and other recollections.

What we are going to do is explore ways of 'varying' these memory images and the advantages of doing this will soon become obvious. In particular the astute reader will be able to make connections between what is said here and the exercises with the swish pattern. New ways of perceiving things here will filter through into your swish techniques. This in turn will increase your mind's 'contrast' points, (which you will recall we dealt with earlier). Your brain works through contrast - comparing where you are now, with where you wish to go to and making the necessary adjustments in order to reach the desired outcome.

The first thing to begin doing is finding out what your real resources are. Re-educating your visual process can at times feel like a major challenge. If you find yourself in state where you feel helpless or lacking in confidence about achieving your new goals, your chances of producing the new behaviours you need to re-educate your visual process and to get the results you want can be a major hindrance. Make a habit of continuously checking your current state so that **you are accessing feelings of confidence and possibility.**

At any moment in your life you owe it to yourself to be able to change any feeling or emotion which is hindering your progress, anything which is preventing you from getting where you want to go to. This applies not only to mastering your visual process but to other areas of your life as well. You may recall earlier that I discussed the importance of how you instruct your brain to carry out your objectives. To begin producing the effective results that you want and so improve your vision, **accept the methods that will produce the change for you.** If you believe for any reason, consciously or subconsciously, that you cannot change your visual process, that is exactly what you will experience. If you believe you cannot benefit from a particular exercise, that is what you will experience. **It is important that you believe in yourself and in your own abilities.**

If at any time you find yourself saying "I can't do this" or "this is not working properly", what you need to do is **change your internal representation** of those circumstances as you are experiencing them, from a negative to a positive representation. A positive internal representation will automatically start to trigger and cause more positive results. **Positive results cause positive results**, so break into that cycle.

Using your memories

Next take the following simple steps. Think of a past memory, an experience that was very pleasant. As you access that memory see what you saw at that time when this pleasant thing happened. Some people find it much easier if they close their eyes as they do so.

What do you see? Describe the picture of the memory to yourself. There are many details that could be there. Is it black and white or full colour? Is it a moving film or a still? Is it near or far away? You can make these types of distinctions no matter what the content of the picture in your mind.

Now describe what you hear. Are the sounds low or high pitched? Near or far? Soft or loud? What about feeling? What do you feel? It may be a heavy feeling or a light feeling, sharp or dull, intense or light. Hot or cold? These are only some of the possible distinctions available to you. We will go on to look at further submodalities in a moment.

Basically submodalities are about the sense experiences. NLP is not the only discipline to have explored the quality of senses. Sense experience goes back to the time of the ancient Greeks and Aristotle.

Think back to the pleasant memory you had a moment ago. As you examine the picture you have of it, do you see the picture through your own eyes (associated) or are you looking at it as though from somewhere else (dissociated)? If you see yourself in the picture, you must be dissociated. Is the image three-dimensional or flat like a photograph? Are there any other distinctions available to you?

Next pay attention again to the sounds that are part of the memory. How do you hear them? Loud or soft? Where do they originate? Are they near or far?

What about feelings or other sensations? How do you feel them? Are they hard or soft? Hot or cold? Where do you feel them?

Some people find these distinctions easy to make. Others find them a little unusual if they are not used to paying them conscious attention. Play around for a moment or two until you **become more aware** of what is available to you.

Try this. Recall the memory you just had and, as you look at that pleasant memory, change the brightness of the mental image and as you do so also notice how your feelings change in response. Make it brighter and brighter. Pause. Now make it dimmer and dimmer until you can barely see it. How do you feel about it now? Now return the image to its original brightness.

For most people making a picture brighter makes the feelings somehow 'stronger'. Increasing brightness can increase the intensity of the feeling and vice versa. So why is this important? **How you feel at any moment in time about a task or objective can have a major impact upon your ability to carry it out.** Your visual process is no different. By learning to take control of how you feel about your visual process you can learn to take control of your sight. Submodalities are the building blocks of human experience and all thoughts and memories, which are our experience, must have a submodality structure. Until now you may have been consciously unaware of the submodality building blocks that make up your experience. The process of sight has as one of its components a submodality structure.

If anyone is able to produce a particular result (in this case 'seeing', and the result is 'normal' vision), then that result is created by specific actions, both mental and physical. Duplicate the exact same actions that someone else produces and you can produce that result. What Dr Bates produced with his technology was a way for you to replicate the results that others have achieved. A knowledge of submodalities will assist you greatly in making the distinctions that you need to be aware of.

"Before we achieve any result or outcome in our outer world, we must first make it happen in our inner world."

Your mental images are formed in your mind's eye. We already know that the complete visual process is made up of the visual element as carried out by the eye and the mental element, which is the memory image and the quality of perception. As we saw earlier with the exercises on shifting, the ultimate goal is simultaneously to have the memory image of what the eye senses at the exact moment of seeing.

The interesting point is that as submodalities change, the way you feel about the experience represented can change. **Some submodalities can be crucial to the whole way we experience a memory.** Change them and we change the way we feel about the experience. It is fair to say that the impact and meaning of particular thoughts or memories is really the result of a number of critical defining submodalities rather than content. What does this mean as far as improving your vision is concerned?

Well there are two things that you can change about an internal representation - either 'what' you represent or 'how' you represent it. There are certain key submodalities that can spur your brain to act in a particular way. Some examples include people who find that making a picture extremely large will provide them with great motivation. Maybe a tone of voice used as they talk to themselves can make a serious difference in their level of motivation and confidence. The point is that *you too* will have certain crucial submodalities within yourself **which stimulate immediate responses** as situations occur. Once you find out what your key submodalities are and how they effect you, particularly those that effect your vision, you are well on the road to normal vision. It is the ability to notice these small distinctions in your experience that will allow you to take control over your mind.

Let's look at an example. 'Seeing' itself is a passive act. Sense information bombards us and things are just seen without any effort. Black letters on a sign will look black and clear, perfectly distinct. When sight is less than perfect the eyes 'chase' the letters in an effort to see them. It is your mind that causes the effort itself to be made by the eye. The process of thinking , even where it is a subconscious thinking of 'effort' to see, causes impulses to be fed to the eye which cause the deviation from normal.

Research has shown that in young children they often see perfectly in the presence of their mothers. Send their mother out of the room and the children at once register a myopic response because of *strain caused by fear*. The interesting point as far as submodalities are concerned, is **isolating at that moment** the nature and structure of the internal representation of that fear that creates the myopic response.

A person may have good vision when telling the truth, yet upon stating what is not true, (even without an intention to deceive or upon imagining what is not true), produce an error of refraction with a decrease at that moment of visual ability. This is because it is not possible to express what is not true without some form of effort and effort produces mental strain. As we know, unfamiliar objects produce eye strain and decrease visual ability, because such objects first produce a mental strain.

Tests have shown that in numerous cases people have been asked to state their ages incorrectly or try to imagine they are a year older or younger. In all cases an error of refraction is recorded. When telling their true ages vision was shown to be normal. What this shows is that although the process has probably so far been unconscious, there is a difference in the submodality structure of the internal representation between something which we know to be true and something which we know to be false. Try the exercise for yourself by simply **paying full attention** to your experience as you state something, which you know to be true. Then repeat the same process with something you know to be a lie. If you can **isolate the difference** between your internal representations, you will have a powerful submodality distinction which you can *consciously* apply to your visual process as a way of eliminating strain and effort. Once you automatically relieve these two symptoms your vision will be normal.

It may be that in order to achieve this some people will require further distinctions about the quality and make-up of submodalities and this is something we will now go on to explore.

An aid to visual acuity

Another benefit of being more aware of your submodality structures is that it allows you to make more distinctions in your visual process and so aids your visual acuity. To be able to control a visual experience you must know more about it. It also helps to be equally aware of the other main representational systems and the distinctions available in them. This is because sometimes we use a process known as *synesthesia*. That is the ability to take in information from the world in one of our senses yet to represent it *internally* in another. An example would be a smell that brought to mind a visual memory. Immediate and unconscious links across the senses are what is known as *synesthesia*.

Referring back to the point I mentioned earlier about mental images and your ability to form them, you can now begin to experiment. A list of some possible submodalities follows so you can begin to become familiar with them. If you already know about submodalities, this is a good opportunity to review them and consider some new distinctions and their impact upon the visual process.

Some common submodalities

VISUAL	AUDITORY	KINAESTHETIC	KINAESTHETIC-PAIN
1 still frame/movie	rhythm	texture	hot-cold
2 colour/black & white	volume	pressure	location
3 brightness	tempo	temperature	duration
4 3-d quality	timbre	intensity	intermittent
5 self in or out of picture	tonality	vibration	pressure
6 distance of picture from self	pauses	steady-intermittent	sharp-dull
7 intensity of colour	inflections	density	tingling
8 distance of central object from self	stereo/mono	location	muscle tension
9 size of picture - life size, larger-smaller	distance from sound	extent	
10 contrast degrees	duration	movement	
11 slow or fast movement?	spatial sound?	weight	
12 focus – are parts in or out?	location		
13 size of central object			
14 steady or intermittent focus			
15 angle viewed from			
16 number of shifts or pictures			
17 location			
18 other?			

Submodalities can be used to change any visual image you have. Have you ever come across people who never seem to let things get them down? How do many of these people manage to do that? When they get an unpleasant thought they 'turn the brightness down'. Try it for yourself now with something unpleasant that you know you have to do. Does turning the brightness down in your mental perception make it seem less unpleasant? Take your time and notice exactly how this can effect you.

Beginning to use submodalities to aid your vision

So how will you really begin to use these submodalities? Let's start by you taking an experience of something you really found visually enthralling. Get a good clear recollection of the event. Work your way first through the visual submodalities and see how each one affects how you feel. For example try making the picture bigger and you should find your response is intensified. Make it smaller and it decreases it. The aim is to find out what works to vary your *own* internal responses, how your brain works, so that you can take more control over your mental process.

How many times do you talk in phrases such as "my mind went blank" or "the future looks dim". You will surprise yourself when you think about it but isn't it a true description of what you are experiencing inside as you say those words?

Can you recall an event that seems a blur to you now? Things are not clear and defined for some reason. What happens as you begin to alter the submodalities of your memory and begin to *sharpen up* the picture. To define the images and give them contrast colour and shape? What's stopping you from having a clear recollection? Change it. What happens?

Once an event has passed in time it is finished. Gone. You cannot go back and physically change the event itself. Each time you recall such an event you are no longer responding to the event but to your *recollection* of the event, your memory of it. The important thing is that your memory of the event can be changed.

As you vary the other visual elements of the submodalities consciously, how does each affect your response? It is important that you actually try the exercises because it will provide you with an appreciation of how you can control your own experience. Controlling your own mental experience is a crucial part of perfecting your visual process. Try each submodality separately. For example, with colour vary the intensity of the colour from intense, vivid colours down to black and white. For 'distance', change the picture from very close to far away. Try changing from a panoramic picture to a framed picture. Take a moment to appreciate the effect of each change you make. In particular give attention to clarity, contrast, focus and fuzzy, misty or hazy qualities. Also pay attention to sharpness and definition. Go in one direction and then another.

Remember that in your own mind anything is possible. You have no limitations and anything you can imagine, you can do! Play with a combination of submodality changes and find out how these effect you. What feels really intense?

As you recall your memories and play with these submodalities how do you perceive yourself? If you normally wear glasses or contact lenses or have some vision impairment, do you perceive yourself as still having that problem as you recall these memories? Were you consciously aware

SUBMODALITIES

of what you thought until I mentioned it? Even as you perceive and recall such events, your subconscious can be working against you as it conflicts with your conscious. While you may not wish to wear glasses consciously, subconsciously your brain may have a mental image of you that includes wearing glasses or contact lenses. This may be a very deeply held image, which is just there - part of your *'deep structure'*.

As your brain is a goal-seeking organism, it will maintain the mental image it has of you. If this image includes you with poor vision and wearing glasses or lenses your conscious desire will never overcome the power of your subconscious, which maintains a different mental image of **who you are.** Conflict between the conscious and subconscious will not produce results. The key point is that if you not aware of the potential conflict, how will you make progress? So ensure that the subconscious image you have of yourself matches the conscious image you have of yourself - someone with normal eyesight who has no need for glasses or contact lenses. Ensure that your memory-recall represents you in the same way. Use submodality changes to your benefit in creating the self-image you want as a person with normal vision.

Some people may say they can't because without glasses they cannot see the world. Well, use your imagination and the power of submodalities. What would it be like if you could? How would you see, what would you see, how would you make it clear, sharp, focused? Remember that in your mind anything is possible. You just need to learn how to use your mind effectively.

Again think of a memory where it was a pleasure to see something. Relax, make yourself comfortable and think back to that time. As you actually step into that experience see what you saw through your own eyes, remembering what has just been said. Remember the events, the colours, and the brightness. the shapes, the definition and the clarity. The 'details' that you can now become aware of. There may also be certain sounds, voices or noises. What were you feeling at that time, emotions, as well as the environment such as temperature, textures etc. Recall and experience fully what that is like.

The next thing to do is to step out of your body while maintaining the rest of the memory. Move away from yourself so that you can see yourself in that experience. It's exactly the same as watching a movie of yourself.

There will have been a difference for you between the two representations of that experience. One will have felt more intense than the other. One is associated experience and one is disassociated. Also in one you will have noticed different things about yourself, particularly about how you sense your visual process within your own perception.

Next go back to that memory and this time your vision is perfect. Everything is clear, sharp and focused. How does that feel? Take the submodality distinctions that you know work for you and manipulate the image. Try making it bigger and brighter. Bring the image closer. Apart from your actual visual process as you represent it in your memory, make the total image more colourful, more intense. Making the image more intense gives it more power and makes it a more pleasurable, desirable state. Aim to make a powerful internal representation of this image. What will it really mean to you when you have normal vision and why do you want to achieve that objective? Only by really giving yourself the required degree of emotional intensity will you **start speeding towards your objective.**

Apart from giving yourself the correct subconscious self–image (for your brain to begin working toward achieving), it provides a contrast point. As already said, your brain works by contrast and so you are providing yourself with the tools your brain needs to achieve its goals. Identifying the difference between where you are now and where you *want* to be.

The emotional intensity of any experience is very important. If you begin to think of yourself in this new way, with an intensity and powerful image of yourself with normal vision, your brain will be drawn toward this representation and will start taking action to achieve it. Only your own experience of what we are talking about will convince you personally of the effects and the difference this can make to you.

Feelings power all success

Remember that your feelings are a powerful factor in achieving success. The cause of an emotion is often outside our conscious awareness but it is controllable just the same. It is a kinaesthetic representation with submodalities that are changeable. You can take control in the process of determining what feelings you want. Emotional intensity is one of the strongest driving forces that will help you achieve your objective. The power of submodalities is the ability to manipulate your own driving forces. Think of any great athlete, and the power of their 'emotional intensity' is often the difference which makes them great - the drive and determination to push them on towards their peak level of performance; the ability to represent their inner worlds in a way which supports their prime objective to the exclusion of all other possibilities. Begin to realise what it means to **have this type of attitude** that is **held deeply in your own subconscious.** Apply this attitude to your visual process.

When I was re-educating my visual process I would often take a scene from the day's events, one I had studied from a visual point of view. I would then play with the submodality distinctions in my mind, for example, examining my memory for a simple thing, such as the colour of grass. What this means is not just generalising it as green, but really appreciating the *different* shades of green, the richness of the colour and the quality of the green itself. Imagine you have the eye of an artist and pay attention to

Submodalities

such details. In your mind, as you recollect scenes from your day, try playing with the colours and shades as they make up your memory. You will find that this has the effect of making you pay attention to the things you look at; you will begin examining the quality of the colour you see and the details of what is available. This is one of the most important exercises you can do. **Mental practice is crucial to the process of seeing correctly.**

As I mentioned earlier, it has been shown that none of us actually see colour in exactly the same way. The modelling process means that the colour red will look different in its qualities and richness to two different people. Red is only a label we give as an identification for that general shade of colour. Each of us actually experiences 'red' as a colour in our own individual way. This is at a deeper level of experience, which we do not normally convey in words because of the limits words place upon us in truly expressing the nature of our total experience. There is always more happening in our experience than we express. **Often we fail to pay attention to certain aspects of experience because it is not represented by a word.** This though is only a reflection of a limitation in our thinking, caused by the words themselves.

So as you practise memory recall of certain events from your day you will come to notice by the quality of the recall you have, how much visual acuity you possess. This will improve without doubt after only a couple of days. Test your recall of a scene with the actual scene itself the next day and see what you remembered and what you had not noticed. You will have remembered a great deal, perhaps more that you imagined but you will also have missed a huge quantity of available information. Do the same exercise for a week and **notice the difference in the power of your recall**. Keep in mind the nature and purpose of submodalities as you do this. You will find without doubt that one will aid the other. Your aim should be a complete recall of your chosen scene in your mind, exactly as it is, as if you were actually there-'live'. Once you have achieved this degree of recall you will find submodality manipulation is easy. Find those submodalities that are strongest for you as you focus in on them.

One thing I found was that it is important to be aware of exactly how you are using your own body as you see the world. All people have access to the three main representational systems, visual, auditory and kinaesthetic, but we all use them to different degrees. Some people access their brains using the visual mode and so they react most strongly to the pictures they see in their minds. Some people are auditory and some kinaesthetic, meaning that they will react to the stimuli in these systems more strongly. What I found was that as I carried out many of these exercises, I began checking my own body for other sensations. I found on a number of occasions that I had a great deal of tension that was running up my back and into my neck. The tension from my neck ran up behind my eyes and finally rested above my left eye. This state had become so natural for me that it was normal. I actually had to concentrate upon relaxing it. I did so by 'letting go' of what seemed like a small ball of tension above my left eye and letting that feeling of relaxation flow right down my neck and into my back and muscles. It is amazing what a difference this had upon me. I noticed immediately that my vision improved and I just felt relaxed. Believe it or not it I found it actually took effort to stay relaxed!

I decided that if I was that tense at normal times without even being aware of it that I needed to pay attention to actually staying relaxed. This I did over the course of a couple of days. I began noticing as I went about my daily activities all the times and places that I could become aware of tension within me and relaxed it. **I decided to make relaxation my natural state.** How many of us want to walk around feeling tense? If that tension is effecting your visual process then it needs to be changed! Pay particular attention to your breathing, as you relax make your breathing longer and deeper. Contrast it with your normal breathing position.

What I did find was that as I learnt to relax and relieve the tensions that I had, my vision showed marked improvements. What this shows is that although we may not realise it, our visual process is connected in with other processes, including the way we feel. Our kinaesthetics. Use what you have learnt about submodalities to identify and become aware of your body sensations as you look at the world. Use them also to **change the way you feel so as to support your aims.** We shall look at some specific physical exercises you can do to support a relaxed state

If auditory cues are particularly important to you, ensure you give yourself encouragement by talking to yourself. Use a confident encouraging tone of voice. Try changing the rhythm and tempo. What type of voice can really get you to do things? As you listen to your internal voice how does it make you feel? If you talk to yourself in a hard, firm, staccato-type voice how does that compare with a smooth, soft, encouraging, coaching type of voice? Try it now. What works for you?

One thing that will be clear as you do these exercises is that all these factors have an effect. They change what you feel and they can change how you perceive. Find the submodalities that will help you the most. Mental practice is the key because after a little while your mind will come to know how you are viewing things in your perception and gradually you will find it translating into your everyday physical viewing of the world. How does this happen? Your brain begins making adjustments to make the state of your actual sight match that as portrayed in your perception. Be alert to the adjustments, however minor they may seem. Use the knowledge that your brain is a goal-seeking organism. Set it going in the right direction and then give yourself the additional changes you need to make through the use of the 'daily eye workout' exercises.

It's also worth bearing in mind the dynamics of relaxation. Whenever there is effort to see, your vision becomes worse. Effort creates tension so be in the position where you can know for yourself what a state of relaxation is. Again noticing the differences is vital. The importance of Chapter 8 and understanding relaxation will again be apparent.

The point to remember is that practice and repetition will pay dividends here. **Practice and repetition are masters of all ability**[2]. As you become more familiar with the submodality shifts that work for you, you will notice the improvements taking effect.

Now that you have learnt how submodalities can improve your vision let's look at two other key components that will drive you forward as you are improving your sight.

---

[1] NLP or Neuro-Linguistic Programming
[2] Use the distinctions you learn here and apply them as you are using the swish pattern.

CHAPTER 17

HOW MEMORY AND IMAGINATION WILL IMPROVE YOUR VISION

Psychologists make a distinction between our memories and our perceptions. Research has shown that memories are generally less clear and detailed than perceptions. Occasionally, however, a remembered image can be complete in every detail. This is known as an *eidetic* image. It is the type of total memory recollection that Magliabechi was famous for.

The brain does not take in sensory experience and then store it in a form that is 'exactly accurate' for later recall[1]. We have already looked at the nature and construction of perception. Memories are recorded and stored on the basis of perceptions, which means they can be subject to similar types of distortion. Research has shown that people can remember things that have not actually happened. This is where imagination plays a role. A piece of one experience can be taken and combined with pieces of other experiences. These can then be combined into what is a false memory. What is important is how you take your experiences and then represent them to yourself and even *how* you go about accessing your past experiences.

Memory plays a key part in your visual process because of the principle of familiarity with given objects and shapes, upon which perception and vision are based. Not all your memories are stored. Short-term memory occurs when an experience is so short that it does not pass into long-term memory. The memory is not then retrievable. Memory is not therefore entirely reliable and this is why it is vital to practise your daily eye work-out exercises and also to ensure you notice even the small improvements you make. Also the importance of the earlier exercises and concentrating upon retrieving memory images will be apparent. The idea is to build by degrees a generalisation of memory both in the conscious and subconscious mind that **your visual ability is normal.** All human memory is a distortion of experience because it is only an internal representation of the real world event. This means that the whole process of experiencing and then remembering is guided and regulated by your previous experiences and your own unique internal building blocks. (You will remember that submodalities are one such component.)

Your memory will be recorded according to a number of variable factors. Included will be what you have decided it is important to notice, your expectations, mood, previous experiences in similar situations and state of your external and internal focus of attention.

You will recall that perception is a complex process that is not entirely understood in all its many aspects. What is clear is that perception and past experience are interlinked because our past experiences exist in our memories. Imagination has its part to play by its ability to combine memories in novel ways. Can you imagine an elephant, which is green and has pink spots? You have never seen an elephant that looks like that but your able to visualise one just the same. It is *not* therefore necessary for you to have directly experienced an event for you to be able to represent it. **Memory and imagination can combine to create new experiences for us.**

We all have the experience of being able to visualise things in our mind's eye. We have already looked at the way in which this is likely to work, the most likely explanation being that it is the eyes that provide the brain with data, which is then translated into neural activity or electrical impulses. The unique pattern of brain activity represents objects that *mean* things to us. Let's look at another example of 'numbers'. The written numbers on a page have certain meanings to us. These meanings have an effect in our brain, represented by a pattern of neural activity that represents the number we view.

One way of understanding what is going on is to accept that the brain has its own special language. The information provided by the eyes is coded into neural activity, the language of the brain. This is then reinterpreted into our experience of the world. The interpretation process is part of what is our perception. Have you ever had the experience of looking at a bonfire and seeing a face in the fire? Maybe when looking at clouds you have seen outlines of faces or other things? Perception is the process at work. We naturally organise information we receive so that it is organised into objects or familiar patterns. Yet it is the brain that does the organising.

The process of seeing is therefore a combination of many sources of information from our various senses. A familiar object is based on our past experience and this gives us the ability to project an object into the future and also helps us recognise objects in the present. It will be obvious that the brain searches for the 'best interpretation' of the information it receives. This can give rise to different interpretations in differing circumstances.

Everyday experience affects your perception. Knowing this and what you have learnt so far should confirm that visual re-education is sometimes necessary where the underlying process is faulty. One view of perception is that we take objects as a model or presupposition and then use our senses to test this model or presupposition. In other words, the senses act by providing us with the necessary evidence for checking our real world visual experience. We will see things best when we have a good base of memories to draw from. The more accurate these memories, the more detailed, then the better your vision will be.

We are dependent upon perception for our understanding of the world because it is the basis of *all* our experience and understanding. The interrelation of perception, memory and imagination and our reliance in varying degrees upon these attributes was the basis of Dr Bates' methodologies. **Your vision can be improved by expanding the power of your memory and imagination.**

Relaxation is the key to good memory

Have you ever had the experience of trying to remember a name or telephone number and the harder you try to remember it the more difficult it becomes to recall anything at all? Yet as soon as you relax and stop thinking about it, the information you want just pops into your head? This is not just a coincidence, as it has been shown that when a normal memory of the colour black is recalled, examination of the eyes shows that all errors of refraction are corrected. If the memory of the colour black is not normal, the opposite is the case and errors of refraction occur. When vision is normal, black in a dim light is the same as black in a bright light. It also the same 'black' at a far point or a near point and whether a large area or a small area. Memory would also seem to work best when you are in a state of relaxation and you can test your degree of relaxation by the accuracy of your recollection of the colour black. The simple test mentioned earlier will show you how close you are. Bring a black letter to a point at which you can see it the best and compare your memory image of black with the real thing. Be aware of the fine distinctions that are available to you.

There are many reasons why someone may not be able to remember. Sometimes a person may not be putting their body in the right position to access a memory properly. Try this. How many windows are there in your house or the place you live? As you accessed that memory for the information and the answer, you may have noticed that your eyes positioned themselves up and to the left, (if you are right-handed). The accessing cue is subconscious and involuntary. Are you aware of it? Your brain stores information in certain specialised places depending upon what you are asking it to do and you can only access the information by correctly using the appropriate accessing cues.

Remembering what was said about perception earlier, it is also interesting to consider that the brain has certain hemispheric functions. Each hemisphere seems to specialise in certain activities. The left hemisphere is usually responsible for language and is known as the dominant hemisphere, while the right, non-dominant hemisphere is responsible for more of the visual functions. The left hemisphere seems to be less well developed with regard to making visual distinctions. It seems that each side of the brain performs a certain set of cognitive tasks. It also seems that the right hemisphere is responsible for constructing our perceptions. It is possible that as we relax, we remember more easily and we access the visual imagery of the right hemisphere of the brain. The increase in our abilities could be due to the fact that we are in a state where we are able to access and use the power of the right hemisphere of the brain.

It has been argued in recent times that we concentrate too much upon the dominant left hemisphere's functions. This is because of the emphasis placed upon left brain functions in the education system. This acts to the detriment of those abilities carried out by the non-dominant hemisphere, which tend to remain underdeveloped.

This is not to be confused with the general principle of contralateral (opposite-side) representation in that each half of the brain controls the movements of the opposite side of the body, so that information seen through the left eye would connect to the right half of the brain. Recent research has included the development of 'neural nets'. These are electronic brains that can learn and identify patterns. This ability to search for and identify patterns is one of the major attributes of our own brains. These neural nets work on the principle of parallel computing and it is thought that our own brains work in a similar way, through parallel processing. The normal computer works in more of a step-by-step sequence. Our own brains have many cross connections and it is this ability which gives our brains such enormous computing power. One theory is that our visual process and final perception is made up of many channels, each dealing with different functions such as brightness, colour, movement, contrast shape, etc. Although each channel is physiologically detached with their own brain locations, and so organised in different areas of the cortex, the brain is able to create our own individual well-formed perceptions.

Sometimes simply remembering something clearly and distinctly will improve your vision, if you are alert enough to notice the difference. In order to develop this ability, various proponents of the Bates' method have used a number of special exercises. What these exercises demonstrate is that it is *'the background'*, i.e. relaxation, under which vision occurs, that creates and results in normal vision. I can confirm that this understanding made a real difference for me. As soon as I began consistently applying this principle, I found that my progress was marked and rapid.

David Marr's book, *Vision: A Computational Investigation into the Human Representational and Processing of Visual Information*, (Freeman, New York, 1982) contains a detailed theory about how we perceive and see. One of his main ideas was that certain simple shapes are 'assumed' by the brain, so it is not necessary for the brain to calculate and re-compute all the numerous possibilities every time it is presented with information.

The assumptions regarding shapes therefore serve to make the brain's problem less complex. The idea is that perceptions are 'internal representations' of the external world. Marr does provide a detailed and interesting analysis of three main components of perception.

On this basis, it could begin to explain the reason why **remembering something clearly and distinctly brings an immediate improvement in vision.** In addition, the principle of re-learning to see things with central alignment, taking into account all aspects of an object and **giving yourself a new accurate memory of the object** would therefore seem to have a solid basis.

A test for relaxation and vision

One interesting finding reported by Dr Bates concerns the case of people who have two eyes with different vision capabilities in each eye. Dr Bates found that the difference between the two eyes could be exactly measured by the length of time a black full stop can be remembered, while looking at a vision chart with both eyes and then with the better eye closed. He reported that a person with normal vision in the right eye and half-normal vision in the left eye could, when looking at the vision card with both eyes open, remember a full stop for twenty seconds continuously. When the better eye was closed, it could be remembered for only ten seconds. The same pattern of results showed up on various occasions including where a person who had half-normal vision in the right eye and quarter-normal vision in the left eye. This person could remember the full stop for twelve seconds with both eyes open, and only for six seconds with the better eye closed. Dr Bates reports a further finding of a person with normal sight in the right eye and vision of one-tenth in the left eye. He could remember a full stop for twenty seconds with both eyes open and only for two seconds with the best eye closed. What Dr Bates found was that if the right eye is better than the left, the memory is better when the right eye is open than when only the left eye is open. The really interesting point is that the difference is in exact proportion to the difference in the vision of the two eyes.

Use the power of your memory with relaxation

The ability to remember true black is a powerful way to begin correcting your visual process. I found that upon practising this technique, once a true memory of black is attained, it gives a real shot of instantaneous relaxation. You will always know for yourself if you are straining and suffering tension, simply by focusing upon your ability to remember black. As you focus upon a memory of *'true black'*, if you do it fully, you will be aware of a feeling of relaxation throughout your body. **The feeling is very noticeable. Be alert to it.** Once you have achieved this it will then be easy for you to carry with you a memory of some small black area, like a full stop. One can generally see a smaller area of black better than a large one because for some reason it seems 'blacker'. Black is not affected by light as a colour. It is either black or it is not. Ensure that you become aware of this distinction and focus upon a small area of a larger black object or letter and notice the difference. When you have done this you can move on to imagine a black full stop as part of a larger area of black. Stop and think about how that would appear for a moment.

Imagine a perfect full stop and remember when you did the exercise of seeing part of an object or letter best. What you are doing here is the same except with colour and shade. Imagine that you see 'one small part' of the black letter on a vision card best. This is your full stop. If it is easier, think of some other black object. Some people think of a full stop initially as a full stop on a page with a white background. Resist the temptation to do so and practise as already outlined. In order to remember the full stop perfectly as true black, it needs to be remembered *against a black background*. Using this as a contrast point, particularly for the feelings generated, you will recognise and so be able to repel times when you start to become aware of a build-up of tension and strain. Being aware of the type and nature of the feeling that accompanies the attainment of the memory of true black helps you to achieve the same state more easily, as you can combine both the visual memory and the feeling. If you find it easier, you can lead into the state of relaxation by finding the feeling first and then beginning to remember black. You may find it easier to remember a larger area of black at first, gradually progressing until the area remembered overall becomes smaller while still maintaining its quality and intensity. As the area becomes smaller your level of relaxation will increase. There are a number of other exercises referred to below, which have been developed by various followers of Dr Bates as ways of achieving the objective.

One point to mention is that as you remember true black, let the memory of it just flow into your mind. Do not start to concentrate upon what you can see or how well you can see. Just let it happen and pay no real attention to what you can see. It's the same as taking the focus away from what you can see but only temporarily. The reason for is that if you begin concentrating upon how much your vision is improving, at the same time that you focus upon remembering black, you may find that you unintentionally produce strain and tension. This will defeat the object and spoil the quality of the memory recall of the colour black.

This exercise can be done almost anywhere and almost at any time. Once you achieve a level of relaxation that allows a good memory of a black full stop, you will notice the difference. **Expect these conditions and actively seek them**. Your level of relaxation will become greater and you will begin to increase the time period over which it is maintainable. Eventually it will become a subconscious skill again.

Representational systems

One useful distinction to be aware of is the difference in the way certain people use their 'representational systems'. You will recall that we all use three main ways of coding information to make sense of the world. These are seeing (visual), hearing (auditory), and feeling (kinaesthetic). A further distinction can be made between those stimuli that are generated in the external world and those that we generate ourselves internally.

We all use all of these three primary systems although we may not be aware of them. It is normal for different people perhaps to favour one system in preference to another. Although we are involved here with correcting the visual process, the way in which you use your own representational system is important.

For example, when you think of the exercise that requires you to remember a black full stop, how do you go about remembering that? You may say that is easy because it's a visual image and so that is how and what you remember. Check your own process though. If you are experiencing a vague, unstable image and are experiencing difficulty, this could be due to your lead representational system. Many people have an inner voice that runs in the auditory system creating internal dialogue. You may be generally talking to yourself about what you are trying to do and how you are trying to do it. If your most highly valued representational system is not visual, try shutting down your internal dialogue. Simply stop it and begin to 'focus exclusively upon the quality of the picture' you are accessing, namely the black full stop. It may take a little practice but there will be an appreciable difference. In addition it has been found that there is a distinction between you "imagining a picture " and "seeing a picture". It is a subtle but important distinction to be aware of. The experience of "imagining a picture" apparently uses a verbal, internal dialogue as part of the inner creation process. You will recall that the brain has specialised hemispheres and this would seem to suggest the left dominant hemisphere is being used. In other words the language system is being used to create the picture. As the function is normally one of the non-dominant hemisphere, "seeing a picture" and cutting off the internal dialogue accesses the non-dominant hemisphere and leads to more vivid visualisation. Become aware of your own internal processing and notice the difference. A simple change in the way you are processing your information can make all the difference. If you still find that your ability to create visual images is poor, exercises that generally develop the right brain functions can help.[2] Although no one representational system is better than another, being able to move between systems and move into the visual system has clear advantages for carrying out the black full stop exercise.

When your ability to access your memory of a black full stop is instantaneous you are successful. If you are taking a few seconds, more work is required because accessing should be instantaneous and continuous. It is fair to say that your memory of the full stop is a test of relaxation and the correct accessing of the brain hemisphere that creates your visual images.

There are a number of exercises that can assist you in this area. Generally any process that makes you more familiar with an object that you are trying to see will make it easier for you to see it. This is an established fact. The act of remembering an object increases familiarity with it. In line with Marr's theories, it can be presupposed that anything that helps improve the make-up of our levels of perception will improve vision. Marr proposed that a perception was made up of (1) the 'primal sketch'; this represents the two dimensional intensities and shapes of an image; (2) the '21/2D Sketch' – of the visual surface, which is 'viewer-centred', representations of depth and orientation of the visible surfaces; and (3) the 3-D model representation, which is object-centred and using what he describes as 'volumetric primitives'. This is similar to the idea that we are based upon the shape of cylinders representing our arms, legs, bodies etc., and that we use these to create an object's perception.

Obviously, increasing the accuracy and detail of our own perceptions means that memory and imagination exercises become very important. The first step is to concentrate upon the letters and numbers that form a crucial part of our everyday lives. Once this is achieved the improvement with other more complicated and less familiar shapes will follow naturally.

The ability to remember true black is the first stage of these exercises. As I mentioned earlier the attention should be directed toward the memory of black and the feelings of relaxation that accompany it. Retain this level of relaxation and make it as perfect as possible. The reason for this is because you may find that relaxation is lost when you begin viewing an object at a distance subconsciously thought to be unfavourable. It can best be described as the surprise of being able to determine details of an object or maybe a letter, for however brief a moment, that you are not used to seeing at such a distance. This may be either a near point or a far point. The surprise leads to a loss of relaxation because you may find yourself actively 'seeking greater detail' for the object in view, which is a natural reaction for the visual process. If you are following the recommendations above and are focused upon a black full stop at the same time, it can become difficult to maintain relaxation, until you have had a little practice.

One exercise to try if you have difficulty is to remember a full stop while looking at the visual correction chart. Look to one side of the chart, (approximately one foot) and gradually decrease the distance to the letters on the chart. You are viewing through your peripheral field of vision without losing the memory of the full stop, and edging yourself closer to the letters on the visual chart. Practise on a few occasions and gradually you will acquire the discipline of looking directly at the letter, without loss of memory of the full stop. Awareness of and **finding that feeling of relaxation** at the same time is a great advantage.

Another variation of the same exercise is to look at only part of a letter on the vision chart. Start with the bottom and imagine that the full stop is a part of that letter. How do you do this? Simply imagine the rest of the letter as less black and less distinct than the area you imagine has the full stop. Once you achieve this, the next step is to note the shape of the letter, starting at the bottom. At the same time maintain the imaginary full stop in the bottom part of the letter you are looking at. Just as soon as you can do this continue with your observation of the shape of the letter by moving to the middle and top of the letter while maintaining the full stop at the bottom. In other words aim to observe the different parts of the letter at first separately and then altogether while keeping the memory of the full stop. Practise, be patient and notice each small improvement.

What I found with this exercise was that at first it was difficult to maintain a memory of true black as a full stop. I started with a far larger area of black in my memory and practised recollecting it at different times, always being aware of the feeling of relaxation that flooded into my body when I remembered true black. I had to be consciously aware of *not* trying to jump at improvements in my vision and just letting them 'come to me'. What I did find was that as time went by, the whole exercise became more familiar and took much less concentration. I found a moment's delay between attaining a memory of true black and the consequent improvements in my vision. Eventually, however, I began to find letters and objects I was looking at in this way started 'coming to me' rather than me 'seeking them out'. It is a subtle but crucial distinction of which to be aware. Whereas before I had found signs in supermarkets and shops took concentrated effort to read, mastering this technique meant that I could not do anything other than see what I looked at. It is a powerful technique and one that will aid improvement of your visual process.

More advanced exercises

You will recall in Chapter 3 that we dealt briefly with the process that we go through in order to read. Reading is in fact one of our main tasks of the day. Letters and figures are everywhere, even though we are not always conscious of how much we rely upon them. Many people in the forty plus age range begin to notice that with age, sight at the near point becomes more difficult and this is when they turn to glasses as an aid for reading. Age does not and need not affect your ability to regain good sight. There have been many reports of people of various ages correcting their vision. Remember the earlier case I referred to of a man of seventy who had worn glasses for forty years for distant vision and twenty years for reading and desk work? Using the Bates' principles he was able to regain normal vision. **Age is not a barrier to success!** Remember that you only can't, if you believe you can't! Other people have already achieved the result you want and you can do the same.

Improve your memory of the alphabet

Stop for a moment and think about your memory of the alphabet. How good is it? You probably know the alphabet and can recite it forwards and maybe backwards and you recognise the letters you see printed on the page in front of you, but exactly *how good* is your memory of the individual letters that form the alphabet?

In the past, various teachers of the Bates' method have reported that many people's memories of the alphabet is not good, in that they do not have **a clear mental picture** of the letters of the alphabet. Again, stop and think for a moment, about how accurate your memory of the alphabet is, first capital letters and then small or lower case letters. It is usually the lower case letters of which people find they have a poor mental image.

It is important to distinguish between feeling insulted at the suggestion that you do not 'know' the alphabet and the fact that it is your visual memory of the actual letters themselves that is being examined. From what has already been said it will be obvious that it is memory and your perception that is being re-trained.

It is because our world is so filled with letters, words and numbers that we find ourselves generalising them away. We move through this world much like a bird flies through the air. We pay it no regard. The whole process of reading depends upon our ability to see the letters that form the words. If the memory of those letters is perfect, this interrelates with the power of our perception and thus our resulting, and measurable, improvements in vision.

Sometimes it is necessary to go back and re-examine what we think we know, in order to see what else we can become aware of. Here you will focus upon a different element of your sense of the alphabet. Spending a few moments reviewing your memory images of the alphabet will be well worth the small effort involved. The aim is to attain clear, distinct and accurate images. In carrying out the process remember to use your ability to look in detail at all the micro-elements that comprise the letter. It is these micro-elements that form the image, so pay them the attention they deserve. Remember to shift your focus of attention from one point to another to avoid staring. Repeat this going through all letters of the alphabet and then do the same with numbers. Sometimes it is easier to see each letter of the alphabet in a different colour first and then change the colour to black. Do what ever you find easiest.

What happens when you do this exercise and imagine a sparkling, almost glowing white background with the black letters against it? Does this alter your perception? Pay attention to this background as it immediately surrounds the letters and those areas included within the letters. Does it make the letters look more striking as you think about them now? Are they more interesting? Try picturing the black letters as an interruption against this background. What is the pattern of blackness that you can see, the lines and curves? Do you find that in your imagination the emphasis has changed and the black stands out more? Experiment, play and find what works for you. Pay attention to the visual submodalities of contrast, brightness, size, etc. that we looked at earlier and find a combination that really makes blackness a true contrast that you can remember. This is where you will find that being aware of the submodality distinctions can make a difference for you. There is always a submodality that will change how things are for you. Use them. Make it fun, because your brain will remember things that are fun much more easily than things that it regards as a chore or boring. Use your imagination to make this whole learning a magical adventure.

Imaginary swinging shifts

This exercise involves a simple use of your imagination. Imagine that you have a clean sheet of white paper in front of you. Next imagine you have a black felt tip marker. Take this marker and make a round black dot. In your imagination, pay attention to the area of white background on the paper to the right of this dot. Next do exactly the same to the area immediately to the left of the dot. Speed the process up by alternating the attention from side to side, right and left. Make it a rhythmic swing backward and forwards. What happens? Do you see the imaginary dot appear to move, first to the left as you pay attention to the right and then it moves to the right as you pay attention to the left?

The next exercise is very similar. Again on an imaginary sheet of paper make two black dots at a distance of about four inches apart. Next imagine between these two dots and one inch below them a circle half an inch in diameter. The outline of this circle is very black, yet the centre within the outline is brilliant white. Now pay attention to the dot on the right in your mind's eye. Next to the dot on the left and build up a rhythmic motion as you repeat the process. What happens to the movement of the circle? Do you find that it moves in the opposite direction to the place where you are paying attention?

Practise with these exercises, as they are good at helping to develop your visualisation process and for accessing a state of relaxation. It also demonstrates your brain's remarkable ability to organise patterns that are only imaginary. The exercises also help form the mental discipline of small-scale swinging shifts.

---

[1] You will recall that the likelihood is that the brain stores 'symbols'.
[2] Tony Buzzan and Raymond Keen's *Book of Genius* provides an excellent introduction to developing right brain skills.

CHAPTER 18

IMAGINATION - THE POWERHOUSE OF GOOD VISION

"Imagination rules the world!"

Napoleon

What is our imagination? We all have an imagination and we can all use our imagination. Have you ever worried about how some future project or goal will turn out, imagining all the things that could go wrong? Have you ever had an important meeting or interview and worried in advance about how it would turn out and if you would get the result you wanted? You probably created a picture in your mind of the possible scenarios, things that could happen. That is one simple way in which we use our imagination.

The important thing about your imagination is that like your other behaviours, it is affected by the information you allow it to have. The human modelling processes of generalisation, deletion and distortion actually filter the information that you receive. This is reflected through your attitudes, values and beliefs. These are the tools you use to interpret any situation, they determine how you will assess any problem or challenge that you face. These are the same tools that you will use in correcting your visual process. You will be making assessments of what you think is possible for you, in accordance with how you are interpreting this information. The limits you apply for yourself will prescribe the area of what is possible, for you.[1]

If you have progressed this far, then you have already proved to yourself that you have an excellent imagination, as many of the exercises so far involve a creative use of your imagination. Accessing your true resources and creatively experiencing through your imagination simply involve "acting as if" a set of circumstances are true - rehearsing it in your imagination. Acting out new behaviours and doing things differently, including how you will "see" the world, simply means deciding to do it. Using your imagination to portray how it could be, and then following through with these new ways of doing things, instead of blindly and habitually doing what you have always done.

The importance of noticing even the smallest of improvements is crucial here. If there is one key principle that I used in correcting my own vision it was this one. How you interpret the results you get back from your decision to improve your own vision. You know that your brain works using contrast. If you have imagined yourself with normal vision and you make a few attempts or try a few exercises, what will happen if you fail to notice the improvements you are getting? Your brain will use the difference between what you *imagine should* be happening and what you are actually achieving, and interpret this as failure. Your imagination will work against you, instead of for you. So correcting your vision is not only about using your imagination in the right way. It is also about using your ability to 'interpret' information.

Your imagination is closely linked as a mental process to your perception and memory, yet it is beneficial if you think of it as a distinct ability for purposes of your visual process. Memory is the recall of previous experiences, while imagination involves you in creating ideas and concepts or relationships you have not experienced before. It is possible for you to have a real perception of the world that you simultaneously confuse with an imagined perception. The imagined perception can in cases be erroneous and mistaken for the true perception. One example is where a person may say "that looks comfortable". This is a mixing of sense information by representing something visual in the kinaesthetic representational system, (also known as synesthesia). In reality it is allowing the imagination to take over the function of real world perception. This can work to your advantage or against you, so it pays to be aware of the differences.

> "The faculty of imagination is the great spring of human activity, and the principle source of human improvement…"

Douglas Stewart, Scottish philosopher

Learn to use your imagination and let it begin working for you and you will soon notice improvements. Dramatic improvements can occur very quickly when your imagination is used correctly.

Try a simple experiment. Close your eyes and remember a black letter or number that you are familiar with. Remember it as perfectly as possible. Once you have done this remember the same letter, only this time *make it imperfect*. How do you do this? Make the edges fuzzy, the background hazy or cloudy, make the boarders jagged. What's the difference? Was it easy to imagine a perfect letter that you probably recalled fairly quickly? Were you able to maintain the image as a constant for some considerable time? What about the imperfect letter? Was this harder to imagine and did it vary in its location in your visual field? Was it hard to hold the colour and shape steady? Although you are only doing this in your imagination, did you notice any similarities with a letter or number that you might physically see *imperfectly?* When you strain to see imperfectly, straining in your imagination to produce imperfect images produces the same type of results. This is more than just a coincidence.

IMAGINATION - THE POWERHOUSE OF GOOD VISION

As we know, the imagination is linked to the memory and to perception. The way in which you perceive can actually go wrong. With some mental illness people can create alternative realities. Hallucinations are an example of experience diverting from reality. To some degree we all perceive some elements of the real world in a distorted way. The example of synesthesia above is an example.

Many philosophers have addressed this question, "what is reality?" Hallucinations and dreams are not real but they can take on the *illusion* of reality. Most people have had a dream or other experience that gives the impression of reality. It may seem that it is real because things can be sensed or even touched. Yet what we believe is real is often misrepresented.

In one well-known psychology experiment, subjects were asked to imagine a scene or object from a screen. They were unaware that arrangements were made, to project very dimly, the same or a similar scene or object to the one the subject was imagining. In a majority of cases the subject believed the projected image to be created by the subject's own imagination. This was the case even when the images were not an exact match. What this tells us is that our own imaginations can play strange tricks upon us if we are unaware of what may be happening. The same principles apply to our visual process.

As referred to earlier, Wilder Penfield the brain surgeon from Canada, found that when operating upon patients, he was able to create hallucinations when particular parts of the patient's brains were stimulated. Patients (who were awake during the surgery) reported 'experiences that seemed real'. Hallucinations can be caused by other things as well, such as drugs like LSD. When these things happen our perceptions are stimulated not by real world sensory experience but by some different form of central stimulation. It becomes possible to experience both the real world and a hallucinogenic world together. Both can seem equally real. I am not suggesting that people with defective vision are hallucinating, only pointing out a known principle upon which the brain seems to 'interpret' information.

What you understand to be the power of your own imagination is very important to you because you will always act, feel and perform according to what you 'imagine' to be true about yourself and your environment. Your behaviour is governed not by your will power but by the power of you imagination.

Have you ever wondered how hypnotic subjects respond so easily to suggestions about their situation? The hypnotic subject is in an altered state of consciousness in which the hypnotist has free access to the subject's imagination. When a hypnotic subject is told that it is cold and snowing, the subject will not only shiver and look cold, his body will respond 'just as if' he were cold, with shivering and goose bumps. It is now a well-established principle that your nervous system cannot tell the difference between a real experience and an 'imagined' experience. In both cases the brain reacts and responds to the information it receives. It will respond to what 'you' think or imagine to be true. This applies not only to facts from the external environment but also to 'facts' that you imagine to be true about yourself. Such facts take on the power of beliefs and belief is one of the most powerful driving forces of human behaviour.

It is strange that some distortions are perceived by all of us and in exactly the same way. The fact that a figure or object is not complex does not affect the fact that distortion still takes place. The arrow illusion is a very good example. The arrow with the outgoing 'v' looks longer than the normal arrow. Both are in fact of equal length. Until one is measured against the other, it is easy to believe that one is indeed longer than the other.

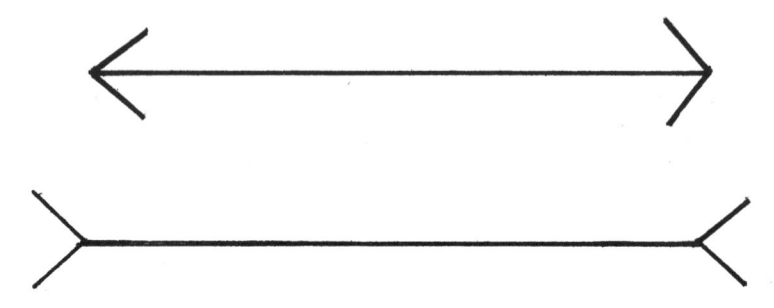

Belief

Let's look at belief. It is a common belief that it is not possible to walk on fire. This is based upon past associations we all hold that come to form our beliefs of what is possible. The fear of walking on fire and its projected consequences, if one attempted it, are however held in our imagination. Many people have heard of Tony Robbins and his seminars in which he teaches fire walking. Tony Robbins takes the fear that arises from the belief that it is not possible to walk on fire and uses the fire walk as a vehicle for turning fear into power. He alters the perception of what is possible and in so doing alters the picture in the participants' imagination. The fire walk, being such a well-known example, demonstrates how our perceptions about the world are originally formed and more importantly, how they can be changed. *We are not stuck with our perceptions.*

It is true to say that we see largely with the mind and only partly with the eyes. This is because **the process of vision itself depends upon the crucial process of interpretation**. It is true that the eyes provide sensory information that is transmitted to the retina, but it is the 'interpretation' of that image which is crucial. It will be clear now that we do not see the image or impression itself *but the mind's interpretation of it.* The earlier exploration of the process of our perception showed some of the factors at work such as colour, size, depth, distance etc. Your behaviours, including the way you see, are not governed according to what things are really like. They are determined according to the image your mind has of what they are like. It is a fact that you have certain mental images of the world, the people in it and yourself. You act and behave as though these images are the truth. The truth is that these images are not reality, they only 'represent' reality. If your ideas and mental images of the world and yourself are distorted or blurred, then the way you respond to that information will be inappropriate. People who have a normal visual process use their memory and imagination to aid their sight. It has been demonstrated that when sight is not normal, then memory and imagination themselves are also not being used correctly. This means that the mind begins to add imperfections to the imperfect retinal image as it 'interprets' the information it receives.

The point has already been made that no two people view the same object in exactly the same way because of differences in the way each of us sees colour and the other elements that make up sight. In effect when sight is imperfect, the interpretation that results out of the complete visual process is also far more variable. This means that as you begin to regain control over the power of your interpretation, you will attain more mental control and **this is the key to rectifying errors of refraction.** Mental control is not about intellectual ability or intelligence. It is about your power of focus. **The power to focus your mind in a state of rest and relaxation with control over your imagination.**

In one reported case, a physician and surgeon, (and obviously a man of some intellect), had a collection of glasses issued by a variety of eye specialists. All differed in their qualities and gave no benefit to him in rectifying his sight. Examination revealed no organic defects of his eyes and no error of refraction. His symptoms however were double vision and only three-quarters normal vision with each eye. He also suffered from illusions, hallucinations and attacks of blindness.

This man also had a very poor memory as it was reported that he was unable to recall the colour of the eyes of any member of his family. This was despite seeing each of them on a daily basis. He did not know the colour of his own house or the number of rooms it had. In this particular case, it was reported that this man's intellect actually hindered progress with his treatment because he insisted everything was debated and discussed. He would argue about how he should be treated and put forward logical, yet incorrect arguments. In particular he argued that when he saw a letter he must see it as "being as 'black' as it was," because he was not colour blind. It apparently took this man eight or nine months to make any progress whatsoever. When asked to remember black with his eyes closed he was unable to do so. Through a number of different exercises he was eventually able to make progress and it was his change in belief that "black required an effort to remember it", that finally brought him immediate improvements. He is reported, when finally being able to respond to the exercises, to have been able to read 20\10 at age fifty-five years, his attacks of blindness ceased and his memory improved. These improvements were permanent, as years later, the report says there had been no relapse.

This man was able to regain control over his focus and the power of his imagination. His intellect had, however, actually slowed down his progress, as his ideas about physiological optics and how he interpreted them hindered his treatment. **It was the change in his belief about what was possible and *how*, that finally brought his improvement**. Once he was able to change his belief, he changed what he imagined and his behaviour, feelings and visual process followed on.

"The imagination is man's power over nature"

Wallace Stevens, 1879-1955

Achieving normal vision will first be realised in your imagination before you actually achieve it in reality. You are a goal-seeking organism and your brain is the controlling component that will steer you toward your objective. The key is to use your own natural processes to provide yourself with a well-formed objective. See clearly how you want to be and be aware of the things you know you will have done when you have achieved this goal. **Align yourself for successful accomplishment.** See the new you, with your new abilities of normal vision and then see yourself in this new way as your life will develop. Once you see yourself as you will be, with these new abilities and skills in your visual process, you will find that changes come quickly. It's like building a bridge between the old you with defective sight and the new you with these new skills and abilities. Once the bridge is constructed it is easy to run across. Practise every day creating the picture of how your life will be and what it will mean to you to have normal vision. Enjoying life without the inconvenience of glasses or contact lenses. Knowing that together with all the other improvements you will notice in other areas of your life, your health will be better. No longer will you be reliant upon optical crutches. Allow yourself to create the positive image of yourself that you need, **as a master of the art of sight**. The image you hold of yourself is the strongest force within you!

Build a bridge to normal vision

The importance of the imagination cannot be over-emphasised. You have already learnt that your perception has been built out of your own interpretations and evaluations, which are themselves, based upon your experience. 'Experience' is very important because it tells you what you can and can't do, what you will attempt and what is possible for you. The great thing is that **your experience can be changed by using your imagination.** Ask yourself the question, "What if...?" any time you start to ask yourself negative questions or find yourself making negative statements associated with your visual process. The best way is just to reverse the statement or question by asking yourself the "what if" question.

"Great sight begins with a picture, held in your imagination, of how you would like your sight to be."

Stephen Y Bohdan

Understanding the difference between those parts of the visual process that are the responsibility and function of the eye itself and those that are due to imaginary phenomena is of major importance. Illusions are created in the imagination and once you are aware of those elements of your vision that are likely to be illusions, created by your own interpretation and imagination, you can begin to regain control over these functions.

An exercise first credited to a Dr Arnau is an excellent exploration into your imagination. It also has the effect of physically stimulating the eye although the exercise is in the imagination. Imagine a ring of strong rubber. The kind that will retain its shape of a circle when not pulled. The rubber is of a type that will however change its shape to form an ellipse shape when squeezed. This is similar to the shape of a rugby ball or an American football in outline.

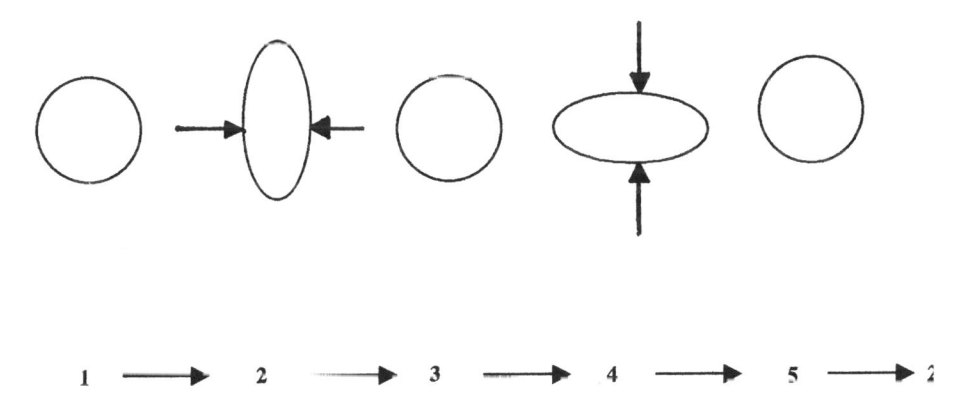

Follow each shape returning again to number 2 after 5 and continue

Next close your eyes and imagine this ring and view all around the outline of the ring. Now imagine that you are squeezing the ring with your hand so that the ellipse shape is vertical, the long axis running from top to bottom. If it were compass points you would be squeezing east and west together. View the shape as it is for a moment and allow the ring to return to its circular shape. Next change the position from which the pressure is applied. Imagine squeezing from top to bottom, or if they were compass points north and south. This will have the effect of creating an ellipse shape with its long axis running horizontally. As you allow the ring to return to its normal circular shape as you release the pressure, take a moment to see that the ring is perfectly circular again. Now repeat the whole process and watch the circle transform itself into a vertical ellipse, then a circle, then a horizontal ellipse, then a circle. Do this ten or twelve times and notice what happens as you watch in your imagination. This is also a good exercise in becoming aware of the type of things you can notice when you pay attention. Did you find that as each transformation of the circle takes place into an ellipse that your eye muscles respond as though pushing the shape of the ellipse into place? As the ring goes back into its circular shape the eyes relax again?

If you have not noticed it before, this demonstrates clearly the function of the eye muscles in the visual process and this is an exercise that will help to strengthen them. As you move through the rhythm of these muscular contractions appropriate to each visualisation you may notice that the sensations are very similar to the adjustments made when looking first at a distant object and then quickly looking at a near object.

Myopia

Many people are reported to have found this exercise very good, no matter what the visual defect. This is probably due to the fact that the eye muscles are given a good workout, so do add this to your 'daily eye workout'. It has also been reported that it is a particularly good exercise for those suffering from myopia or short-sightedness. I found this exercise to be very beneficial in helping to strengthen my own eye muscles and after a short while the improvements became noticeable as I found my long distance vision improving.

The speed with which you are able to improve your own sight obviously depends upon the exact nature of your problem and how quickly you are able to adapt properly the understandings available to you. The thing to remember is that the whole process is a wonderful dynamic, which means that improvement in one area stimulates improvement elsewhere. Taking the exercise above with the ellipse, as you feel your eye muscles working and strengthening you will come to notice improvements in the quality of your vision. Again be aware of even minor changes. Use these in conjunction with the picture you hold of yourself, of how you will be when your sight is normal. It is evidence that you are moving toward your objective.

> "hold a picture of yourself long enough and steadily enough in your mind's eye and you will be drawn toward it".
>
> **Dr H M Fosdick**

You will remember the swish pattern you did in Chapter 10. This is a specific way of visualising yourself and the goal you are moving towards. Research has shown that all people do not think about themselves in the same way. You will remember the distinction between associated and dissociated images. Associated is where you see an event through your own eyes, as though inside the experience and dissociated is where you are not in the experience, but you are seeing it and hearing it from the outside. Let's return to this exercise and find out what else can be learnt.

Imagine sitting in front of a large picture screen and on that screen you see a motion picture of yourself. See yourself carrying out your favourite activity. How does that differ from stepping into that activity and seeing it 'as you do it', experiencing it through your own eyes? There is a marked difference in intensity if you pay attention to the differences that you notice.

This distinction can form the basis of a number of changes that can be made to the way you experience and remember an event. It is often used in a more detailed form as a phobia cure. So how does this help with your sight correction? The answer is to find which of the two ways of representing your experience work best for you. Which helps you to notice the most distinctions and improvements?

There are two ways of considering the impact of these two distinctions. For some people looking at an image of how they see themselves to be, with particular skills and abilities (in this case with normal vision), means they are drawn toward the image. Your brain will contrast the difference between where you are now and where you want to be and start making the adjustments necessary to achieve the desired state.

For other people experiencing the event in an associated way is more effective because of the intensity of the experience. You will remember that it has been shown that your nervous system cannot tell the difference between an "imagined" experience and a "real" experience. This means what you imagine to be true. This has held true in a number of psychology experiments, the most famous of which is the sinking basketballs exercise. In this experiment the effect of mental practice as a way of improving skill was tested.

What happened was that one group of students practised throwing the basketball every day for twenty days and was scored on the first and last days. A second group was also scored in the same way but had no practice at all. The third group was also scored on the first day and then had no physical practice. Its members did, however, spend twenty minutes a day imagining that they were throwing the ball and sinking the basketball. When they missed they would imagine that they corrected their aim appropriately.

The fascinating result of this experiment was that the first group which physically practised twenty minutes a day improved by twenty-four per cent in its scoring. The second group, who had no practice, showed no improvement. The third group who practised in its imagination improved its scoring by twenty-three per cent!

No matter how **you decide to progress** the important thing is to give your images fine detail. Make the experience as vivid and detailed as possible. Have your mental pictures approximate real experience as much as possible. By real experience for your visual process, it means paying attention to all the details that have been pointed out in the exercises so far. If you imagine yourself looking at a billboard, notice the sharpness of the letters and their outlines. The clarity between the colour of the letter and the background. The blackness of any letters. The way it is when your sight is normal. In addition notice all the other things that are not solely to do with your visual sense - the environment around you, the temperature, and textures of things you touch. What noises can you hear and what are you saying to yourself? What is the tone of voice? Noticing the small details in your imagination makes the experiences real. This is a practice experience just the same as the basketball exercise.

If your imagination is vivid enough and detailed enough this imagination practice will be indistinguishable from real experience, your neural system will equate it with reality. The key is practice. Forget how things have been for you and the defects of vision you may have suffered from. Concentrate upon the now. Create the perception of how you will be with normal vision and then see yourself being that person with those abilities. Acting and feeling just how it will be and let yourself feel good because of the results you have gained.

If you are the type of person who does something once and then can always do it, fine. This exercise will give immediate results. If you are not like this then gradual progression and practice are the keys to progress. If you have ever mastered any new skill it takes a time before you become aware that you should be doing different things, at different stages in the skill building process. You have practised consistently, albeit unconsciously, to get whatever results you are currently achieving. Defective vision is a result. It may not be a result you want, but it is a result none the less. Think about it; you probably achieved it even with out trying. It is a fact that with a little practice, you will automatically begin to notice new results and begin becoming aware of new distinctions in your visual process. Soon you will do this too "without trying". You will soon have a store of memories of how things 'should' be in your visual process and you will find that your subconscious moves you quickly toward matching your perceptions.

---

[1] Subject to those conditions that physically or through disease make any improvement in sight impossible.

CHAPTER 19

PRESBYOPIA — OLD SIGHT: CAN WE STOP ITS MARCH?

Presbyopia merits a special mention because it is estimated that between the ages of forty-four and sixty-five years the condition effects up to eighty-five per cent of the population. The problem is with the eyes' accommodative power, which gradually begins to fade until many people become totally reliant upon glasses for vision at the near point. The reason given within traditional theory is that the condition is simply a fact of life we must all live with because presbyopia is reflective of the ageing process.

You may have been told that because the lens of your eye hardens with age, this prevents the eyes from accommodating at the near point. There are however always exceptions to this rule. We all know older people who have excellent sight and who do not need to wear glasses for reading. This condition does not affect everyone. What is the difference between those who find that their eyesight deteriorates with age and those who continue with normal vision without ever needing glasses? Can presbyopia be cured?

The answer to the last question is 'yes'. We shall examine how this is possible and at the same time look at the difference between those whose eyesight remains normal and those who find their eyesight failing with age. The model of possibility in this area is Dr Bates himself. He showed us that presbyopia is not an inevitable result in our lives and does not have to correspond with the ageing process. Dr Bates demonstrated upon himself that **presbyopia can be prevented and eliminated.** There were many others whom Dr Bates treated and they also regained the ability to see at the near point without the aid of glasses. Reports include patients who had suffered from the condition for fifteen and twenty years who made a full recovery back to normal vision.

Other reported observations have shown that the hardening of the lens can occur from any age and cases as young as ten have been known. The condition is not therefore solely dependent upon age although it is fair to say that as a general observation the lens of the eye does tend to 'harden' with age. This also corresponds however with other changes that take place in the body as we age.

You will recall from Chapters 1 and 2 that in any event, the general conclusion is that the lens in the eye is *not* the primary factor in the process of focusing and accommodation. What this means is that this observation regarding the lens 'hardening' becomes unimportant so far as the question of how you remedy the condition is concerned. Weakness in the ciliary muscle is equally unimportant because of its minor role in the accommodation process.

The cause of presbyopia is 'strain'. By being more specific, we can say that it is a strain to see at the near point. There are specific characteristics associated with strain at the near point. These are, however, only the symptoms which are derived from the same root causes that we have already looked at. An example that illustrates the point is that of observations carried out upon a group of dressmakers. The reported findings were that dressmakers, who complained about their sight, could thread a needle with the naked eye and examination with a retinoscope showed their eyes to be in focus while carrying out this task. The same people were however unable to read or write without their glasses on.

Dr Bates was able to conclude:

> "Presbyopia is, in fact, simply a form of hypermetropia in which the vision for the near-point is chiefly affected, although the vision for the distance, contrary to what is generally believed, is always lowered too."[1]

Here is another very telling point. It has been reported that when the eye 'strains' to see at the near-point, the point of focus is always pushed further away than it was before. This means that if you have presbyopia and try to read fine print at a close-up point and fail, your focus is actually being pushed further away than before you attempted to read in this way. The resulting failure is caused by strain within the visual process.

If you suffer from presbyopia try this. Read text close up at about six inches. Palm your eyes for a few moments. Immediately after, but in a relaxed manner, read the same print from six inches. Are you now able to read the fine print or at least see 'flashes' of perfect vision, even if only for a few moments? This is reported to be the common experience for most people. The question is, if you can do it for a few moments under those conditions, what stops you from doing it all the time? Obviously the physical and mental abilities are still in place. This is a classic example of the effect of 'strain' within the visual process and exactly the same principles apply in curing it that we have already examined.

If we take a closer look at the facts in Dr Bates' own personal case, he reported that:

> 'I was then suffering from the maximum degree of presbyopia. I had no accommodative power whatsoever..."

The retinoscope showed that when he tried to see anything at the near point his eyes were focused for the distance and when he tried to focus

PRESBYOPIA - OLD SIGHT: CAN WE STOP ITS MARCH?

anything at the distance they were focused for the near point. In effect, this was the opposite of how his eyes 'should' have been working.

How did Dr Bates cure the problem? He used his imagination in a specific way to achieve the result he wanted. We have already seen how your imagination will improve your visual process when you use it in the correct way. What Dr Bates found in himself and in his research with others who had the same condition, was that 'black letters' no longer looked 'black'. The letters looked more 'grey' and without distinction. The letters all looked alike. Check now if your own sight is like this with letters as you read them?

At this stage do not confuse what you *'know'* with what you can see. You may 'know' that the letters in print are 'black' but how do they look? True black or grey? The fact is that if you have this problem, there is a conflict between your internal representation of the way the letter looks as you remember it and what you see. Use your imagination to 'imagine' the typed letters you see as 'true black'. Imagine how the letters on the page would look 'in your imagination' as true deep black. Hold that image. Retain it and now contrast what you see on the page. Are the two images identical in every way?

Once you see the difference you have the answer. Maintain that thought process by reinforcing that thought using the techniques of anchoring, which we will look at in the next chapter. Completely normal sight will be achieved. Practise with the smallest types of print you can find and become aware of exactly what you can see. Use all the principles you have learnt so far. Do not strain. Ensure you are totally relaxed and do not try to read the print. Let the print come to you. Do this by focusing upon the white background area and notice how the shape of the letters impacts the white background. Remember that good sight is nothing more than a state of mind. When you begin to notice the blackness almost jumping out at you and into clarity, do not be greedy. Continue exactly the way you have been and gradually you will find the improvement happens all by itself and quite naturally.

Do not be a sheep which follows the flock blindly and simply accepts what others have said about presbyopia. Glasses are not the inevitable consequence if you choose to do something about presbyopia. Take the pathway that will keep your eyes free from glasses and help yourself to maintain your eyes in a good healthy condition. Keep your prime sense of sight working at its most effective. **If the world looks good, you will feel good.**

---

[1] Dr Bates, *Better Eyesight Without Glasses* (Souvenir Press), 132,

CHAPTER 20

APPLYING *CAPE* AS A PRINCIPLE OF GOOD VISION

"We are what we think. All that we are arises with our thoughts. With our thoughts we make our world."

The Buddha

Some people consider it a tragedy of life that we seem to be constantly urging and pushing ourselves forward toward successive goals; the pursuit of ever increasing satisfaction for our lives. The opposite is an attitude of resignation where we allow our reason to control our striving so that it ceases. So how does this affect your visual process? How did you come to accept defective vision in the first place? Did you just become resigned to it as an inevitable fact of life?

What I found was that my own sight had deteriorated over time and I never questioned what *I thought was inevitable,* until the day I noticed my sight become worse again. It has been one of my principles in correcting my own sight and maintaining that improvement as a permanent feature, that I adopted the attitude of **"CAPE"** This is an easily remembered mnemonic which stands for *C*onstant *A*nd *P*ermanent *E*nhancement. This refers to my attitude toward visual improvement. I am always looking for new ways to improve my sight. Even though I now consider my sight to be good, I am constantly finding new ways to enhance my vision permanently and make it better. I constantly challenge myself with new tests of my visual ability. I know my vision can always get better, as there is actually no limit to the ability of the human eye to see. In one reported case, a young girl had such excellent eyesight that she was able to see the moons of Jupiter with her naked eye! Some primitive tribes' people have also demonstrated a far greater ability to see objects at great distances. This is probably due to cultural differences in the way we live and our differing requirements for survival. It also shows how we can and do adapt to our environments.

There are many reported cases of people having corrected their sight and doing nothing further in order to maintain the correction. I take the view that it is usually a failure to strive for something better coupled with simply accepting the circumstances of poor sight, which leads into the spiral of deteriorating eyesight in the first place. Adopting the attitude of

CAPE prevents the possibility of any such relapse. It is really like a quality check that you carry out on your visual process. A way to push your visual abilities forward and on to the next level.

I have talked throughout of noticing small improvements that you make in your ability to see. **CAPE** sums up this attitude because it is the gradual and consistent improvements that you make over time that develops the art of seeing. The answer to the question of how long does it take to correct eyesight, depends upon the level to which you wish to improve it. Obviously there are externally accepted measures which say that eyesight is normal at a particular standard. Some people will carry out one or two exercise for visual correction and gain immediate benefit. Others will not believe that improvement can happen so quickly or that their problem can change so easily into a solution. You will **feel secure with your own improvements** when you recognise your progress and know that every day you are seeking constant and permanent enhancement of your visual abilities. I stopped worrying about maintaining the improvements I had made in my sight when I began focusing instead upon *how to enhance them*.

Manchester United and the Ryan Giggs principle

Manchester United is a football club that is famous throughout the world. It has won the English premiership three times in four seasons up to 1996. It won the title again in 1997, despite tough competition and a general increase in the quality of the opposing teams. What makes Manchester United so good? - a dedication to excellence and always wanting to achieve more. Its manager, Alex Ferguson, has demanded a five per cent increase in the team's performance level for the next season. He knows well, that in order to remain the best football club in England, it is a requirement that he must always look to improve performance. There is always room for improvement, even when current performance is already providing admirable results. It is a principle from which we can all learn.

Manchester United also has a very talented young player called Ryan Giggs. He is a winger in the style of George Best and although he is now only in his early twenties he is regarded as one of the best players in the world in that position. How did Ryan Giggs get to be so good? It's fair to say that he has natural talent but this is not the only thing that makes him great. Ryan practises hard at his skills, always looking to refine and improve them. Each small improvement gives him further belief in his own ability. Small improvements are achievable and believable. It has created a success loop for Ryan Giggs that makes him one of the great footballers of our time.

What can we learn from this as far as sight and vision are concerned? It's simple, really. Ryan Giggs did not become the footballer he is today by just walking out onto the pitch and playing. He has put in lots of practice to get to the level he is at today. He may have natural talent but he has honed and focused this talent. Apart from people suffering some disability, we are all born with an ability to see. We all have that natural talent. One question that people still ask is whether we have to 'learn' how to see. There is evidence that human beings continually go through a form of perceptual learning, even as adults. The work of Dr Bates would also seem to lead us to the conclusion that the art of seeing is indeed one which we learn and which we can be constantly developing.

Defective vision is in many cases, (excluding those of disease or physical restrictions) simply a reflection of having forgotten 'how to see correctly'. Dr Bates' methods are evidence that it is possible to re-educate your visual process. Do so by using the proven strategies of winners. Remember that small improvements are believable and consequently achievable. Alex Ferguson does not look for massive unattainable improvement. He looks for **small but manageable improvements**. You follow the same approach with correcting your vision and over time these improvements will all add together to transform your ability to see.

If you suffer, for example, from extreme short-sightedness, you may only be able to see a matter of feet in front of you without optical aids. Expecting immediately to double or triple your sight range may be totally unrealistic. Your eye muscles may be in an extremely weak condition. Using the exercises in this book you will notice improvements. Watch first for increases in your range of vision in inches or centimetres. Each new improvement becomes a new foundation for the next improvement to rest upon. It is the strategy of success. Nurture your own sense of certainty in your own ability to achieve small improvements. This will spur the desire within you to take those actions that result in yet further improvement. Adopt an attitude that reflects **CAPE** and make it part of your program.

Anchoring - a tool to help you develop CAPE

Modern psychology has developed many useful tools that can help us to improve our lives. I believe that many of these tools have in the past been very general in their application. This has meant that their usefulness has been limited for many ordinary individuals. Anchoring is one specific technique that I have profitably adopted in correcting my own vision. When anchoring and the results it achieves are applied to the principle of **CAPE,** a powerful tool is created in aiding the correction of defective vision.

What is anchoring?

You may never have heard of anchoring before. An anchor is the term used to describe a sensory stimulus that is linked to a specific state or set of states. It is really a development of the "stimulus-response" concept used in behaviourist models of psychology. Most people are familiar with the Pavlov's dogs' experiment where the dogs were conditioned to respond by salivating upon hearing a bell ring. There are some distinctions between the reasoning to each approach but in essence the power of anchors is that they can instantly access very powerful emotional states and sensations. Have you ever been driving along and suddenly looked in your rear view mirror to find a police car behind immediately behind you with its blue lights flashing? What is the immediate response it generates within you? That is an anchor - feelings and sensations linked and associated to a particular event. We are all responding to anchors all the time even though we are not aware of many of them. An internal response, such as saying something to yourself, or forming a picture or feeling is a response to an event or stimulus in just the same way.

Have you ever noticed a situation in which you felt perfectly fine until a particular person that you have had unpleasant dealings with walks into the room? Maybe someone you work with, perhaps a boss or supervisor? You may not always be aware of it but your internal feelings and responses begin to alter almost automatically. The way you respond and communicate when this person is around is based upon a previous association. Perhaps you feel uncomfortable when this person is around, maybe inferior, mistrusting or you simply lack confidence in what this person says and tells you. We can all think of situations when people have had this type of effect upon us. The feelings and responses we make in such situations are generated by the anchors we associate to the situation.

In the same way there can be totally subconscious anchors in our everyday environment that generate certain responses in us totally automatically. To a degree, defective vision relies upon certain anchors in your environment that maintain your state of defective vision. Just when, how and why these anchors came to have these associations for you is probably totally unconscious. In one respect everything that is contained in this book is about breaking the power of negative anchors and installing new positive visual anchors that will help correct your vision.

Anchors are powerful because they can give any experience permanence. This is where the link with **CAPE** arises. What will happen if each improvement you make can be anchored? The result is that you can create the best visual conditions for yourself automatically without having to think about it. It's a way to gain some control over your powerful unconscious reactions. Using anchoring you can make those reactions work for you, instead of the unconscious defective visual program responses that have occurred in the past. Establishing an anchor requires the setting up of a synesthesia pattern. You will remember from what was said earlier that this is where two different sensory systems have become linked in time and space. The meaning to you of any particular 'stimulus' depends upon the response that it generates within you. For example, you look at a sign and automatically say to yourself, "I can't see the letters". Alternatively, it may mean, by you **'noticing'** small improvements, that it may trigger a new response, such as "the outline of the letters is less blurred and the shapes have more definition".

There are certain characteristics that will help to make any anchor more effective.

a) Conditioning an anchor over a period of time will contribute to the establishment of the anchor, but pay attention to initially powerful positive and successful experiences. These are the strong foundations for building an anchor.

b) Reinforcement will contribute to the establishment of an anchor. This means repeating the association between the anchor and the response. Consistency of a stimulus is a powerful way to anchor. Let's take the example of radio advertising, where if you hear an advert often enough, you soon only have to hear only a small part of it, perhaps the music, to know what it is. Use the same principle with your visual process so that where you have made a successful improvement you anchor it and achieve the same effect upon the next occasion with out thinking about it.

c) Be aware of your own internal experiences at the time an anchor is created, as these have a significant effect. In creating anchors to aid your visual process much of the substance of the anchor will in fact depend upon your internal experience.

d) The stronger the intensity of the way you feel when a stimulus is simultaneously provided, the stronger the anchor will be. When you notice the improvements that occur in your sight, allow yourself to *feel good about them!* Even if they are small improvements. **Feel excited** about the progress you have made and what it will mean to you if you continue to achieve such progression. Imagine that you have an internal success monitor with a scale that goes all the way up to one hundred. This scale is a measure of the intensity you attach to each improvement. **Increase the intensity of what each improvement means to you**. You can then start to anchor successfully.

I used anchors to increase the distance over which I could see. I knew that when I was practising improving my vision I would make improvements and I was very alert to these improvements. With each improvement I noticed I would create an imaginary still frame or snap shot of the improvement in quality of my vision and at the same time I would say to myself *"hold that clarity"*. I would say this with a special tone in my voice to reflect the achievement. As it was always a moment of improvement when I said this, I always felt excited at the progress I was making with the improvements in my vision. I had the three essential elements of a good anchor. In other words I had an anchor in each representational system, visual, auditory and kinaesthetic, which was combined to work simultaneously.

"Hold that clarity" is a particularly effective phrase, as it is a direct instruction to your brain to do just one thing. It does not matter what defect you are remedying because 'clarity', whether at the near point or the far point is always the objective.

Try this for yourself because it is guaranteed to work if you get the anchoring techniques correct. Like anything that is new, it may take a little practice but with familiarity comes improvement. The great benefit of anchoring is that if done correctly, you will be able to almost relive the key moments when you have made improvements in your vision. Review each day's progress at the end of the day and use your power of visualisation to recreate these moments. By thinking back to the improvement you have made and re-accessing the anchor, repeating the words you said at the time and feeling exactly how you felt at that time, it can feel almost as if you are stepping right back into the experience. You will be able to relive the moment that you noticed the improvement in your sight. This is a highly effective technique.

You will recall that your brain can learn both from a real experience and an imagined experience. By repeating your successes in this way you are actually reinforcing the improvement. This is a method that really works and it is worth the effort taken to become proficient at it. It helps to create the confidence you need to help push yourself forward. You will soon come to associate confidence with your own ability to make improvements in your vision. If there is anything special about the moment you chose to make an anchor, make this part of your anchor. You will recall that anything that is initially positive or unique about an event will help to anchor it. There will be certain milestones that will be particularly memorable for you along the road to correcting your vision. You can use these as contrast points for reviewing your progress whenever the need arises.

It does not matter what your visual defect, once you begin to make improvement you can also start to anchor. I use the power of anchoring to automatically access times when I have made improvements in the quality of my sight, particularly moments when I have extended the distance of my vision. By simply accessing my anchor I am able to get an improvement instantly in my long distance vision.

Repetition

Another essential principle that comes into play here is repetition. Your brain learns by repetition and by repeating this process your brain soon knows what you expect of it. Follow the process enough times, each time anchoring a small improvement and you will soon come to notice that **improvements start happening all by themselves, even when you are not expecting them!** This is the true power of anchoring. Over time you will find that simply thinking about improvements in your vision brings about a similar effect.

Timing is critical with anchoring. Anchors can be used in any number of situations for various things. Limit yourself to perfecting this visual improvement anchor and you will match all the ingredients for making a successful anchor. You can always test an anchor, even just after you have made it. Change what you are thinking about, make it something completely different. Next say the words to yourself, "hold that clarity", use the same voice qualities to say the words to yourself. At the same time re-visualise the quality of the picture you had when experiencing the improvement and also re-accessing that feeling of excitement generated by your progress.

The whole process has a certain dynamic quality, particularly with visual improvements. **Achievement has a built-in intensity with it.** There is going to be an improvement which at some stage is going to have a certain *"wow"* type effect. You almost won't believe what you have achieved. The more intense the anchor is at this moment, the more powerful the result, and the effect will be long-lasting.

Use the auditory stimulus at the peak of the anchor. "Hold that clarity" should be said to yourself at that precise time. Uniqueness is a key feature of a good anchor and the self-generating feeling of excitement at the progress you have just made will give your brain a clear and unique signal. Replicate the anchor exactly and you always have access to the improvements you have achieved. Follow these basics and your visual improvement anchors will be very effective.

In practising anchoring in this way you are already creating an association in your neurology which is linked to improvement and achievement - to success. By the time you have done this specific technique several times you will appreciate for yourself its true value in helping to correct your sight defects.

Another advantage of this specific exercise is that you can stack your improvements. What this means is that you begin to build a volume of visual improvement moments over time and put them together to form something larger. Each improvement, while being unique, is also a platform for the next level of improvement. Whenever you find yourself coming to an impasse you can access all those times of improvement by simply saying the words, "hold that clarity". If you have truly accessed **the state that represents all those improvements**, you will find that you breakthrough to your next objective easily.

When you get good at anchoring and you have the ability to review exactly the specifics of an improvement you have made, it is also an excellent opportunity to ask yourself some new questions about the state

Applying CAPE As A Principle Of Good Vision

of your vision. The improvement you have made is fixed in your mind and anchored. What would happen if you could see something in that remembered picture more clearly, more sharply, more distinctly. How would that look? For example, if a sign formed part of the picture and the letters were there, but they were not quite as bold as they should be and the shapes were not as defined as they would be if perfect. How much improvement is required to make the picture perfect? What type of improvement will be required? What will happen if you need more boldness in the letters and focus in on just this one element? Practise in your imagination. Take your time and when you achieve the result you want, use the anchoring technique. Make it just the same as the real improvements you make and at the right moment, *"hold that clarity"*. Feel the same excitement and create a new anchor. Test for improvement in your vision the next day, by placing yourself in the same circumstances in reality. Use the anchor and what happens? You will **notice an improvement** and your brain will almost immediately recognise that the way you are seeing things is not as it should be. You will find that adjustments start to take place, provided you allow them to.

As with all of these exercises this is not a 'magic' solution. Apply the principle of gradualness and notice *all* improvements. Your sight will become better as your skill develops. You will find anchoring becomes easier and more effective. It becomes a more useful tool every time **you use it.** One thing you can be confident about is that **anchoring works and applying the attitude of CAPE will guarantee that you receive top results from it.**

EPILOGUE

There are certain parts of this book that will give you great advantages in reading and re-reading. The techniques certainly work; however, I believe that to benefit fully from them you must do two things:
   a) be familiar with the techniques and understandings. This means relaxing and taking your time rather than rushing after results.
   b) using the techniques.

The final element in successful completion of your eyesight correction program is simply now *'feeling certain'* that you have a complete overview of what you will do. The final stage must be deciding that you will do whatever it takes to achieve the results you want. Take all the reasons you know you have for wanting to correct your eyesight and **feel certain that you will achieve what you want.** Out of this feeling of certainty action and results will grow and develop.

My own personal experience has shown me that good eyesight is a dynamic process that involves many interconnecting elements, all intricately linked together. Each element is as important as the other. There is no instantaneous 'quick fix' without first having an overview of the whole process. I believe that things do change once you have that 'overview'. You too will then identify for yourself the key components that you know will correct your own vision.

I want to hear about your success

Finally, I hope that you too receive the same marvellous feelings of achievement and accomplishment that I did. As you improve and correct your own eyesight, please let me know about your successes. What do you find works best for you?

I believe that correcting your own eyesight reflects your abilities as an individual to scale new heights and show yourself and others that you can achieve new objectives and goals. Achievement here will always serve as a reminder in the future of what you have achieved in the past. It will stand out in your personal history as confirmation of your commitment to your own personal development and achievement. I wish you every success and I thank Dr W H Bates and the others who have helped develop his methods, for making success in this area of my life possible.

APPENDIX A

VITAMINS: THE FOOD OF GOOD VISION

You will recall in Chapter 2, 'Unravelling the mystery of vision', that we looked at vitamins and the role they have to play in good eyesight. It was not until 1967 that George Wald, an American biochemist, published and received the Nobel prize (together with two others), for research into the physiology of vision. The important part of his work concerning sight was the isolation and demonstration of the substance retinal, in the retinal rods and how they react to light. This research was significant for explaining the changes that actually take place within the eye during differing light conditions of light and dark. An insufficiency of retinal, (which is formed from vitamin A), results in night blindness. A crucial piece of research, this directly shows the link between diet deficiency and health. **Good vision is also the result of good diet and receiving the correct amount of the required vitamins.**

The correct vitamin intake to strengthen your visual process and capabilities is therefore vital.

Further information about the qualities of vitamins

The human body is generally unable to make its own vitamins. There are a couple of exceptions, but the crucial one as far as your own vision is concerned, vitamin A, is not produced naturally by the body.

Everything that lives needs vitamins in order to survive. Vitamins are required elements of good health, growth and reproduction. The real use of vitamins by the body is in the regulation of chemical activities that occur within the body.[1] Basic ingredients from food are generally the source for these requirements. Alternatively, and in order to ensure that correct amounts are received, supplements have been developed. In total there are thirteen different types of vitamins that have been identified.

RDA

If you have ever wondered what the 'RDA' is, this is the daily 'recommended dietary allowance' for vitamins. In other words, if acquired daily, these essential nutrients will meet the known nutritional needs for a healthy person.

Vitamin A

Let's take a closer look at vitamin A. Also known as 'retinol', it is destroyed when exposed to light, (and also heat and air). You will recall from the chapter that dealt with the eyes reaction to light, how this vitamin now becomes of vital importance. Vitamin A has a direct part to play in your visual process and it is actually a constituent of the pigment that is found in the retina.

What happens if you do not have enough vitamin A?

Be concerned about your level of vitamin A intake because deficiency does result in eye disorders. It has been shown that early symptoms include the development of night blindness and a continued deficiency will result in a loss of sight.

Apart from the visual problems, other problems that can result from a deficiency include skin problems and deficient mucous membranes' linings on inner body surfaces.

Excessive intake of vitamin A can cause a toxic condition

Before swallowing all the vitamin A you can find, be aware that incorrect dosage can lead to a toxic condition. This can cause scaly skin, loss of hair, fatigue, and even drowsiness. Blurred vision can also be a symptom and sometimes headaches.

Vitamin energy providers

It is a chemical process of reaction between carbohydrates, fats and proteins that create energy and tissue within our bodies. These reactions take place at different parts of our body as enzymes are produced from specific vitamins. The vitamins themselves are conveniently divided into two types:
1) water soluble and
2) fat-soluble.

Vitamins B and C fall into the first category while A, D, E, and K, fall into the second category.[2]

Generally vitamins work together to control the different body functions, although the fat-soluble vitamins are more selective in their functions. The lymph system deploys the vitamins to the different parts of the body after they have been absorbed by the intestine. These fat-soluble vitamins keep cell membrane structures healthy and are responsible for the synthesis of certain enzymes. This is important for good vision.

Compared to the other type of water-soluble vitamins, the fat-soluble vitamins are stored in larger quantities, mainly in the liver.

Keep your body in balance

A lack of vitamins can therefore result in upsetting the body's natural balance and metabolic reactions, which are so important for good vision. While vitamins are available naturally from the food we eat, they are unevenly allocated within these natural resources. Some vitamins are only found in plants, while others like vitamin D are made only by animals.

Appendix A - Vitamins: The Food Of Good Vision

The good news is that all vitamins can be 'synthesised' or made commercially. You may have noticed that a number of foods are actually supplemented with vitamins where these may have been lost in the food processing system.

Vitamin supplementation can be unnecessary for an otherwise well nourished individual but taking care of the specific requirements of the visual maintaining vitamins, when you suffer from defective vision, makes good sense. It may be that your body's requirements have increased due to any one of a number of changes, (maybe illness, age or other causes of imbalance), so supplementation is then essential. Again remember that excessive intakes are to be avoided because of the risk of toxicity. **So what is the correct measure?**

The correct amount of vitamin required is dictated by the official RDA referred to above. The amount of a vitamin required to produce a certain effect in the body, based upon its strength has been determined by the United Nations Agencies, (Food and Agriculture and World Health Organisation) and can be expressed either in IUs, (International Units) or directly in metric weight.

Most pharmacists will advice upon the correct measure of vitamin A for your daily requirements.

---

[1] Chapter 1 The chemical process of neural, rod and cone activity.
[2] Vitamins do not provide significant body mass nor do they provide a source of calories.

Appendix B

DRY EYE

The eye is kept moist by a continual washing of the eye with tears to keep it clean and help avoid infection. Your tear fluid actually contains proteins that are antibacterial.

It seems that tear production can diminish with age. A loss of water from the tear film means that the tear film becomes more concentrated. As this concentration increases it pulls water from the surface of the eye. The result is dryness as the 'osmolarity' increases.

The result is eyes that become sore and more susceptible to infections. Sufferers experience a sandy gritty type of sensation causing irritation.

One possible solution is 'Teratears'. Claimed to 'create an environment needed to promote natural healing and provide dry eye relief' – details can be found on the internet at:

http://teratears.com./index.html.

Appendix C

A SELF- INDUCED STATE RELAXER

Use the following suggested script to prepare your own audio-tape. If you wish to order a professionally prepared tape see the order details at the back of the book. The professional tape is recommended because it has the advantage of taking you down in to a deeper state of relaxation and contains suggestions (not contained in this script), that will aid you in correcting your eyesight. If you are not used to preparing scripts of this nature attention to voice control and delivery are crucial to the success of the instructions.

When you use your tape ensure you are in a quiet place and ready to relax without any disturbances. It is best lying down on your bed.

>"Close your eyes. You are going to enter into a deep and comfortable state of relaxation. I want you to begin examining your body so that you can guarantee to yourself that you will become totally relaxed...as you begin to relax your muscles simply let your mind relax also...begin with your feet...as you feel your toes...stretch them... feeling the texture of what your feet are resting upon...begin to tighten your calves...now relax them and let that relaxation move and spread up past your ankles, up the back of your legs to the back of the knee...feel those muscles relaxing and easing comfortably...now your thighs, tense them and make them tight...become aware of the tensing feeling in your thigh muscles...now relax those muscles...feel them loosening, lengthening and resting comfortably...feel your legs as they sink even deeper into the bed as you relax even more...and as you find yourself relaxing...start thinking how it is to be totally relaxed...and begin to tense the muscles in your stomach, pull them together gently...now let them expand and relax comfortably.
>
>   Your back muscles and shoulders...twist and expand your shoulders...feel the muscles as they pull...now let your shoulders slump as you relax those muscles...noticing how your back sinks deeper into the bed as you are relaxing even more deeply...now your fingers, and hands, clench them and feel the tension...now relax them, and allow the relaxation to move through your arms and up to your neck...notice how effortless

and easy your breathing is...and how deep and regular it is becoming...and as you think about this tighten your neck muscles...now loosen them again and as the muscles relax...allow your whole body to rest in a comfortable position.

Draw a deep breath, hold it for a moment and then let it out slowly...now tighten up your face muscles, squeeze them and feel the tension...now relax those muscles and feel them extending and slackening...relaxing even more than ever before. As you allow the relaxation to reach your scalp, you know that you are relaxed throughout your whole body...from the top of your head to the bottom of your toes. Your body is now completely relaxed...it is loose...limp and heavy...and very, very, relaxed. Notice that your body is sinking deeper into relaxation and as you breath in deeply...you sink down further into relaxation...In a moment I will count slowly from one to 10...and as you hear each number you will drift deeper and deeper into calm relaxation. 1...2...3...4...5...6...7...8...9...10...(counting is done slowly and resolutely).

As you sink into deep relaxation you find it easy to focus your attention and imagine things very clearly...I want you to imagine that you are standing on a garden patio that has steps leading down to a wonderful garden...as you view the garden you see it is bordered by lovely trees and the garden is tranquil, private and secluded. To the side of the garden is a waterfall flowing into a stream...you listen to the sound of the water...and looking around you see flower beds full of beautiful flowers...a faint sound of a bird in the trees is adding to your feeling of deep relaxation...which permeates your whole being.

The garden is a wonderful sight...and as you look more closely you see there are three steps leading down to the garden and then a pathway that leads to the waterfall. In a moment you will walk down the steps and with each step you will go deeper and deeper into relaxation. As we begin with the first step and you place your foot onto the step...you feel yourself going deeper into relaxation...down onto the second step...and as you do so you feel a deep sense of relief as you drift down deeper into relaxation. Down onto the third step and you feel so...so...relaxed. A wave of relaxation moves easily through your whole body and you are now standing on the grass... a little further ahead is the waterfall and next to the waterfall is a garden chair...it looks very comfortable...in a moment you will walk toward the garden chair and sit in it...when you sit in the chair you will find it very comfortable and relaxing...and then

Appendix C - A Self-induced State Relaxer

you will be even more relaxed than you are now... so walk over to the garden chair...now sit down in it and as you do so breath in deeply...and upon breathing out you experience a wave of relaxation going through your whole body relaxing every part of your body...every muscle and every nerve...and as you breath in...you breath in positive thoughts about good vision and as you breath out you breath out negative thoughts about your vision...so leaving you with even more room for positive thoughts about good vision...

Continue to enjoy the peace and tranquillity of being so relaxed for a few more minutes...and when you return to your normal waking state you will bring with you all the calm and peaceful feelings of deep relaxation...and you will remember the quality of the feeling of deep relaxation...each time you do this exercise you will find it easier to do and you experience a deeper feeling of relaxation upon each occasion...the effects of spending time in deep relaxation will become stronger and stronger and will last longer and longer...and you will remain relaxed and confident about your capabilities more and more each day...and you will feel a desire to repeat this exercise each day...

In a moment I will count from 10 to 1...and at the count of 1 you will fully open your eyes...and feel fully aware and alert...10...9...8...7...coming up now...6...5...4...3...you are more and more aware...2...1...eyes open".

The more you perform this exercise the better. Try it three times on the first occasion with increasing states of relaxation upon each occasion. Be sure to use it on a daily basis. Finally, you will have a contrast point from which you can measure the state of your relaxation at any time. The closer you can get to this state of relaxation during your normal activity the better your sight will become.

Whenever practising any visual correction technique be aware of the levels of stress you are generating within yourself. You will be surprised at the way in which concentration and effort can reduce your relaxation level and increase your stress level. This is a very simple exercise but it is highly effective and very powerful as the atmosphere and the feeling to step into and surround yourself within for sight correction.

GLOSSARY

ACCOMMODATION — when the eye is able to focus upon far or near points by changing the focusing mechanisms within the eye.

ASTIGMATISM — Occurs when focusing differs in two planes or meridians. In other words the vertical and horizontal cannot be in focus at the same time. Focusing takes place in an irregular way. In order to rectify the problem both planes need to be seen in sharp focus

CATARACT — Opacity in the lens

CYCLOPHORIA — Squint due to weakness of the eye muscles.

DIOPTER — The unit of measurement of the power of an optical lens.

DIPLOPIA — Double vision. Usually due to lack of co-ordination of movements of the eyes.

ECCENTRIC FIXATION — Where central fixation/alignment is lost, other areas of retina are stimulated to compensate.

EMMETROPIA — The condition of the normal eye when parallel rays are focused exactly on the retina and vision is perfect.

FAR POINT — The farthest point a person can see clearly. The eye is unable to focus a sharp image beyond this point. For the normal eye it should be infinity.

GLAUCOMA — A condition where pressure inside the eye is raised abnormally as excess fluid accumulates. Urgent treatment is required if suspected.

HYPERMETROPIA — Far-sightedness.

LAZY EYE — Also called 'amblyopia'. A dimness of vision when occurring in one eye without apparent physical defect or disease.

MIOTIC — A substance that causes constriction of the pupil.

Glossary

MYOPIA Short-sightedness

NEAR POINT The closest point to the eye at which an object may be seen clearly. For the normal eye about twenty-five cm moving away with age.

OPHTHALMOSCOPE Instrument for examining the eye. Looking at the interior and the retina. A mirror that reflects light into the eye and a central hole through which the eye is examined.

PRESBYOPIA Is an error of refraction (see below - refraction) a rigidity of the lens, due to faulty reactions in the actions of the muscles on the outside of the eyeball.

REFRACTION A term which means the variations that take place in light waves as they enter the eye. Defective sight occurs when light waves are not being focused in the way they should be to produce perfect vision.

RETINOSCOPE An optical instrument for examining refraction of light in the eye.

SQUINT OR STRABISMUS A condition in which one eye deviates in any direction.

TRANSDUCTION The process by which light energy is converted into nerve impulses.

BIBLIOGRAPHY

The author acknowledges the following unquoted materials used in preparation of this work where references are not shown in the text.

'The effect of an interrupted daily period of normal vision stimulation on form deprivation myopia in chicks', Napper, Brennan, Burrington, Squires, Vessey, Vingrys, Elsevier Science Ltd, UK

NLP Personal Profile, Engel & Arthur

Yoga Of Perfect Sight, Dr R S Agarwal

ADDITIONAL ITEMS AVAILABLE

For a full listing of visual correction aids, please send a large, stamped addressed envelope.

1) Professionally prepared audio tape- State Relaxer
2) Additional visual correction charts
3) White on black visual correction chart
4) Details of private lessons/tuition and availability

Address to write to:

Verso Research Publishing
World Trade Centre
8 Exchange Quay
Salford Quays
Manchester M5 3EJ
United Kingdom

DO YOU HAVE A BOOK TO PUBLISH?

If you have a manuscript for publication, particularly in the following areas, we would be pleased to hear from you. Please send a letter of enquiry first.

- Self-help
- Alternative medicine
- Health & Beauty
- Pyschology
- UFOs
- Paranormal
- Sales
- Marketing
- "How to" computer titles
- "How to" internet titles

Address to write to:

Verso Research Publishing
World Trade Centre
8 Exchange Quay
Salford Quays
Manchester M5 3EJ
United Kingdom